Amendments for: **Physical Management of Multiple Handicaps—Second Edition**

Page 23, Figure 3.2: The third sentence s
flexion activates upper extremity flexion and lower extremity extension if a
STNR is present (see Figure 3.3)."

Page 25: Please replace the paragraph on Tonic Labyrinthine Reflex (TLR) with the following.

Tonic Labyrinthine Reflex (TLR)

The TLR appears to be triggered by the position of the head in relation to gravity. The TLR has two components that involve the head and trunk when the body is in a prone or supine position. For example, a prone TLR is exhibited by resistance to an attempt to lift the head into extension. If a prone TLR is present, head flexion produces shoulder girdle protraction and leg flexion (Capute et al., 1984). A supine TLR is exhibited by resistance to an attempt to lift the head and flex the trunk from a supine to a sitting position. If a supine TLR is present, extension of the head produces shoulder girdle retraction and leg extension (Capute et al., 1984). (In sidelying, the TLR activates extensor muscle activity on the weight-bearing side and flexor activity on the non–weight-bearing side.) It also limits initiation of a segmental roll. In sitting, the TLR compromises balance and posture (see Chapter 8). Often head extension elicits total body extensor response. A straight sitting position (with the trunk and head as neutral as possible) minimizes the effects of prone and supine TLRs. Normally the TLR is present at birth and integrates around 5–6 months. The purpose of the TLR is to allow muscles to begin working in a reciprocal manner to overcome gravity. This is accomplished by sensory feedback in the neck muscles that offers a gravity assist-resist contrast. During normal development, the TLR strengthens the trunk and head for antigravity postures. Persons with multiple handicaps have weakness that prevents them from overcoming the pull of gravity. In these individuals, the TLR keeps them "pinned" in either a prone or supine position. Therapeutic positioning minimizes the effects of the TLR. For example, a sitting position in which the head and trunk are well supported in a neutral position best limits the muscle imbalance between trunk and neck flexors and extensors. In supine, positioning that supports the head, shoulders, and hips in flexion helps decrease extensor muscle tone.

Page 76, paragraph 5, line 4: Please delete "(see Figure 8.4)."

Page 83, paragraph 2: The correct figure citation is Figure 12.8.

Page 250, paragraph 2, line 7: The correct figure citation is Figure 15.6.

Page 275: Please change the spelling of "Comesis" to "Cosmesis."

Page 276: The following definition should be substituted for encephalopathy. Encephalopathy   An unclassifiable brain dysfunction.

Physical
Management
of Multiple Handicaps

Physical Management of Multiple Handicaps
A Professional's Guide

Second Edition

by

Beverly A. Fraser, M.A., P.T.
Doctoral Student
Special Education
Temple University
Philadelphia, Pennsylvania

Robert N. Hensinger, M.D.
Professor of Surgery
Section of Orthopaedic Surgery
University Hospital
Ann Arbor, Michigan

and

Judith A. Phelps, O.T.R.
Occupational Therapist
Wayne County Intermediate School District
Wayne, Michigan

with contributions by
Dean S. Louis, M.D.
Lawrence W. Schneider, Ph.D.
Glenda Atkinson, P.T.
Judy C. Arkwright, M.A., CCC-SLP
Carol L. Topper, C.O., O.T.R.
Steven R. Taylor, C.O.

·P·A·U·L·H·
BROOKES
PUBLISHING CO.

Baltimore • London • Toronto • Sydney

Paul H. Brookes Publishing Co.
Post Office Box 10624
Baltimore, Maryland 21285–0624

Typeset by The Composing Room of Michigan, Inc., Grand Rapids, Michigan.
Manufactured in the United States of America by
The Maple Press Company, York, Pennsylvania.

Library of Congress Cataloging in Publication Data
Fraser, Beverly A., 1938–
    Physical management of multiple handicaps : a professional's
guide   /   by Beverly A. Fraser, Robert N. Hensinger, and Judith A.
Phelps, with contributions by Dean S. Louis . . . [et al.].—2nd ed.
        p.   cm.
    Includes bibliographical references.
    ISBN 1–55766–047–6
    1. Physically handicapped—Rehabilitation.   2. Self-help devices
for the disabled.   I. Hensinger, Robert N.   II. Phelps, Judith A.
III. Title.
RD797.F723   1990
617—dc20   89–48308
                                                                              CIP

Contents

About the Authors

Beverly A. Fraser, M.A., P.T., has authored numerous textbooks and journal articles concerning physical management of persons with severe multiple handicaps. She has presented at many national and international professional meetings. For 16 years with the Wayne County Intermediate School District, she provided physical therapy services to students with severe multiple handicaps and conducted several research and grant projects. Presently, Ms. Fraser is a doctoral student in special education at Temple University in Philadelphia.

Robert N. Hensinger, M.D., is Professor of Surgery at the University of Michigan Medical School and Chief of Pediatric Orthopaedics at the University of Michigan Hospitals. He is a widely published and lectured surgeon. Dr. Hensinger has received international acclaim for his contributions to the fields of pediatric spinal surgery and technology for multiply handicapped students. Dr. Hensinger has served as president of several national orthopaedic societies.

Judith A. Phelps, O.T.R., is an occupational therapist with Wayne County Intermediate School District who has specialized in working with persons with severe multiple handicaps for 11 years. She has consulted on state-funded grant projects and with group homes and various mental health agencies in the metropolitan Detroit area. Ms. Phelps is the coordinator of a project to develop age-appropriate learning instructional materials for adults with severe multiple impairments. She is a frequent presenter at professional conferences.

Acknowledgments

Under the auspices of the Wayne County Intermediate School District in southeastern Michigan, we have worked with classroom and administrative staffs to enhance the educational programs and physical well-being of special education students with severe multiple impairments.

We thank the administrators of Wayne County Intermediate School District and the University of Michigan Hospitals. The flexible work environment that they fostered enabled us to develop our coordinated medical/therapeutic/technological approach to the physical management of students with multiple handicaps. We are especially grateful to Dr. Sally Vaughn and Ms. Nancy Nagle of the Grants, Planning, Research, and Evaluation Center of the Wayne County Intermediate School District for sponsoring the Photographic Documentation of Abnormal Body Posture Project and other product development research mentioned in this book.

Much of our work centered around the Riley School, which provides special education programming for students with severe mental and physical impairments. Our appreciation is extended to the total Riley School staff, under the direction of William Holdsworth, who helped us develop and refine our physical management program. We offer a very special thank you to the parents or guardians of the Riley School students whose photographs appear in this book and to the Riley school staff who shared their creative and innovative work with us. It is their hope and ours that others will be helped by the experiences of Riley's students.

We are grateful to occupational therapist Anna Wise, nurse Sylvia Schuster, school psychologist Kathy LaCombe, speech-language pathologist Patricia Cunningham, physical therapist Jackie Bruno, and equipment specialist Mark Dittmer for reviewing portions of the manuscript. Also, we appreciate the photographic consultation of Duncan Cole, Phyllis Cole, and Terri Rachford.

We are especially indebted to Beverly Rainforth, Ph.D., P.T., Assistant Professor of Special Education, State University of New York at Binghamton, for reviewing our former work and making valuable suggestions for the revision of *Physical Management of Multiple Handicaps: A Professional's Guide*. Dr. Rainforth and her special education students provided information and insights that helped us organize this text for classroom use. Our thanks are also extended to the readers who wrote to us to share comments and constructive criticisms about the first edition of this book.

On countless occasions, Bob McDermott and the Allen Park Kiwanis Club have provided financial assistance and moral support for our projects. We owe them a special thanks. Also, special recognition is due to Genevieve Galka, Mary Lou Dawson, Dr. H. Sidney Heersma, Mary Paquette, Lynne Morris, Vivian Zoma, Marge Haver, Ella Treloar, Kleah Jacques, Sandi Schmidt, Paula Kerrigan, Carol Lacey, Jerry

Fylonenko, Veronica Blackman, Collette Cullen, and Katie Palmer for sharing their expertise with us.

Finally, we extend our appreciation to Melissa A. Behm, Vice President, Paul H. Brookes Publishing Co., for guiding us during the development of this book.

Introduction

This work reflects a physical management philosophy developed throughout a 16-year period by Beverly A. Fraser and Robert N. Hensinger, joined in recent years by Judith A. Phelps, and Dean S. Louis and Steven R. Taylor. Since the publication of *Physical Management of Multiple Handicaps: A Professional's Guide* in 1987, the body of knowledge concerning persons with multiple handicaps has expanded and become more complex. Thus, the second edition of this book features contributions by authors Judy C. Arkwright, Glenda Atkinson, Lawrence W. Schneider, and Carol L. Topper.

Physical Management of Multiple Handicaps: A Professional's Guide (2nd ed.) presents a coordinated approach to the physical management of severe multiple handicaps. These handicaps occur, for the most part, as a result of extensive, diffuse brain damage that affects the total body, causing persistent primitive postural reflex activity, vastly abnormal muscle tone, low cognitive functioning, nonverbal communication, sensory deficits, and progressive musculoskeletal deformities. The physical management process described in this book reflects the authors' areas of interest—orthopaedics, physical and occupational therapy, specialized seating, orthotics, transportation safety, and adaptive devices for function and communication. Equipment essential to the physical management process is discussed and pictured throughout the book.

The book is intended for professionals in the fields of health and education who promote the physical well-being and educational development of persons with multiple handicaps. It should be particularly helpful to those first entering this specialized area and to those who provide occasional service to such persons.

Physical Management of Multiple Handicaps (2nd ed.) is divided into five sections: Section I: Life-Styles and Physical Management of Persons with Multiple Handicaps; Section II: Management through Orthopaedics; Section III: Management through Seating Systems, Orthotic Devices, and Transportation Safety; Section IV: Management through Therapeutic Positioning and Adaptive Equipment; and Section V: Management of Activities of Daily Living.

The first section of the book describes the role of physical management of persons with multiple handicaps in a comprehensive program of home and school care. A coordinated approach is described that reflects the input of physicians, therapists, equipment specialists, transportation research scientists, special educators, and parents. An overview of postural abnormalities and therapeutic goals and techniques is presented. A coordinated orthopaedic management philosophy is introduced.

Section II highlights orthopaedic conditions associated with severe multiple handicaps and discusses orthopaedic examination and treatment of these conditions. Specifically, orthopaedic treatment (surgical and nonsurgical) of spinal curvatures, lower extremity deformities, and upper extremity deformities are presented.

The third section is devoted to the role played by seating and orthotic devices in the management process. Appropriate seating equipment provides a foundation upon which a management program can be built to meet the person's home, school, transportation, orthopaedic, and therapeutic needs. Specialized seating includes commercially available wheelchairs and other seating devices, as well as custom seating systems. A classification system and overview of seating systems is presented along with a discussion of adaptations that often are necessary for persons with multiple handicaps. State-of-the-art custom seating and orthotic devices appropriate for persons with multiple handicaps are described and pictured. Therapeutic principles pertinent to seating and orthotics are presented throughout this section.

Section IV describes various uses of positioning and adaptive equipment in the physical management process. This section features adaptations designed to enhance the posture and function of persons with multiple handicaps. State-of-the-art devices are pictured and described along with new products that show promise. Positioning techniques are described that are important in the use and selection of equipment. Therapeutic considerations pertaining to the trunk and lower extremities and upper extremities are presented, followed by a discussion of adaptive devices designed to increase function.

Section V is devoted to the management of activities of daily living. The Feeding and Eating chapter (Chapter 15) focuses on feeding evaluation, the use of videofluoroscopy to detect aspiration risks, and therapeutic handling and positioning tailored for specific eating conditions. A discussion on tube feeding also is included. The Hygiene chapter (Chapter 16) addresses adaptive clothing, toileting aids, and grooming and oral hygiene products appropriate for persons with multiple handicaps.

Eight appendices are also included for the reader's reference and convenience. Appendix A references physical and occupational therapy service delivery model resources appropriate for educational settings. Appendix B presents a list of manufacturers/distributors of seating equipment. Appendix C contains a glossary of medical, therapeutic, educational, and technical terms used in the text. Appendix D presents an overview of normal body motion including skeletal and joint range of motion illustrations. Appendix E lists current related readings according to major subjects that are discussed in this book. Appendices F, G, and H respectively include information about sources for adaptive clothing, adaptive devices, and wheelchair tie-down/restraint systems approved for transportation.

In writing this book, we emphasize a coordinated, and often integrated, approach to the physical management of severe multiple handicaps. We are not recommending a specific course of treatment for general use with this population. Persons with multiple handicaps have extensive physical abnormalities that present complex challenges to health professionals. Solutions can come only through careful evaluation, management, and monitoring of each individual, and through sharing information among all those involved in the physical management process.

This book is dedicated to
John L. Marchello
in appreciation of the time and effort
he has devoted to developing new products
for persons with multiple handicaps.

SECTION

I

Life-Styles and Physical Management of Persons with Multiple Handicaps

Chapter

1

——— . ———

Personal and Environmental Considerations for Persons with Multiple Handicaps

Persons with multiple handicaps face obstacles in every aspect of their lives. Severe medical, neurological, and orthopaedic conditions make such persons appear to be "trapped inside a body that doesn't work." In the past, multiple physical abnormalities coupled with apparent low cognitive functioning have limited, and in many cases prevented, these persons from receiving what presently is considered appropriate medical attention and educational opportunities, as well as denied them opportunities for interaction with nonhandicapped persons other than family members and caregivers.

The advent of mandatory special education legislation and the concept of least restrictive environment that emerged during the 1970s focused the attention of educational and health professionals on this formerly "forgotten" population. During the last two decades, a great deal has been learned about physical and educational needs of persons with multiple handicaps.

COGNITIVE AND BEHAVIORAL CONSIDERATIONS

Typically, persons with multiple handicaps are nonverbal and appear to function on a profoundly low cognitive level. In fact, the cognitive levels of such persons may range from very low to normal and above. However, this book is geared toward persons with severe mental impairments (i.e., IQ falls within the

0–30 range). Persons with multiple handicaps also experience deficits in adaptive behavior (Valletutti & Sims-Tucker, 1984). Adaptive behavior is defined as the "effectiveness of degree with which the individual meets the standards of personal independence and social responsibility expected of his age and social group" (Grossman, 1977, p. 5). Self-abusive behaviors, such as scratching, hitting, biting oneself, and head banging, often are present. Low cognitive function, severe deficits in adaptive behavior, and the possibility of inappropriate or self-abusive behavior, combined with physical and medical problems, necessitate close and constant supervision of these persons.

PHYSICAL CONSIDERATIONS

Persons with multiple handicaps usually have total body involvement that results from damage to or deterioration of the central nervous system. Commonly, they have a neuromuscular diagnosis, such as severe cerebral palsy, hydrocephalus, microcephalus, neonatal sepsis, meningitis, viral encephalopathy, cerebrovascular accident, or brain trauma, that leads to orthopaedic deformities (Fraser, Galka, & Hensinger, 1980). Persons with multiple handicaps may be described as "developmentally disabled," a popular generic term used to describe a wide range of cognitive or psychological impairments and mental retardation (Valletutti & Sims-Tucker, 1984). However, these persons do not develop normally and should not be confused with "slow developers," since their physical condition typically worsens with growth and development. The majority of persons with multiple handicaps have skeletal systems that are normal at birth (Fraser et al., 1980). Deformities develop during the growth process in response to abnormal neurological influences and secondary muscle imbalances.

Most persons with multiple handicaps function motorically at less than a 1-year chronological age level, with the majority unable to assume or maintain an unsupported seating position. A few are capable of assisted standing, standing transfers, and limited ambulation. Usually, movement, when possible, is accomplished in abnormal and/or nonpurposeful patterns, severely limiting functional skills. Realistically, little can be expected in the way of significant motor or functional gains beyond the early years of development (Gordon, 1985). In fact, a decrease in function and movement may be anticipated as deformities develop, especially during periods of rapid growth. However, appropriate physical management significantly improves the quality of life of these persons.

MEDICAL CONSIDERATIONS

In addition to motoric limitations, persons with severe handicaps often suffer from a staggering array of medical conditions. DuBose (1976) described persons with multiple handicaps as a "diagnostician's challenge" because of the multiplicity, severity, and complexity of their handicaps. Chronic respiratory infections, pneumonia, and aspiration are common. Persons with multiple handicaps also experience oral-motor dysfunction that causes extended feeding times and inadequate nutrition. Most are incontinent and wear diapers. Bowel impaction and urinary tract infections are common. Seizure activity may be present, and often medication to control seizures limits function. Cardiac and lung function may decrease as spinal deformities develop. Hearing and visual impairments often accompany other physical handicaps. The combination of severe physical deficits and frequent infections require persons with multiple handicaps to receive lifelong medical and nursing care.

Some persons with multiple handicaps may be "medically fragile." An individual who is medically fragile has a condition that is extremely disabling or life-threatening. Usually such persons are dependent on life-support equipment such as ventilators, feeding tubes, or apnea (i.e., breathing) monitors for survival. Persons who are medically fragile usually require prolonged or intermittent hospitalization, institutionalization, and homebound school services (Kent Intermediate School District, 1987).

LIFE-STYLES

Most persons with multiple handicaps need help with even the most basic elements of self-care, such as feeding, toileting, dressing, and mobility. They live in protected environments, such as private family units, group community homes, nursing homes, and institutions.

It has become quite common for persons with multiple handicaps to remain in their homes during the first several years of life. Advancements in home care equipment, coupled with the availability of respite care facilities, financial aid, and school programs, have helped ease the burden of having a child with handicaps reside in the home.

However, many parents reach a point where full-time placement of their child outside the home becomes necessary. Parents become physically less able to care for an individual with multiple handicaps in the home as the child ages. Handling and lifting become more difficult as the child grows and deformities develop. A child easily handled by one person during infancy and early childhood may become a two-person lift during preteen years and a three-person lift during adolescence (Fraser & Hensinger, 1983). Many persons with multiple handicaps require around-the-clock skilled nursing care, best provided in a medically supervised program. These programs may be located in community-based group homes, intermediate care facilities (ICFs), nursing homes, hospitals, or institutions.

Since the 1970s, when individuals' rights were reexamined, a movement has been underway to deinstitutionalize all persons with handicaps (Certo,

Haring, & York, 1984; MacMillan, 1977; Mulliken & Buckley, 1983; Turnbull & Turnbull, 1979; Valletutti & Sims-Tucker, 1984). While this concept has merit, some professionals, including the authors, question whether it is appropriate for *all* persons with multiple handicaps. A nursing home may be the most appropriate setting for persons who require extensive medication supervision, frequent physicians' examinations, and specialized nursing equipment and care. Some parents also feel more comfortable placing their child in a nursing home that provides skilled care than they do releasing their child to a foster care parent or group home. Parental feelings, along with medical recommendations and care requirements, plus the qualifications and merits of the program being considered, should be taken into account when considering out-of-home placement for this population. Various levels of care may be required throughout the life of a person with multiple handicaps, and flexibility is needed when planning for this care.

Regardless of residence, persons with multiple handicaps now enjoy many experiences of community life. Persons who live in group homes, nursing homes, or institutions no longer are restricted to that setting for endless days. Improved seating and transportation systems make it possible for them to attend community-based recreational activities and educational programs.

SPECIAL EDUCATION

PL 94-142 (Education for All Handicapped Children Act), enacted in 1975 and implemented in 1977, entitles every school-age child to a free appropriate education regardless of the type or severity of handicap (*Federal Register*, 1977). What constitutes an "appropriate" education varies with a person's physical condition and cognitive functioning level.

PL 94-142 states that special education programs and services must take place in the *least restrictive environment* to encourage maximum interaction with nonhandicapped students. Thus, a continuum of educational settings is provided to meet the needs of students with mild to severe handicaps. The continuum includes instruction in regular classes, special classes, and special schools, at home, and in hospitals and institutions (Petovello & Sullivan, 1981).

Persons with multiple handicaps fall under the educational diagnostic category of "multihandicapped." This category refers to persons who have physical and cognitive problems that cannot be appropriately served in regular education programs or in a special education program designed solely to meet the needs associated with one impairment. The "multihandicapped" population is diverse and ranges from persons able to achieve a fair degree of independence to those who are totally dependent (Wilcox & Bellamy, 1982). Options appropriate for students with the types of multiple handicaps described in this book range from full-time special class placement in the same building with regular education classes (least restrictive) to hospital and institution instruction (most restrictive). The majority of students with multiple handicaps now are able to attend classes in a special school for handicapped students that is located relatively close to home. A few students attend special classes located in a regular education building, and a small number require home or hospital/institution instruction.

Special school settings allow buildings to be specially designed to accommodate wheelchairs and other essential equipment. They facilitate delivery of support services, such as therapy and nursing care, since support personnel are more likely to be present on a full-time basis. They also encourage physicians, equipment specialists, and other consultants to make on-site visits that may not be feasible with separate classrooms that are located in regular education buildings.

Curriculum Modifications

Persons with multiple handicaps are unable to participate in either a traditional academic curriculum or one that develops functional skills needed for independent living or working. Instead, an appropriate curriculum for this population focuses on developmental skills—gross motor, fine motor, perceptual, cognitive, social, and self-help, to the extent possible (Wilcox & Bellamy, 1982). This developmental curriculum continues throughout the school experience, but modifications occur as the student ages. For example, early intervention efforts are directed at encouraging normal movement and development and preventing "learned helplessness." Elementary years are devoted to preventing and limiting deformities and developing skills within the confines of existing deformities. Secondary education focuses on maintaining the student's physical condition and preparing him or her for adult life without school support. In terms of realistic physical management, "maintaining" represents "progress" with this population during the teen years.

Classroom and Building Modifications

Classrooms and buildings used by persons with multiple handicaps should be barrier free. Features such as ramps, wide doors, ground floor classrooms, adapted bathroom facilities, and bus unloading areas should be provided. Classrooms for persons with multiple handicaps usually are equipped with floor mats, water beds, special floor chairs, therapy equipment, and hydraulic lifts, instead of desks and chairs. Sufficient space is needed to maneuver several wheelchairs. Lavatories are desirable in each classroom for the convenience of students who are capable of being toilet trained and for use by staff members who change diapers or handle students with communicable diseases. Screens are needed to provide privacy for students who require diaper changes. Life-saving equipment, such as oxygen and suction machines, should be readily available.

Transportation Modifications

PL 94-142 requires that transportation be provided as a part of school programming for students with handicaps. Unlike regular education students who sit on a vehicle seat, most persons with multiple handicaps must be transported in wheelchairs that are adapted or that contain specialized seating systems. Ideally, wheelchair users should be transferred out of the wheelchair onto the bus seat and secured with appropriate passenger restraints. However, transfers are not possible or practical for many persons with multiple handicaps and they must remain in the wheelchair during transportation. Transportation safety concerning such situations is discussed in detail in Chapter 10.

CLOSING THOUGHTS

Extensive physical and cognitive deficits dictate the nature of education and life-styles of persons with multiple handicaps. They require the care and attention of many specialists—including health professionals (e.g., physicians, therapists, nurses), educational professionals (e.g., administrators, teachers, behavior specialists), and equipment experts (e.g., rehabilitation engineers, designers, manufacturers, sales personnel). It is through the dedicated work of these specialists, functioning in coordination with parents and caregivers, that persons with multiple handicaps are able to realize their maximum potential.

REFERENCES

Certo, N., Haring, N., & York, R. (Eds.). (1984). *Public school integration of severely handicapped students: Rational issues and progressive alternatives.* Baltimore: Paul H. Brookes Publishing Co.

DuBose, R.F. (1976, April). *The multiply handicapped child: The diagnostician's challenge.* Paper presented at the 64th annual international convention of The Council for Exceptional Children, Chicago (ERIC Document Reproduction Service Nos. ED 122 486 and EC 082 866).

Federal Register, 1977, Education of Handicapped Children, Implementation of Part B of Education of the Handicapped Act, 42 (163), Washington, DC: U.S. Department of Health, Education and Welfare, Office of Education.

Fraser, B.A., Galka, G., & Hensinger, R.N. (1980). *Gross motor management of severely multiply handicapped students, Vol. I: Evaluation guide.* Austin, TX: PRO-ED.

Fraser, B.A., & Hensinger, R.N. (1983). *Managing physical handicaps: A practical guide for parents, care providers, and educators.* Baltimore: Paul H. Brookes Publishing Co.

Gordon, J.H. (1985, Spring). Treating profoundly handicapped children. *Totline (Publication of the American Physical Therapy Association Section of Pediatrics), II(1),* 26–27.

Grossman, J. (Ed.). (1977). *Manual on terminology and classification in mental retardation.* Washington, DC: American Association on Mental Deficiency.

Kent Intermediate School District. (1987). *Guidelines for identifying and meeting the needs of medically fragile students within the Kent Intermediate School District: A special report.* Coordinated by The Kent Intermediate School District, MI.

MacMillan, D.L. (1977). *Mental retardation in school and society.* Boston: Little, Brown.

Mulliken, R.K., & Buckley, J.J. (1983). *Assessment of multihandicapped and developmentally disabled children.* Rockville, MD: Aspen Publishers Inc.

Petovello, L.R., & Sullivan, N.A. (1981). *Special education: An advocate's manual.* Lansing: Michigan Protection and Advocacy Service for Developmentally Disabled Citizens.

Turnbull, J.R., & Turnbull, A.P. (1979). *Free appropriate public education: Law and implementation.* Denver: Love Publishing Co.

Valletutti, P.J., & Sims-Tucker, B.M. (Eds.). (1984). *Severely and profoundly handicapped students: Their nature and needs.* Baltimore: Paul H. Brookes Publishing Co.

Wilcox, B., & Bellamy, G.T. (1982). *Design of high school programs for severely handicapped students.* Baltimore: Paul H. Brookes Publishing Co.

Chapter

2

Physical Management

Physical management is recognized as the foundation upon which to build effective educational experiences and an improved quality of life for persons with multiple handicaps (Fraser & Hensinger, 1983; Trefler, 1984; Ward, 1983). This text emphasizes those aspects of physical management that are provided chiefly through orthopaedic and physical and occupational therapy intervention—that is, orthopaedic treatment, therapy, handling techniques, seating systems, orthotic devices, and adaptive equipment. These reflect the authors' work and interest. This emphasis is not intended to negate the importance of other aspects of physical management.

PERSONS INVOLVED IN PHYSICAL MANAGEMENT

The skills of a number of people, both professionals and nonprofessionals, are involved in providing physical management to persons with multiple handicaps. Professionals include physicians, therapists, nurses, teachers, orientation and mobility specialists, social workers, psychologists, and administrators. Nonprofessionals include parents, family members, and caregivers. The following discussion describes briefly the function of each with respect to persons with multiple handicaps.

Primary Care Physicians

Primary care physicians—family practioners and pediatricians—often are the most actively involved members of the medical profession in examining and treating persons with multiple handicaps (Fallen & McGovern, 1978). Primary care physicians consult other specialists, such as orthopaedists, physiatrists, neurologists, ophthalmologists, otolaryngologists, psychiatrists, and dentists, as required, to provide specialized care for persons with multiple handicaps.

Orthopaedists

Orthopaedists are medical doctors specializing in the surgical and nonsurgical treatment of bones, joints, and muscles. They are the medical specialists most likely to be involved in the management of persons with multiple handicaps. Persons with severe physical impairments develop extensive muscle, bone, and joint abnormalities that require orthopaedic evaluation and treatment, including surgery. Often their work is supplemented by physical and occupational therapists (Rubin, 1985).

Physiatrists

Physiatrists (i.e., doctors practicing physical medicine) also treat persons with multiple handicaps. To some extent, their role is interchangeable with the nonsurgical role of orthopaedists. For example, physiatrists conduct seating and equipment clinics for persons with multiple handicaps in some settings. In other situations, such clinics are under the auspices of orthopaedists. In many locations, the question of whether an orthopaedist or a physiatrist leads in providing medical supervision for these persons is resolved on the basis of availability and personal interest.

Therapists

Physical therapists, occupational therapists, and speech-language pathologists each bring a specific expertise that can help persons with multiple handicaps to achieve their maximum physical potential. Physical therapy service for these persons includes prescribing and supervising gross motor and weight-bearing activities, positioning, range of motion, relaxation, stimulation, postural drainage and pulmonary therapy, and other physical manipulation and exercise procedures; supervising therapy/gross motor and orthopaedic equipment; and establishing and maintaining physician contact. Generally, heat, sound, and electrical treatment modalities are not used with persons with multiple handicaps.

Occupational therapy for this population includes positioning for functional activities, oral-motor assessment and programming, training activities of daily living and prevocational skills, and prescribing and supervising use of adaptive devices and equipment. Occupational therapy intervention, in conjunction with nursing, dietary, and speech-language pathology, provides a life-sustaining service for persons with multiple handicaps by establishing a feeding program that prevents malnutrition.

Speech-language therapy consists of evaluation and program planning for receptive and expressive language, often using nonverbal communication systems (e.g., picture cards, signing, electronic communication devices). Speech-language pathologists work in close cooperation with audiologists when an individual experiences hearing impairment. In some settings, speech-language pathologists (while working with an occupational therapist) conduct feeding programs.

Areas of overlap exist in therapy for persons with multiple handicaps, especially between physical and occupational therapy. Shared responsibilities include positioning to incorporate gross and fine motor skills into functional activities; wheelchair and equipment prescription, assessment, and repair supervision; and contact with parents, educators, equipment providers, and medical staff. Occupational therapists and speech-language pathologists often share oral-motor assessment and therapeutic techniques related to oral speech production. Both physical and occupational therapists may aid a speech-language pathologist in positioning an individual to operate a communication system. A speech-language pathologist, in turn, offers information that can help other therapists to communicate effectively with a person with multiple handicaps.

Nurses

Registered nurses who work with persons with multiple handicaps supervise medication, perform specific nursing procedures, and administer first aid. In addition, nursing entails assisting others to recognize symptoms of diseases specific to the population, offering counseling to families regarding individual health and nutritional needs, and providing other professionals with pertinent information about patient care. Nurses work in cooperation with physicians, dentists, school personnel, persons with handicaps and their families, and community agencies to promote and maintain optimal health.

Teachers

Teachers of persons with multiple handicaps provide instructional training and develop cognitive, affective, and psychomotor skills to the extent possible. They conduct periodic educational evaluation of each student, often in conjunction with therapists and other support staff. Teachers also implement orthopaedic and therapeutic related activities for students within the classroom.

Orientation and Mobility Specialists

Orientation and mobility specialists seek to teach persons who are visually impaired how to move effectively, efficiently, and safely in familiar and unfamiliar environments. Mobility specialists often work in consultation with therapists and teachers.

Social Workers

Social workers are charged with improving a multiply handicapped individual's relationship with society. They identify problems and situations that interfere with a person's ability to make optimal use of educational experiences and to promote improved quality of life. School social work focuses on interactions among students, school personnel, family, and community in order to enhance the problem-solving and coping capacity of all concerned. Social workers also help secure funding for necessary equipment and medical care.

School Psychologists

The major contribution of school psychologists to physical management is modifying and controlling, and teaching others to control, inappropriate and/or self-abusive behavior. Behavior control is a prerequisite to effective physical management. School psychologists also assist in developing relaxation techniques, in training appropriate behaviors, and in lending understanding of cognitive levels (K. LaCombe, personal communication, June 6, 1989).

Equipment Providers

Equipment providers include designers, rehabilitation engineers, manufacturers, orthotists, and sale representatives. These specialists work with one another and with therapists, physicians, and educators to provide equipment that is suitable for use by persons with multiple handicaps.

Administrators

Administrators supervise those who interact directly with persons with multiple handicaps in a hospital, nursing home, group home, foster care home, or school environment. They oversee related expenditures and are accountable for overall program effectiveness. Administrators should recognize the need for interaction among personnel from various agencies who also serve persons with multiple handicaps (e.g., medical, educational, caregivers) and schedule time for appropriate interactions.

Nonprofessionals

Nonprofessionals who are intimately involved with persons with multiple handicaps include parents, other family members, school bus drivers and aides, and caregivers. They come into contact with the individual who is handicapped every day, are emotionally close, and provide direct and constant care. Parents may be overwhelmed with the number of professionals involved with their child. They must become familiar with various professionals' disciplines and technical jargon and learn to communicate with these people—while simultaneously dealing with the realities of caring for a child with severe handicaps. They have the unenviable task of assimilating the advice of many professionals and carrying out physical management techniques taught to them by various professions.

METHODS OF PHYSICAL MANAGEMENT

There is general agreement that a coordinated approach is desirable to physical management of persons with multiple handicaps. Under such an approach, responsibilities for diagnosis, equipment selection, program planning, and physical management implementation are shared. A check-and-balance system results that provides built-in monitoring of the contributions made by the various professional specialists, thereby discouraging professional "tunnel vision," eliminating treatment fragmentation (Thompson, Rubin, & Bilenker, 1983), and developing collective wisdom. Three methods exist for coordinating physical management with persons with multiple handicaps: multidisciplinary, interdisciplinary, and transdisciplinary.

Multidisciplinary Method

Multidisciplinary refers to representatives of several professional disciplines interacting with an individual. Professionals using the multidisciplinary method work directly with an individual and his or her family. Reports written by professionals from various disciplines often are forwarded to one person who interprets the findings. This creates a problem when the person interpreting the findings has superficial knowledge of various disciplines (Buckley, 1983). Also, this method may lead to professional contradiction and client frustration (Sparling, 1980). The multidisciplinary method represents the traditional medical model.

The multidisciplinary method has been used traditionally in the education of students with moderate to mild handicaps. However, it is less appropriate for students with multiple handicaps because it isolates delivery of services and can prevent a coordination or integration of techniques from various specialties into a comprehensive physical management program. It does appear to work well for students who are in local schools where the concentration of persons with handicaps is small. In recent years, the multidisciplinary method has evolved into interdisciplinary and transdisciplinary methods.

Interdisciplinary Method

Interdisciplinary refers to reciprocal interactions between or among disciplines and to a combining of individual elements (Giangreco, York, & Rainforth, 1989). As in the multidisciplinary method, professionals using the interdisciplinary method work in parallel, conducting independent assessments and providing direct service in addition to occasional consultation. However, this method differs from the multidisciplinary method in that informal interactions and exchanges of information among professionals take place at team meetings. Shared planning times decrease fragmentation and unnecessary overlaps of treatment across domains (Copeland & Kimmel, 1989). However, educators and health providers soon realized that a merging of techniques from various specialties was needed to provide a "therapeutic day" for persons with multiple handicaps. This thinking led the way for the transdisciplinary method.

Transdisciplinary Method

Transdisciplinary refers to interaction that extends across or beyond traditional disciplinary boundaries (Giangreco et al., 1989). The transdisciplinary method is a relatively new approach that employs professionals in diagnosis and program planning and designates a case manager or facilitator to be responsible for carrying out the program in consultation with the various specialists. It is similar to the other methods in that each specialist remains accountable for his or her portion of the program. This method differs from the other methods because another person or persons implement the prescribed program. In the school setting, the case manager usually is the teacher. The teacher does not implement "a therapy session" but conducts an instructional program that combines methodology (Campbell, 1987a). This method works particularly well in special school programs where large numbers of persons with handicaps are located in the same building and professionals are involved in ongoing service delivery to these persons. It offers an opportunity for professionals in one discipline to understand and appreciate the work of those in other fields. Many practioners agree that the benefits of the transdisciplinary model are enormous for children with multiple handicaps (Bates, Renzaglia, & Wehman, 1981; Campbell, 1987b; Meyer, 1987; Meyer & Eichinger, 1987; Mulliken & Buckley, 1983).

Within the transdisciplinary method, the concept of "integrated therapy" is developing (Giangreco et al., 1989). Integrated therapy requires members of several disciplines to share goals and to integrate therapeutic techniques with other instructional methods. This allows for the teaching of cluster skills and does not separate students from classroom activities and other students. Information regarding integrated therapy is beginning to appear in professional literature (Campbell, 1987b; Campbell, McInerney, & Cooper, 1984; Giangreco, 1986; Horner, Meyer, & Fredericks, 1986; McEwan & Karlan, 1987).

IMPLEMENTATION OF PHYSICAL MANAGEMENT

Regardless of the method of coordinating physical management, role changes and flexibility are required among professionals and nonprofessionals who work with persons with multiple handicaps. In the past, physicians tended to work in relative isolation, sharing information only with medical specialists and other health professionals. Physical therapists, occupational therapists, and speech-language pathologists usually worked in hospital settings. Seldom did they see patients who were multiply handicapped. An isolated approach existed with respect to treatment, with little communication between therapy disciplines. Parents of children with handicaps often were expected to follow the advice of health professionals with little or no information provided about the nature of the handicaps and the reasons or objectives of the treatment. PL 94-142 (Education for All Handicapped Children Act, 1975) was instrumental in changing that situation.

Effects of PL 94-142

The advent of PL 94-142 gave parents the right to inspect and restrict access to records, obtain independent evaluation, be informed about school programs, consent to evaluations and placement, and receive impartial due process hearings (*Federal Register,* 1977). The legislation also specified that physical therapy, occupational therapy, speech-language pathology, and other ancillary or support services had to be reasonably available. Protection of parents' rights guaranteed under PL 94-142 increased awareness among health and educational professionals concerning the responsibilities of parents in making decisions about their handicapped child's education and physical management. Parents, family members, and caregivers have come to expect an open and honest relationship with professionals. In return, they help professionals understand the parents' own needs along with those of the individual who is handicapped. The result is better coordinated care.

PL 94-142 also stimulated changes in thinking among physicians, many of whom came to recognize that a conflict can arise between treating a "patient" and caring for a "person" (Fraser & Hensinger, 1983). A disease-oriented approach to treatment of physical handicaps has given way to a more functional approach to patient care that emphasizes achievement of overall physical management goals, and respects social, educational, and recreational aspects of the individual's life (Bleck, 1987).

Similarly, therapists found that resourcefulness, adaptability, and innovation were essential to providing meaningful therapy for persons with multiple handicaps. They came to recognize that collaboration among physical therapists, occupational therapists, and speech-language pathologists encouraged a synthesis of techniques that is fundamental to sound physical management. Therapists, also, began to depart from centralized service delivery models (typical of the medical model) and to explore ways to deliver therapy services in the least restrictive, most integrated manner. Expanding on the concept of "least restrictive environment" (discussed in Chapter 1), Giangreco et al. (1989) describe this effort as pursuing the "least restrictive option" and present a hierarchy of therapy delivery systems that are increasingly less restrictive than the centralized model.

Equipment providers, too, were affected by changes precipitated by PL 94-142. Traditionally, equipment development was initiated in rehabilitation engineering departments of universities. Providers have come to recognize that professionals and nonprofessionals working with persons with multiple handicaps in such settings as schools, nursing homes, group homes, foster homes, and private homes have valuable suggestions for product design and adaptation (Bergan & Colangelo, 1985; Fraser & Hensinger, 1983; Margolis, 1983). A need remains for equipment to be safety tested by engineers under real-life situations (Schneider, Melvin, & Cooney, 1979).

Teachers inherited an expanded role as a result of PL 94-142. In addition to teaching duties, they have become curriculum coordinators who work with support staff (e.g., therapists, psychologists) to design and implement a program incorporating appropriate educational and physical management objectives.

Health and education administrators found their roles changed by a need to facilitate cooperation among parents, professionals, and interagency personnel. The focal point for the change became individualized education programs (IEPs) and related assessments, development and regular updating of which became a program requirement.

CLOSING THOUGHTS

Physical management of persons with multiple handicaps requires cooperation among and between professionals and nonprofessionals. The growing number of professionals involved in the physical management process includes physicians (e.g., primary care physicians, pediatricians, orthopaedists, physiatrists, dentists), therapists (e.g., physical, occupational, speech-language pathologists), nurses, teachers, orientation and mobility specialists, administrators, and equipment providers. PL 94-142 had established a need for interaction among all concerned with the physical management process, which results in an improved quality of life for persons with multiple handicaps.

REFERENCES

Bates, P., Renzaglia, A., & Wehman, P. (1981). Characteristics of an appropriate education for severely and profoundly handicapped students. *Education and Training of the Mentally Retarded, 16,* 142–149.

Bergan, A.F., & Colangelo, C. (1985). *Positioning the client with central nervous system deficits: The wheelchair and other adapted equipment* (2nd ed.). Valhalla, NY: Valhalla Rehabilitation Publications, Ltd.

Bleck, E.E. (1987). *Orthopaedic management in cerebral palsy.* Philadelphia: J.B. Lippincott.

Buckley, J.J. (1983). Roles of the professional. In R.K. Mulliken & J.J. Buckley (Eds.), *Assessment of multihandicapped children* (pp. 63–67). Rockville, MD: Aspen Publishers Inc.

Campbell, P.H. (1987a). The integrated programming team: An approach for coordinating professionals of various disciplines in programs for students with severe and multiple handicaps. *The Journal of the Association for Persons with Severe Handicaps, 12*(2), 107–116.

Campbell, P.H. (1987b). Integrated programming for students with multiple handicaps. In L. Goetz, D. Guess, & K. Stremel-Campbell (Eds.), *Innovative program design for individuals with dual sensory impairments* (pp. 159–188). Baltimore: Paul H. Brookes Publishing Co.

Campbell, P.H., McInerney, W., & Cooper, M.A. (1984). Therapeutic programming for students with severe handicaps. *American Journal of Occupational Therapy, 38* (9), 594–602.

Copeland, M.E., & Kimmel, J.R. (1989). *Evaluation and management of infants and young children with developmental disabilities.* Baltimore: Paul H. Brookes Publishing Co.

Fallen, N.H., & McGovern, J.E. (1978). *Young children with special needs.* Columbus, OH: Charles E. Merrill.

Federal Register, 1977, Education of Handicapped Children, Implementation of Part B of Education of the Handicapped Act, 42 (163), Washington, DC: U.S. Department of Health, Education and Welfare, Office of Education.

Fraser, B.A., & Hensinger, R.N. (1983). *Managing physical handicaps: A practical guide for parents, care providers, and educators.* Baltimore: Paul H. Brookes Publishing Co.

Giangreco, M.F. (1986). Delivery of therapeutic services in special education programs for learners with severe handicaps. *Physical & Occupational Therapy in Pediatrics, 6*(2), 5–15.

Giangreco, M.F., York, J., & Rainforth, B. (1989). Providing related services to learners with severe handicaps in educational settings: Pursuing the least restrictive option. *Pediatric Physical Therapy, 1*(2), 55–63.

Horner, R.H., Meyer, L.H., & Fredericks, H.D.B. (1986). *Education of learners with severe handicaps: Exemplary service strategies.* Baltimore: Paul H. Brookes Publishing Co.

Margolis, S.A. (1983, October). *Seating and positioning: An overview.* Paper presented at the annual meeting of the American Academy of Cerebral Palsy and Developmental Medicine, Chicago.

McEwan, I.R., & Karlan, G.R. (1987). *Effects of position of communication board use by students with cerebral palsy.* Paper presented at the 14th Annual Conference of The Association for Persons with Severe Handicaps, Chicago.

Meyer, L.H. (1987). *Program quality indicators: A checklist of most promising practices in educational programs for students with severe disabilities* (rev. ed.). Syracuse, NY: Syracuse University, Division of Special Education and Rehabilitation.

Meyer, L.H., & Eichinger, J. (1987). Program evaluation in support of program development: Needs, strategies, and future directions. In L. Goetz, D. Guess, & K. Stremel-Campbell (Eds.), *Innovative program design for individuals with dual sensory impairments* (pp. 313–346). Baltimore: Paul H. Brookes Publishing Co.

Mulliken, R.K., & Buckley, J.J. (1983). *Assessment of multihandicapped and developmentally disabled children.* Rockville, MD: Aspen Publishers Inc.

Rubin, J.H. (1985). Treating profoundly handicapped children. *Totline* (Publication of the American Physical Therapy Association Section on Pediatrics), *II*(1), 26–27.

Schneider, L.W., Melvin, J.W., & Cooney, C.E. (1979). *Impact sled test evaluation of restraint systems used in transportation of handicapped children* (SAE Technical Paper Series No. 790074). Warrendale, PA: Society of Automotive Engineers, Inc. (400 Commonwealth Drive, Warrendale, PA 15096)

Sparling, J.W. (1980). The transdisciplinary approach with the developmentally delayed child. *Physical and Occupational Therapy in Pediatrics, 1*(2), 3–15.

Thompson, G.H., Rubin, I.L., & Bilenker, R.M. (1983). *Comprehensive management of cerebral palsy.* New York: Grune & Stratton.

Trefler, E. (1984). *Seating for children with cerebral palsy: A resource manual.* Memphis: The University of Tennessee Center for the Health Sciences, Rehabilitation Engineering Program. (682 Court Avenue, Memphis, TN 38163)

Ward, D.E. (1983). *Positioning the handicapped child for function: A guide to evaluate and prescribe equipment for the child with central nervous system dysfunction.* St. Louis: Author.

Therapeutic Considerations

This chapter presents an overview of therapeutic considerations as an introduction for nontherapist professionals or as a review for therapists who work with persons with multiple handicaps on an occasional basis. The chapter is divided into three sections. The first section describes postural abnormalities resulting from obligatory postural reflexes, pathological muscle tone, and basic upper and lower extremities synergy patterns dysfunction that commonly affect persons with multiple handicaps. In the second section, appropriate therapeutic goals are set. Therapeutic approaches and techniques including postural drainage, joint range of motion, positioning, therapeutic handling, and relaxation are discussed in the third section. Therapeutic positions that are mentioned throughout the book are defined, and a related readings list is provided in Appendix E for readers desiring more detailed information.

POSTURAL ABNORMALITIES

Obligatory postural reflex activity, pathological muscle tone, and synergy patterns dysfunction are key factors in creating postural abnormalities found among persons with multiple handicaps. Other contributing factors such as sensory, motor, and musculoskeletal dysfunction are addressed in various chapters of this book.

Obligatory Postural Reflex Activity

Postural reflexes (sometimes called attitudinal reflexes) are normally present in infancy and are integrated into the central nervous system before the 6th month of life. They provide a postural base upon which controlled movement is dependent (Ward, 1983). Such reflexes also serve to balance muscle groups. For example, an infant is born in a flexed position with flexor muscle groups stronger and shorter than extensor muscle groups. Postural reflexes stabilize the infant in positions that allow for strengthening and shortening of extensor muscles. These reflexes normally integrate when antagonistic flexor/extensor muscle group balance is achieved. Typically, this occurs when a child is able to maintain a sitting position, at which time righting responses develop to allow vertical head orientation in space, body symmetry, and midline hand orientation to occur. Normally, as reflex maturation continues, equilibrium responses develop that promote recovery of midline vertical orientation and body symmetry when a loss of balance occurs. Righting and equilibrium responses, unlike postural reflexes, persist throughout life.

Many persons with multiple handicaps are affected by and, in many cases, ruled by postural reflex activity. Four postural reflexes that most commonly interfere with functional posture are the asymmetrical tonic neck reflex (ATNR), the symmetrical tonic neck reflex (STNR), the tonic labyrinthine reflex (TLR), and the Galant reflex (Ward, 1983). While other reflexes are mentioned and described throughout this book, a general discussion of these four reflexes in warranted because of their extensive influence in limiting postural control and movement.

Asymmetrical Tonic Neck Reflex (ATNR)

The ATNR is activated by lateral head rotation that causes extension of the arm and leg on the side of the body toward which the face is turned (face side) and flexion of the arm and leg on the side of the body toward which the back of the head is turned (skull side). This posturing is often referred to as a "fencing position." The ATNR usually is easily elicited when the person with the handicap is supine, and is often observed in seating positions (Figure 3.1). The ATNR interferes with feeding, visual tracking, midline use of hands, and body symmetry. Prolonged presence of the ATNR may lead to skeletal deformities such as scoliosis, pelvic obliquity, and hip subluxation and dislocation (Fraser, Galka, & Hensinger, 1980).

Symmetrical Tonic Neck Reflex (STNR)

The STNR is similar to the ATNR in that head position influences extremity flexion and extension. However, unlike the ATNR, lateral asymmetry does not result (Palmer, Shapiro, Wachtel, & Capute, 1983). The STNR is activated by neck flexion and extension. When the neck is extended, the upper extremities extend (Figure 3.2) and the lower extremities flex. Conversely, when the neck is flexed, the upper extremities flex (Figure 3.3) and the lower extremities extend. The effects of the STNR in sitting may be controlled by an appropriate seating system (Figure 3.4). In prone, the STNR interferes with upper extremity weight-bearing activities (e.g., prone on elbows or hands) and prohibits lower and upper extremity weight-bearing activities that require reciprocal arm and leg movement (e.g., creeping, crawling). In sitting, the STNR interferes with functional use of the arms and hands on a tray or table.

Figure 3.1. Asymmetrical tonic neck reflex (ATNR). This seated child demonstrates an ATNR. As her face turns toward the right, her right arm extends and her left arm flexes. Often, similar movement of the lower extremities may be observed. The ATNR interferes with feeding, visual tracking, midline use of hands, and body symmetry. This child is wearing a vinyl-coated foam helmet to protect her head in the event of seizure activity.

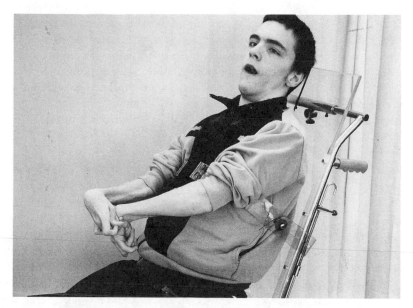

Figure 3.2. Symmetrical tonic neck reflex (STNR). Neck extension causes this person's upper extremities to extend and lower extremities to flex. Conversely, neck extension activates upper extremity flexion and lower extremity extension if a STNR is present (see Figure 3.3). (A clear plastic back was inserted into a wheelchair frame to demonstrate a relatively unsupported sitting position.)

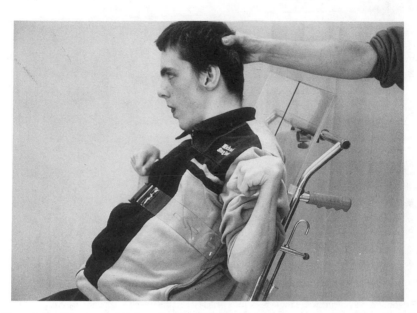

Figure 3.3. Symmetrical tonic neck reflex (STNR). Neck flexion causes the upper extremities to flex and the lower extremities to extend. The STNR interferes with upper extremity weight-bearing activities in prone and functional use of the arms, and prohibits weight-bearing reciprocal arm and leg movement.

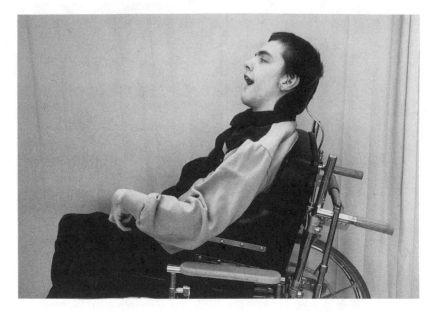

Figure 3.4. Seating position limits effects of symmetrical tonic neck reflex (STNR). A seating system that provides adequate trunk support and maintains the head in a midline position allows the upper and lower extremities to rest in a relaxed position.

For example, the arms usually rest in a semiflexed position on a tray for hand activities to occur. This may be possible when the head is forward. However, as the individual raises his or her head to look up, the upper extremities straighten, pushing the hands away from the activity. In addition, extension of the lower extremities during neck flexion may cause an individual to thrust out of the chair.

Tonic Labyrinthine Reflex (TLR)

The TLR appears to be triggered by the position of the head in relation to gravity. The TLR has two components that involve the head and trunk when the body is in a prone or supine position. For example, a prone TLR is exhibited by resistance to an attempt to lift the head into extension. If a prone TLR is present, head flexion produces shoulder girdle protraction and leg flexion (Capute et al., 1984). A supine TLR is exhibited by resistance to an attempt to lift the head and flex the trunk from a supine to a sitting position. If a supine TLR is present, extension of the head produces shoulder girdle retraction and leg extension (Capute et al., 1984). (In sidelying, the TLR activates extensor muscle activity on the weight-bearing side and flexor activity on the non–weight-bearing side.) It also limits initiation of a segmental roll. In sitting, the TLR compromises balance and posture (see Chapter 8). Often head extension elicits total body extensor response. A straight sitting position (with the trunk and head as vertical as possible) minimizes the effects of prone and supine TLRs. Normally the TLR is present at birth and integrates around 5–6 months. The purpose of the TLR is to allow muscles to begin working in a reciprocal manner to overcome gravity. This is accomplished by sensory feedback in the neck muscles that offers a gravity assist-resist contrast. The TLR strengthens the trunk and head for antigravity postures. Persons with multiple handicaps have weakness that prevents them from overcoming the pull of gravity. In these individuals, the TLR keeps them "pinned" in either a prone or supine position. Therapeutic positioning minimizes the effects of the TLR. For example, a sitting position in which the head and trunk are well supported in a vertical position best limits the muscle imbalance between trunk and neck flexors and extensors. Also, a supine position with the head, shoulders, and hips flexed helps decrease extensor muscle tone.

Galant Reflex

The Galant reflex is elicited by a tactile stimulus applied to the skin over the paraspinal muscles from shoulder to hip level. Stimulation is applied to each side of the spine separately. If the Galant reflex is present, lateral flexion of the trunk occurs with concavity toward the stimulated side (Figure 3.5). This response may be present at birth and normally integrates around 2 months of age. Persistence of this response may lead to trunk asymmetry and may prevent cocontraction of trunk muscles needed for posture stabilization. Trunk

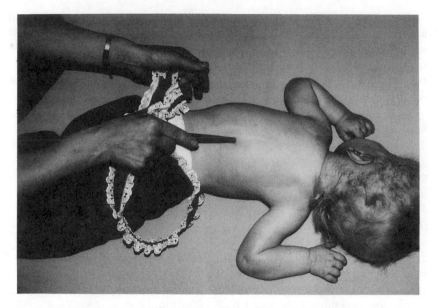

Figure 3.5.   Galant reflex. This reflex is elicited by a tactile stimulus applied to the skin over the paraspinal muscles from shoulder to hip level. As shown in this photograph, lateral flexion of the trunk occurs with concavity toward the stimulated side.

instability and asymmetry are precursors of scoliosis. In this case, the aim of therapy is to prevent scoliosis formation by supporting the trunk in sitting positions and symmetrically aligning the trunk in prone and supine positions.

Pathological Muscle Tone and Movement

Muscle Tone Pathologies

Unfortunately, there is no quantitative method for measuring muscle tone. Instead, muscle tone abnormalities are determined by observation of how the muscles affect body posture and movement. Hypertonia is characterized by too much resistance to movement of a limb or body part, hypotonia by too little resistance to movement of a limb or body part, and fluctuating tone shifts between the two.

Hypertonicity

The majority of persons with multiple handicaps develop hypertonicity that usually involves spasticity, resulting in muscle imbalances and soft tissue contractures and eventually leading to bony deformities. Hypertonicity limits posture to positions in which spastic muscles assume a shortened position. Such positions usually render a person with multiple handicaps unable to shift weight within a posture or move out of a posture. Muscles of the upper and lower extremities often form contractures that severely limit joint range of motion and create additional positioning difficulties.

Hypotonia

In persons with multiple handicaps, hypotonia is characterized by an inability to support the trunk in an antigravity posture and by unstable hypermobile joints. Caution must be used in handling such persons to prevent joint subluxation. The shoulders are especially susceptible to subluxation. Adequate trunk support should be provided if a sitting position is under consideration (see Chapter 8).

Fluctuating Tone

Fluctuating muscle tone often is associated with athetoid cerebral palsy and severe seizure disorders. Persons with athetoid involvement usually have muscle tone that alternates between hypotonic and hypertonic (e.g., tension athetosis). Such individuals often have a limited ability or lack the ability to hold postures needed for control of limb movement. In such cases, it may be necessary to provide trunk stabilization to enhance controlled distal movement.

Movement Pathologies

Athetosis is characterized by involuntary ceaseless slow movement of the limbs or head. These usually are especially severe in the hands. Some persons with multiple handicaps experience tension athetosis that is usually associated with extensor patterns (Bleck, 1987). Ataxia (i.e., failure of muscular coordination) is a common problem for individuals with multiple handicaps. Those capable of ambulation usually demonstrate a wide-base, swaying gait.

Obligatory Synergy Patterns

Synergy patterns allow muscles to work together to perform an action, such as lifting a glass of water, more efficiently than isolated muscle function. The ability to move in and out of synergies and use various components of the synergies to perform tasks is a necessary part of normal human function. However, persons with multiple impairments tend to lock into synergy patterns that interfere with postural control and movement. Spasticity is a major cause of obligatory synergy activity (Ward, 1983). Flexion and extension synergy patterns involving upper and lower extremities are quite common to persons with multiple handicaps. Such synergy patterns are pictured and described in Chapters 11 and 12. Experience indicates that positioning to control and counteract pathological synergy patterns is an effective therapeutic intervention.

THERAPEUTIC GOALS

Therapy in young children and those with mild to moderate pathology involves movement to encourage functional muscle cocontraction and balance that allows an individual to stabilize a posture and then relax and move into another posture. Reflex-inhibition positions are used to facilitate integration of postural reflexes. When spasticity develops to the point where movement is severely limited, therapy is directed at preventing deformities (usually by relaxation techniques designed to reduce muscle tone, range-of-motion exercises, and positioning to minimize the effects of postural reflexes). Once deformities become established (usually by age 7), emphasis changes from prevention to therapeutic management (Fraser & Hensinger, 1983). The goals of such a management program are to prevent or minimize further deformity and to assist the individual in developing function within the confines of his or her deformities (Bleck, 1987).

Therapeutic goals should be set for each person with multiple handicaps on an individual basis. The goals of promoting normalcy and independent function are unrealistic for this population. Generally, therapeutic management goals for these persons are:

To prevent or minimize deformity
To maintain or improve joint flexibility
To promote function within the limits of existing pathology
To maintain surgical corrections
To provide mobility through appropriate seating and transportation systems
To help the person adapt physically to varied environments
To improve general health

THERAPEUTIC INTERVENTION

In the past decade, traditional therapy treatment has given way to management intervention (Bleck, 1981; Fraser & Hensinger, 1983; Schmoll, Downey, Carlson, & Darnell, 1987). Traditional therapy (especially physical therapy) consisted of treatment directly administered by a therapist under a detailed physician's prescription. Contemporary therapeutic intervention involves a more demanding skill level with the therapist serving as analyst, catalyst, adviser, and manager rather than technician (Bleck, 1987).

The change from traditional therapy treatment to management intervention requires flexible service delivery models that will vary according to the needs of the individual with multiple handicaps and the intervention program. Service delivery may include general consultation and individual intervention (Schmoll et al., 1987). General consultation requires communication between the therapist and professionals, paraprofessionals, parents, and administrators based on the therapist's expertise and judgment. General consultation is not client specific and includes inservices, advice regarding environmental adaptations, and long-range program planning. Individual or client specific intervention includes a continuum of service delivery including direct, monitored, and individual consultation. Direct service involves intervention for an individual or small group of individuals with the therapist assuming primary responsibility for the intervention. Monitored service consists of specific training and supervision of personnel who conduct the intervention program. The therapist, however, remains responsible for the program and monitors it. Individual consultation requires a therapist to share perspectives and knowledge regarding a specific individual with others. Occupational and physical therapy school service delivery model resources are listed in Appendix A.

Intervention Approaches

Specific treatment approaches such as Neurodevelopmental, Rood, Brunnstrom, and Proprioceptive Neuromuscular Facilitation (PNF) are commonly used with children with developmental disabilities, very young children with motor impairments, and those with mild to moderate pathologies (Connolly & Anderson, 1978). These treatment approaches, often identified with an individual's contribution or philosophy, are confusing to the nontherapist and require a historical review of therapeutic history to be understood. A clear way of organizing this material was needed. Schmoll et al. (1987) summarize various treatments into four intervention approaches: neuromotor, functional, psychoeducational, and orthopaedic. The neuromotor approach emphasizes neurophysiological and developmental sequences as the foundation for motor learning. The functional approach stresses improving an individual's functional skills within his or her environment. The psychoeducational approach is based on the theory that sensorimotor development is an important foundation for learning. The orthopaedic approach employs orthoses, splints, casting, and surgery to improve musculoskeletal structure and function.

The population with severe multiple handicaps who are described in this text appear to benefit from a functional approach combined with appropriate orthopaedic intervention. The neuromotor and psychoeducational approaches are less desirable because persons with multiple handicaps do not follow a normal developmental sequence, develop deformities, and are noncooperative due to cognitive limitations and/or behavioral problems.

Techniques

Specific therapeutic techniques are helpful in managing abnormalities of persons with multiple impairments (Galka, Fraser, & Hensinger, 1980). Such techniques often incorporate key principles and philosophies from various intervention methods. These techniques include postural drainage, joint range of motion, positioning, therapeutic handling, and relaxation. A brief discussion of each follows. (Many of these techniques are described in detail in connection with equipment mentioned in various chapters of this book.) Tailoring of techniques is often necessary to meet the needs of an individual with multiple handicaps.

Postural Drainage

Persons with multiple handicaps commonly suffer chronic respiratory infections. Most are unable to understand the concept of coughing and often lack the muscle control to cough effectively. Since these persons are unable to cooperate actively in a postural drainage program, passive postural drainage techniques are employed. Such techniques (e.g., positioning, clapping, vibration) are performed to help clear mucus from the lungs and tracheobronchial tree (Reinisch, 1978). Usually, congestion in persons with multiple handicaps is general in nature, and it is not necessary to identify specific lung areas for drainage. Postural drainage positions include prone, supine, and sidelying, in combination with head and trunk elevation or inversion. Such techniques are most effective when administered in the morning and evening and at least 1 hour after eating or medication is given.

Joint Range of Motion

Spasticity, soft tissue changes, unbalanced length of antagonistic muscles, and bony deformities often render individuals with multiple handicaps unable to actively perform range-of-motion exercises. Therefore, passive joint range of motion is an especially appropriate management technique for persons with hypertonia. At a minimum, passive joint range of motion provides the individual with the sensation of body parts being moved, and at a maximum, helps prevent further loss of motion. Exercises should be performed slowly and within a range of comfortable movement (Galka et al., 1980). Generally, stretching to the point of eliciting a stretch reflex should be avoided (Eldred, 1967; Rood, 1956). Range-of-motion exercises, combined with relaxation techniques, are especially effective in reducing muscle tone and increasing or maintaining range of motion, at least on a temporary basis (Galka et al., 1980). Straight and diagonal plane motions may be used in a general range-of-motion program. Range of motion may be incorporated into an individual's daily care routine. For example, a caregiver may passively abduct scissoring legs during each diaper change (Fraser & Hensinger, 1983).

In cases of muscle contracture, range of motion may include carefully applied muscle stretching. This involves prolonged holding at the point of maximum tolerated muscle length (Griffin, 1974). This technique serves to desensitize the muscle's stretch receptors (Harris, 1978a,b). Since persons with multiple handicaps usually are unable to indicate discomfort orally, it is important to observe and palpate tendon tension to determine the maximum length tolerated. Although range of motion that involves passive stretching has been used for many years to maintain or increase passive motion, there is little clinical documentation of success in preventing contracture and deformity. Methods and frequencies of stretching techniques need further investigation to determine efficacy in gaining passive motion. Miedaner and Renander (1987) conducted a study to determine if straight plane passive range of motion in children with severe motorical involvement was more effective when provided five times versus two times per week. The results showed no significant difference between the two frequencies. Passive range of motion must be augmented by positioning to be effective in gaining range at joints that have no active motion (Cherry, 1980).

Positioning

Positioning has been recognized as an adjunct to therapeutic handling directed toward persons who are younger or mildly to moderately handicapped (Bergan & Colangelo, 1985; Ward, 1983). However, positioning may be used effectively in conjunction with a range-of-motion or gross motor program. Ashmore and Holly (1983) demonstrated that a passive stretch must be sustained for a minimum of 20–30 minutes per muscle or muscle group to be effective in maintaining plastic elongation of connective tissue. Studies (Nwaobi, 1986; Nwaobi, Brubaker, Cusick, & Sussman, 1983) have shown that positioning is effective in inhibiting specific muscle activity. Positioning equipment may include splints for the extremities and orthoses or devices to support the trunk in desired recumbent, sitting, or standing postures. Also, equipment may be used to position an individual in order to strengthen the lengthened agonist as well as passively stretch the antagonist. For example, in the case of slight knee flexion contracture, supported standing in a stand-in box helps strengthen the quadriceps muscles in order for the individual to balance muscle pull of the shortened knee flexors.

In a more general sense, positioning through the use of adaptive equipment is fundamental to physical management of multiple handicaps. Proper positioning maintains the body in the most symmetrical alignment possible; reduces the effects of abnormal reflex, muscle tone, and synergy activity; and provides a base from which functional activity may occur. Wheelchair and seating systems have become some of the most important positioning devices. For the individual with multiple handicaps, positioning becomes the foundation upon which an effective therapy or physical management program can be built.

Sections III and IV of this book describe in detail positioning equipment used with persons with multiple impairments. In the past, basic supported body positions have not been uniformly named or described by therapists. The following paragraphs establish positioning terms that are used throughout the book.

Recumbent Positions Recumbent positions are those in which the body is horizontal. They include supine, prone, and sidelying. Recumbent positions also include variations of supine, prone, and sidelying in which the head and trunk are either elevated or inverted. This is usually accomplished by positioning on a wedge. Combination positions in which the head and trunk are elevated or inverted are designated by the word elevated or inverted preceding the position (e.g., inverted prone, elevated supine). Recumbent positions are particularly useful with persons with multiple handicaps since they are conducive to relaxation and require minimum postural control. Equipment used in conjunction with recumbent positioning usually is static (i.e., stationary) or dynamic (i.e., flexible). Mats, wedges, and sidelyers are examples of static positioning devices. Water beds and air mats are dynamic because they have built-in responsiveness to shifts in posture and movement. Recently, dynamic positioning aids are being used in combination with static equipment.

Vertical Positions Vertical positions are those in which the trunk and head are supported upright. They include sitting, kneeling, and standing postures. Supported within a vertical posture, the trunk and head may be inclined forward or reclined slightly. Vertical positioning equipment includes chairs (e.g., wheelchairs, classroom chairs, floor sitters), prone standers, kneel standers, and stand-in boxes. To date, most vertical positioning equipment is static.

Therapeutic Handling

A variety of positions should be included in an individual's every shift in posture and mobility. Increasingly, physical therapists are teaching parents and caregivers to provide such therapy to their children who are handicapped. In a study conducted in Sweden, parents reported few difficulties in performing treatments and children received intensive physical therapy as a result of their parents' participation (von Wendt, Ekenberg, Dagis, & Janlert, 1984). Therapeutic handling is especially important for children who are developing righting and equilibrium responses. However, most persons with multiple handicaps do not reach this level of development. Also, therapeutic handling techniques are difficult to perform on many persons with multiple handicaps because of the extensive deformities and rigid postures that are common in older children, adolescents, and adults.

For this population, the definition of therapeutic handling may be altered to include lifting methods and body mechanics taught by the therapist to those handling the person on a daily basis (Fraser & Hensinger, 1983). Emphasis should be placed on handling techniques that prevent injury to the individual who is handicapped and to the caregivers. Techniques for handling young children with cerebral palsy are described by Finnie (1975). Some of these techniques may be used with adolescents and adults with severe impairments. However, as the individual with the impairment grows and develops deformities, often techniques must be modified to accommodate his or her size and condition. For example, one person lifts may no longer be possible and two and three person and hydraulic lifting techniques are required. While general lifting and handling guidelines are helpful, they do not take the place of ongoing instruction and supervision provided by the attending therapist that is specifically directed to meet a particular individual's needs.

Therapeutic handling of persons with multiple handicaps may also include therapeutic techniques such as postural drainage, passive joint range of motion, and positioning. Therapeutic techniques may be delegated to parents, educators, and caregivers provided the techniques are prescribed, demonstrated, and monitored by an attending therapist for a specific individual (Galka et al., 1980). A pilot study conducted on students with multiple impairments compared the effectiveness of direct physical therapy service to a monitored service in which intervention was provided by the educational staff under a therapist's direction (Sommerfeld, Fraser, Hensinger, & Beresford, 1981). Study results indicated that there was no significant difference between the two service delivery models in improving students' physical skills. Although further studies are needed to determine the most beneficial form of physical therapy for students with multiple impairments, a monitored service delivery model appears to be cost effective and appropriate for this population. This model enables a therapist, whose principal value and expertise lies in evaluation and program planning, to provide service to a large number of persons with handicaps (Bleck, 1987).

Relaxation

Relaxation techniques are useful in decreasing muscle tone and allowing a person with handicaps to achieve temporary active or passive movement in a more controlled manner. Relaxation may be provided by environmental stimuli or by specific handling techniques. Environmental factors, such as visual, auditory, gustatory, and olfactory stimulation, may help to create an appropriate relaxing atmosphere. For example, the use of cool colors; soft, low music and voices; warm beverages; and foods with pleasant taste and odor help lessen tension.

Relaxation techniques commonly used to reduce spasticity include slow rocking, rhythmical rotation of the trunk or pelvis about the body axis, gentle shaking of limbs, and neutral warmth. Slow rocking motions provide a low-frequency vestibular stimulation that inhibits the central nervous system, producing a calming effect (Ayers, 1972). Other techniques such as slow rotation (i.e., holding the person over a slowly moving surface such as a ball, bolster, or vestibular board) and inverted positioning may be effective but are not well described or explained in therapeutic literature (Cherry, 1980). Specific relaxation techniques are especially effective in reducing muscle tone and allowing for increased movement when combined with therapeutic handling and range-of-motion techniques (Galka et al., 1980). Although the value of relaxation techniques in achieving a prolonged or permanent lessening of muscle tone is questionable, such techniques do promote handling and facilitate increased movement on a temporary basis.

CLOSING THOUGHTS

Obligatory postural reflex activity, pathological muscle tone, and synergy patterns dysfunction are key factors in creating postural abnormalities found among persons with multiple handicaps. Therapy, mainly through positioning and handling, is directed toward minimizing the effects of these postural abnormalities. Realistic therapeutic goals for this population generally include preventing or delaying and minimizing deformity, maintaining or improving joint flexibility, promoting function within the limits of existing pathology, maintaining surgical corrections, providing mobility through appropriate seating and transportation systems, aiding adaptation to varied environments, and improving general health. In order for these goals to be accomplished, therapeutic techniques representing various intervention approaches should be tailored for persons with multiple handicaps on an individual basis.

REFERENCES

Ashmore, R., & Holly, R. (1983). The effects of graded duration of stretch in normal and dystrophic skeletal muscles. *Muscle Nerve, 6,* 269–277.

Ayers, A.J. (1972). *Sensory integration and learning disorders.* Los Angeles: Western Psychological Services.

Bergan, A.R., & Colangelo, C. (1985). *Positioning the client with central nervous system deficits: The wheelchair and other adapted equipment* (2nd ed.). Vallhalla, NY: Valhalla Rehabilitation Publications.

Bleck, E.E. (1981). C.P. abroad: Winds of change. *American Academy for Cerebral Palsy and Developmental Medicine News, 101,* 7 –9.

Bleck, E.E. (1987). *Orthopaedic management in cerebral palsy.* Philadelphia: J.B. Lippincott.

Capute, A.J., Palmer, R.B., Shapiro, B.K. Wachtel, R.C., Ross, A., & Accardo, P.J. (1984). Primitive reflex profile: A quantitation of primitive reflexes in infancy. *Developmental Medicine and Child Neurology, 26*(3), 375–383.

Cherry, D.B. (1980). Review of physical therapy alternatives for reducing muscle contracture. *Physical Therapy, 60*(7), 877–881.

Connolly, B.H., & Anderson, R.M. (1978). The severely handicapped child in public schools: A new frontier for the physical therapist. *Physical Therapy, 58,* 433–438.

Eldred, E. (1967). Functional implications of dynamic and static components of the spindle response to stretch. *American Journal of Physical Medicine, 46,* 129–140.

Finnie, N.R. (1975). *Handling the young cerebral palsied child at home.* New York: E.P. Dutton.

Fraser, B.A., Galka, G., & Hensinger, R.N. (1980). *Gross motor management of severely multiply impaired students: Vol. I. Evaluation guide.* Austin, TX: PRO-ED.

Fraser, B.A., & Hensinger, R.N. (1983). *Managing physical handicaps: A practical guide for parents, care providers, and educators.* Baltimore: Paul H. Brookes Publishing Co.

Galka, G., Fraser, B.A., & Hensinger, R.N. (1980). *Gross motor management of severely multiply impaired students: Vol. II. Curriculum model.* Austin, TX: PRO-ED.

Griffin, J.W. (1974). Use of proprioceptive stimuli in therapeutic exercise. *Physical Therapy, 54,* 1072–1079.

Harris, F.A. (1978a). Correction of muscle imbalance in spasticity: Inappropriocep-tion, part IV. *American Journal of Physical Medicine, 57*(3), 123–138.

Harris, F. A. (1978b). Muscle strength receptor or hypersensitization in spasticity: Inapproprioception, part III. *American Journal of Physical Medicine, 57*(1–6), 16–28.

Miedaner, J.A., & Renander, J. (1987). The effectiveness of classroom passive stretching programs for increasing or maintaining passive range of motion in non-ambulatory children: An evaluation of frequency. *Physical & Occupational Therapy in Pediatrics, 7*(3), 35-43.

Nwaobi, O. (1986). The effects of body orientation in space on tonic muscles activity of patients with cerebral palsy. *Developmental Medicine and Child Neurology, 28,* 41–44.

Nwaobi, O., Brubaker, C., Cusick, B., & Sussman, M. (1983). Electromyographic investigation of extensor activity in CP children in different seating positions. *Developmental Medicine and Child Neurology, 25,* 175–183.

Palmer, R.B., Sharpiro, B.K., Wachtel, R.C., & Capute, A.J. (1983). Primitive reflex profile. In G.H. Thompson, I.L. Rubin, & R.M. Bilenker (Eds.), *Comprehensive management of cerebral palsy.* New York: Grune & Stratton.

Reinisch, E.S. (1978). Functional approach to chest physical therapy. *Physical Therapy, 58*(8), 972–975.

Rood, M.S. (1956). Neurophysiological mechanisms utilized in the treatment of neuromuscular dysfunction. *American Journal of Occupational Therapy, 10,* 220–224.

Schmoll, B., Downey, J., Carlson, C., & Darnell, R. (1987). *Physical therapy: Management of cerebral palsy.* Flint, MI: Mott Children's Health Center.

Sommerfeld, D., Fraser, B.A., Hensinger, R.N., & Beresford, C.V. (1981). Evaluation of physical therapy service for severely mentally impaired students with cerebral palsy. *Physical Therapy, 61*(3), 338–343.

von Wendt, L., Ekenberg, L., Dagis, D., & Janlert, U. (1984). A parent-centered approach to physiotherapy for their handicapped children. *Developmental Medicine and Child Neurology, 26*(4), 445–447.

Ward, D.E. (1983). *Positioning the handicapped child for function: A guide to evaluate and prescribe equipment for the child with central nervous system dysfunction.* St. Louis: Author.

Chapter

4

—●—

Orthopaedic/ Therapeutic/Neurosurgical Management Philosophy

An orthopaedist, working alone, can be overwhelmed by the degree of pathology and deformity—or potential for deformity—exhibited by persons with multiple handicaps. Sorting out musculoskeletal abnormalities and attempting to identify treatment approaches or management techniques that will be most helpful to an individual can seem an almost impossible task. Among this population, deformities do not occur in isolation; they affect the total body (Bleck, 1987). Usually they are residual effects of severe cerebral palsy, hydrocephalus, neonatal sepsis, meningitis, viral encephalopathies, and cerebral vascular accidents (Fraser, Galka, & Hensinger, 1980) with conditions often overlapping. It is not easy to categorize or classify underlying causes by traditional disease definitions or syndromes. In fact, the exact nature of the neurological injury may never be known.

Diagnosis, examination, and treatment are further complicated because persons with multiple handicaps exhibit cognitive, expressive, and behavioral deficits that make them either passively or actively unable to cooperate. Unlike a person with mild or moderate handicaps, most persons with multiple handicaps are not capable of indicating pain, orally expressing concerns, or cooperating during an examination or treatment procedure. These problems make the input of those who deal with the individual on a regular basis invaluable before orthopaedic recommendations are made. Parents or caregivers can provide information about the person's social, emotional, and motor functions; about how the person exhibits pain; and about communication methods. They also indicate their areas of particular concern.

Because of the complexities involved, repeated observation and extensive assessment are advised before a management plan is developed. Orthopaedists should expect physical and occupational therapists to provide information that will help establish a diagnosis, determine a prognosis, and formulate a physical management plan (Goldberg, 1975). These therapists routinely assess and monitor postural abnormalities and functional abilities of persons with multiple handicaps in school, hospital, and clinic settings.

This chapter presents a philosophy of orthopaedic treatment tailored to meet the needs of persons with multiple impairments. It also describes principles of coordinated orthopaedic/therapeutic observation, assessment, examination, goal planning, and prognosis that have proven effective in the authors' work with persons with multiple handicaps.

PHILOSOPHY OF ORTHOPAEDIC TREATMENT

The musculoskeletal system of most persons with multiple handicaps is normal at birth. Deformities develop in response to abnormal neurological influences and secondary muscle imbalances. Therefore, episodial orthopaedic care, often appropriate for other patient populations, is not adequate for persons with multiple impairments. Instead, orthopaedic intervention consists of long-range continuum care with surgery sometimes being required. There are three phases to orthopaedic management of persons with multiple handicaps: 1) prevention, 2) control/support, and 3) correction. Prevention is important in the management of very young children, control/support usually becomes necessary when predeformity pathology is obvious, and correction is indicated (in many cases) when deformities are present, usually by age 7 (Bleck, 1987).

Prevention Phase

In a very young child with multiple handicaps, early intervention, such as therapy and positioning to promote normal movement to the extent possible, may, at least, delay development of skeletal deformities. At present, there is a scarcity of research with this population aimed at determining whether it is possible to prevent deformities. Because most children with multiple handicaps eventually develop some degree of physical deformity, preventive techniques should be viewed as a way of delaying the onset of them. They should not be represented as an absolute means of prevention. A preventive physical management plan should be tailored to each handicapped person's home and school situation. Parents, caregivers, and others involved with the child play a vital part in carrying out the plan.

Control/Support Phase

The control/support stage of orthopaedic treatment should be implemented when a child shows evidence of asymmetrical posturing or abnormal muscle tone. For example, such a child may need a travel chair or wheelchair equipped with special postural control features (e.g., scoliosis pads to prevent slumping sideways in the chair, an abductor pommel to prevent scissoring legs). In today's environment, emphasis is placed on control equipment that is cosmetically appealing and not "handicapping" in appearance. For example, it may be preferable to prescribe a brace (i.e., orthosis) that is worn under a shirt to hold the trunk upright instead of a visible chest support.

Surgical Correction

Surgery is the only correction for most deformities. Candidates for surgery include persons who are beginning to develop a deformity, are experiencing pain, are losing mobility, or have deformities that interfere with personal hygiene care. Soft tissue procedures (e.g., the surgical lengthening of muscles and tendons, the releasing of tight structures such as ligaments and capsules of joints) are preferable over bony procedures (e.g., surgical cutting of bone to realign or fuse a joint) for this population. Soft tissue surgery generally requires less surgical and anesthetic risk, shorter or no cast time, and a faster return to normal activity. If surgery is not a viable option—usually because of respiratory conditions or parental refusal—elaborate support systems may be used to slow progression and maintain function. If deformities become too severe for surgical correction, emphasis is placed on providing comfort and support and avoiding life-threatening conditions.

Within the context of this philosophy of orthopaedic management for persons with multiple handicaps, certain patterns of interaction are desirable among health professionals. These interactions are discussed in the remainder of this chapter.

PRELIMINARY THERAPEUTIC SCREENING AND ASSESSMENT

In a school setting, preliminary therapeutic screening and assessment may be conducted by the therapy staff to identify individuals whose physical abnormalities appear to warrant review by an orthopaedist (or other physician). The nature of these screenings and assessments is likely to vary, depending on the therapeutic specialty involved and the state in which they occur. Occupational therapists are permitted to make detailed evaluations of an individual's activities of daily living skills and to program without a physician's prescription. Many states' physical therapy practice acts, which mandate conditions for licensure, require a written referral by a physician for physical therapy services to be initiated and implemented. Some states permit evaluation without a medical referral and a few permit provision of services without a referral. While it appears likely that a restriction on evaluation only upon referral will be removed during the next several years, such a step will occur on a state-by-state basis and physical therapists are cautioned to keep advised of legislative change. In the meantime, physical therapists may, prior to medical referral, perform general observation to identify candidates for further evaluation.

OBSERVATION

Observation of a person with multiple handicaps in a familiar and comfortable environment is recommended to obtain an accurate overview of the person's motoric, social, and cognitive abilities. Watch how the person moves about on a mat, the way in which caregivers handle the person, and the manner in which a person sits in a wheelchair. Look for answers to the following questions: How is movement accomplished within the confines of the person's deformities? Is presently used equipment generally appropriate for the person's needs? Does the person interact with adults or peers? How does the person communicate? To what degree is the person motivated? Do behavior problems interfere with purposeful activities? Will behavior problems interfere with physical management or treatment? Informal observation provides an excellent opportunity to become acquainted with an individual with multiple handicaps and to screen for potential or existing orthopaedic abnormalities.

Physician visits to a patient's school are ideal, since they allow for observation of a patient in a familiar environment and for consultation with attending staff. PL 94-142 requires physical and occupational services in schools. Thus, consultation is possible with therapists who work with students in a "real world" situation. Similar input often is not possible when working with a patient in the isolation of a clinic or hospital. In a hospital setting, a physician usually has the first contact with a person with handicaps and may be called upon to refer that person for therapeutic assessment and possible intervention based solely on his or her own observations.

School therapists are in a unique position to assist an orthopaedist by providing background information about the patient and by presenting a realistic picture of his or her functioning level and needs. Also, school visits acquaint a physician with the school's physical plant and equipment— important in planning a realistic physical management program. Physician visits to schools usually are feasible from a time and cost containment standpoint in special (e.g., center-based) school programs or settings where relatively large numbers of persons with multiple handicaps are located in one building.

Observations of family members, caregivers, therapists, and school faculty can provide an excellent source of supplemental information about a person with multiple handicaps. Especially in cases where school-based observation by the physician is not possible, an attending occupational or physical therapist should accompany a person during his or her first clinic or office visit along with a parent or caregiver.

ASSESSMENT

Joint orthopaedic/therapeutic and photographic assessments are recommended wherever feasible because such assessments improve understanding of the complexity of pathology and the needs of persons with multiple impairments. Each discipline tends to focus on specific problems, with combined knowledge contributing to the most accurate assessment. For example, orthopaedists are concerned with bone maturity, soft tissue contractures, joint capsule integrity, dislocations, scoliosis, pelvic obliquity, upper and lower extremity joint deformities, and the effects of unbalanced muscle pull on bones and joints. Therapists usually approach assessment principally from a developmental, neurological, and functional standpoint, with emphasis on determining activity of daily living and movement abilities and limitations. Relationships among orthopaedic and therapeutic factors should be considered in order to obtain a meaningful assessment.

Therapeutic Assessment

Therapeutic assessment yields baseline data. Generally, a *functional* assessment is often more helpful than a *developmental* assessment. A functional assessment is activity related. This type of assessment identifies specific tasks or skills that an individual can presently perform. A developmental assessment identifies the state of an individual's maturation (i.e., adaptive, motor, or social functioning in relation to normative patterns). Persons with multiple handicaps cannot be expected to develop normally. While it is helpful to determine and approximate developmental age, such assessments do not provide a base for realistic physical management. A functional assessment provides a picture of the person within the confines of severe pathology and acts as a starting place from which to plan an appropriate physical management program.

Physical therapy assessment normally includes motor function, muscle tone, muscle strength, joint range of motion, movement patterns, postural reflexes, postural analysis, environmental mobility, breathing patterns, and adaptive equipment (Cassidy-Conway & Zawacki, 1983; Satterfield, 1981). Occupational therapy assessment normally includes sensorimotor and perceptual motor performance, activities of daily living, upper extremity function, and adaptive equipment (Lawlor & Zielinski, 1983). Many physical and occupational assessment areas overlap, and joint assessment is desirable, especially in the area of adaptive equipment. By establishing therapeutic baseline data, the physical and occupational therapists provide an orthopaedist with information that aids in diagnostic and treatment planning and serves as a reference point against which future progress or regression may be documented. While the neurological condition of most persons with multiple handicaps may be expected to remain fairly static, with deformities developing gradually over a period of time, sudden changes in condition should be brought to the attending physician's attention. If neurological deterioration occurs, intensive reevaluation is indicated. Sudden changes such as sleepiness, fatigue, or loss of motor skills and coordination may indicate recurrence of an old medical problem (e.g., Holter valve malfunction, seizure activity, medication change) or a new problem (e.g., tumor, metabolic illness, systemic disease).

Orthopaedic Assessment

The primary focus of an orthopaedic assessment is the joints of the spine and extremities. While upper extremity deformities are common to persons with multiple impairments, deformities of the spine and lower extremities usually receive first consideration since they pose serious postural problems that affect total body function and interfere with sitting and standing activities.

An activity-oriented approach is often a more helpful first step than a traditional joint-by-joint orthopaedic assessment. Using this approach, the orthopaedist notes how joint deformities affect the person's activities of daily living and how certain muscle groups are used during play or gross motor activities. Body alignment should be assessed with the person in recumbent, sitting, and standing (if possible) positions. Therapy reports on primitive postural reflex activity should be considered, and the orthopaedist should note how positional changes affect limb movement and posture. Particular attention should be paid to the effect of head position and the position of the body in space since many persons with multiple impairments are ruled by primitive postural reflexes (see Chapter 3).

Following an activity-oriented assessment, the orthopaedist may conduct a traditional joint-by-joint assessment—evaluating active and passive joint range of motion, muscle strength, and muscle tone. Specific tests used with persons with moderate to mild handicaps may have to be modified for individuals with multiple handicaps. For example, the Ely test used to detect spasticity of the rectus femoris muscle usually is performed with the patient in a prone position. It may be difficult for an individual with multiple impairments to tolerate a prone position. An attending therapist may assist an orthopaedist in modifying positioning and testing procedures.

Photographic Assessment of Resting Body Posture

Most persons with multiple handicaps assume static resting postures that are described in extensive, often confusing, medical and therapeutic jargon. An easily understood visual means of documenting abnormal resting body posture was needed to facilitate communication among professionals and caregivers who provide service and equipment for this population. Addressing this issue, a study, under the direction of Wayne County Intermediate School District (supported by ERIA Chapter 2 Mini-Grant 982), was undertaken in 1988 and 1989 (Fraser, Marchello, Hensinger, & Louis, 1989). This study explored the use of photographs to document abnormal resting body posture of severely multiply impaired students. Students were photographed on or near background devices to document sitting, standing, and hand/foot postures. Procedures were established for consistently accurate and reproducible picture taking. The photographs were evaluated by a team comprised of orthopaedists, physical and occupational therapists, teachers, equipment specialists, and parents. Team members agreed that the photographs that were taken provided easily understood visual methods of documenting abnormal body. Photographic documentation provides a means of recording postural abnormalities, tracking postural changes, assessing posture management, and communicating about an individual.

Sitting

Posture assessment chairs were designed for posterior (Figure 4.1), lateral (see Figure 8.1), and anterior (Figure 4.2) views of sitting posture with subjects receiving only minimal support. Such photographs allow physicians, therapists, and others concerned with seating to assess relatively unsupported seating postures and to compare and document postural management provided by appropriate seating systems (see Chapter 8).

Standing

A standing board grid (e.g., consisting of 1 inch squares) was designed to stabilize a subject's standing posture and to provide a background during picture taking. The subject's standing posture was photographed in a lateral view (Figure 4.3) to document anterior spinal curves (i.e., kyphosis) and posterior spinal curves (i.e., lordosis). In addition, anterior and posterior standing posture pictures were taken to show frontal asymmetries and sideways spinal curves (i.e., scoliosis), respectively.

Hand/Foot Postures

Measurement boards were designed to provide a background to picture commonly noted abnormal resting posture of the foot and hand. The board was placed on a camera stand to allow the photographer to position the camera in such a way that the focal point of the lens was fixed over the specified part of the board upon which the hand or foot rests. Valgus (i.e., outward angulation from the midline) (Figure 4.4) and varus (i.e., inward angulation from the midline) resting postures may be documented. Such pictures also serve as

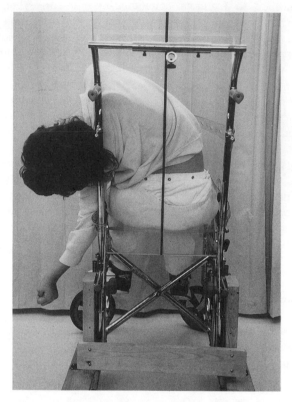

Figure 4.1. Posture Evaluation Chair designed for posterior "see through" view. This modified, fully reclining wheelchair frame features a clear plastic back to permit photographs of spinal and pelvic alignment. This photograph documents a severe collapsing sideways curve of the spine (i.e., scoliosis). Normally, the spine should be aligned with the black center line.

documentation of surgical corrections (Figure 4.5). Hand photographs record flexion (Figure 4.6) or extension and ulnar deviation (i.e., sideways position of the hand away from the thumb) (Figure 4.7) or radial deviation (i.e., sideways position of the hand towards the thumb) postures. Posture pictures offer a visual initial documentation that may be replicated at a later date to track progression of the condition and to evaluate surgical or therapeutic management.

Summary Due to Assessments

Physical management may be planned as a result of orthopaedic, therapeutic, and photographic assessment. Equipment, such as wheelchairs or orthoses may be prescribed. It may be appropriate for the orthopaedist to refer an individual to other specialists for additional assessment, to recommend

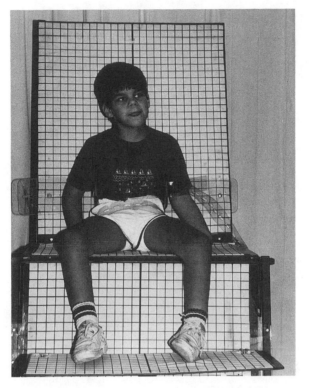

Figure 4.2. Posture Evaluation Chair designed for anterior view. This multi-adjustable chair prototype is covered with a foam cover grid (comprised of 1-inch squares). A clear chest strap secures this individual to the chair, but provides only minimal support. This photograph documents uncorrected resting/sitting posture. Clear plastic postural supports may be added to the head, thighs, and feet to simulate therapeutic wheelchair positioning (see Chapter 8).

orthopaedic examination, or to continue following the patient at a school-based or hospital clinic until such time as more specific orthopaedic examination is needed.

EXAMINATION

An orthopaedic examination is conducted in a hospital or doctor's office setting and usually includes diagnostic tests. Since scoliosis and hip dislocations are common in persons with multiple handicaps, it is recommended that the examination include roentgenographic studies of the spine and pelvis (at least yearly in the early years) to document current status and to serve as a base point for subsequent comparisons. Specific joint-by-joint examination often is repeated, with emphasis on the relationship and combinations of

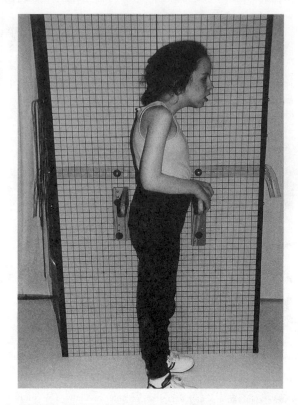

Figure 4.3.   Standing Board Grid. This standing board grid (comprised of 1-inch squares) is imprinted on a soft foam surface. Side supports assist in maintaining standing balance. This photograph documents the beginning of an abnormal backward curve of the upper spine (i.e., kyphosis) and a forward head.

deformities (e.g., kyphoscoliosis, dislocated hips) common in persons with multiple impairments.

It is recommended that the parent or guardian of a person with handicaps attend the orthopaedic examination. At this time, the orthopaedist should discuss the person's condition with parents or guardians and inform the family about the risks, benefits, and technicalities of proposed surgery or other orthopaedic treatment. Therapists may help by talking to the family before the examination and again afterwards to clarify details of the management program. However, therapists should avoid influencing the family's decision regarding surgical treatment (Fraser & Hensinger, 1983). That decision should remain strictly between the patient's family and the orthopaedist.

It is desirable that the results of the orthopaedic examination be shared with team members. If surgery is scheduled, for example, equipment requirements and the degree of therapeutic involvement may change postoperatively.

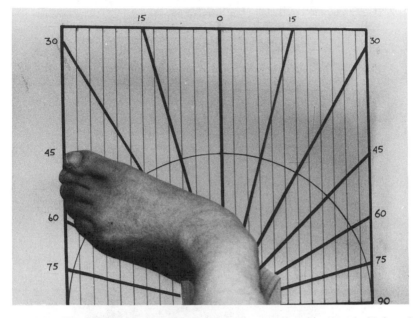

Figure 4.4. Foot Measurement Board. This foot measurement board is covered with foam for comfort. Angles are marked in 15-degree increments. The board includes a heel stop at the intersection of the 90- and 0-degree lines. The focal point is the center of the board, indicated by the intersection of a semicircle at the 0-degree line. This photograph documents a valgus (i.e., outward angulation of the foot) resting posture of about 45 degrees. Normally the second toe should rest on the 0-degree line.

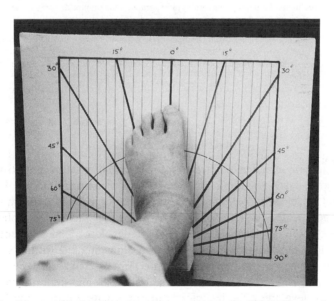

Figure 4.5. Photographic documentation of postsurgical results. This is the same foot pictured in Figure 4.4, six months postsurgical correction. After surgery, the foot rested in an almost normal position on the measurement board.

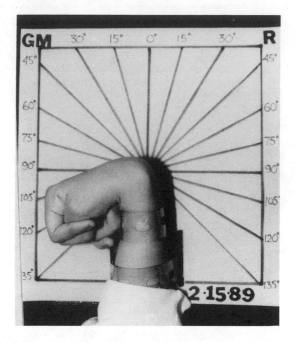

Figure 4.6. Hand Measurement Board documenting flexed wrist posture. Hand measurement boards are covered with foam for comfort. Angles are marked in 15-degree increments. An adjustable positioner stabilizes the forearm, allowing the wrist to be placed at the intersection of 0- and 90-degree lines, the focal point for the photograph. This picture documents a wrist flexion resting posture of about 100 degrees. Normally the index finger should rest on the 0-degree line.

Pending major purchases, such as a wheelchair, should be postponed until surgery is completed. Also, surgery should be planned around the availability of postoperative therapy.

GOAL PLANNING

Coordinate goal planning should be based upon observation and assessment, and, in some cases, examination results. Goal planning should include both long- and short-term goals and should reflect orthopaedic and therapeutic input. Appropriate long-term goals for a young person with multiple impairments may be to progress from one major developmental level to another (e.g., rolling to sitting) and to delay development of deformities. For an adolescent, an appropriate long-term goal may be to maintain the present level of function. Since regression is expected due to progression of pathology or deformities developing during growth spurts, maintenance of physical abilities actually constitutes progress for some persons with multiple handicaps.

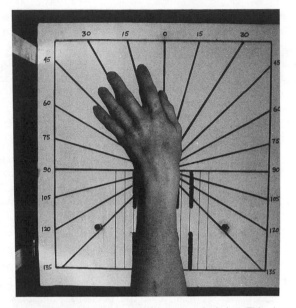

Figure 4.7. Hand Measurement Board documenting ulnar deviation. This picture documents a wrist ulnar deviated (i.e., angulation of the hand away from the thumb) resting posture of about 15 degrees. Normally the index finger should rest on the 0-degree line.

Short-term goals should be realistic. For example, preventing progression of a scoliosis and increasing trunk stability may be achievable through use of an orthosis (i.e., brace). Success may be measured by periodic X-rays. Therapeutic short-term goals may focus on functional activities gained from increased trunk stability provided by the orthosis. In this example, an appropriate short-term therapeutic goal may be to advance the child from sitting using the hands for support to sitting without hand support while wearing the orthosis. Behavior objectives are used by school-based therapists to measure the success or failure of short-term goals. For example, a therapist may measure increased trunk stability provided by the orthosis in terms of observable behavior. Has the child learned to sit without using his or her hands for support while wearing the orthosis? If so, for how long? Is sitting balance improving to the point where the child uses the hands for other activities while sitting? Combining orthopaedic and therapeutic short-term goals provides a functional and measurable approach to physical management.

PROGNOSIS

Caution is appropriate in predicting when an individual will accomplish specific motor skills such as walking. Maximum potential is difficult to determine and requires ongoing assessment. And, excessive optimism or pessimism can be disconcerting to parents and caregivers. It is important that professionals provide factual information about the nature of severe handicaps and help parents and caregivers realize that deformities may occur despite ongoing therapeutic management. Parent/caregiver attention should focus on the use of equipment and on management techniques that allow an individual to function to the utmost of his or her present ability and thereby to experience an improved quality of life.

HOSPITALIZATION

Persons with multiple handicaps pose many special concerns for acute care hospital staff, with communication, feeding, and personal care being the areas of greatest difficulty. Personnel may not be trained in the time-consuming and specialized feeding techniques required for persons with multiple handicaps (see Chapter 15). Also, acute care hospitals may not have appropriate adapted equipment or communication aids on hand. Close cooperation between the hospital staff and those familiar with the person's routine is essential. A parent or caregiver should accompany the person to the hospital and discuss details of the person's care with the nursing staff. Specialized equipment needed by the individual should be taken to the hospital and its use explained to attending staff at the time of admission. Also, a written summary from the school nurse and therapists can help the hospital's staff to provide individualized patient care.

Discharge planning should be completed before hospital admission. Therapeutic and nursing follow-up should be available so that potential problems can be identified early and preventive or corrective measures taken. With the length of hospital time required for surgical procedures being reduced continually, school-age children are returning to school and their normal routines quickly. School-based therapists and nurses, therefore, become involved with postsurgical monitoring. Surgery should be timed so that therapy will be available for the individual postoperatively. All those concerned with the patient should be thoroughly familiar with the goals and procedures necessary for recovery and rehabilitation.

SURGICAL AND POSTSURGICAL CONSIDERATIONS

Orthopaedic Surgery

Procedures that require shorter periods of immobilization, that need less time in casts or shorter casts, and that employ internal fixation to avoid casts are the techniques of choice with persons with multiple handicaps. Ideally, soft tissue surgery should be done when a deformity is beginning to develop. This can avoid need for extensive bony surgery that requires longer time under anesthesia and extended hospital and cast time. It also preserves mobility and avoids the pain that can accompany fixed deformities.

Persons with multiple handicaps have difficulty tolerating casts over weight-bearing joints, such as the hips or knees, because of severe sensory deficits and lack of soft tissue bulk. Casts are difficult for caregivers to handle and present a hygiene problem for incontinent persons. Internal fixation procedures, such as the Luque instrumentation in spinal fixation (see Chapter 5), may avoid the use of prolonged postoperative casting. Also, postoperative care may include therapeutic positioning and night splinting in order to avoid casting. If casting is necessary, it should be limited to the joint or joints directly related to the surgery. Persons with multiple handicaps are especially prone to osteoporosis and joint stiffness as a result of prolonged immobilization.

There is a scarcity of studies concerning orthopaedic surgical procedures performed on persons with severe multiple handicaps as a group. For this reason, a retrospective study of 34 surgical procedures performed during a 12-year period was conducted on a select population of students with severe multiple handicaps who attended Riley School in Wayne County Intermediate School District (Louis, Hensinger, Fraser, Phelps, & Jacques, 1989). The purposes of this study were to identify the surgical procedure performed and to have school staff evaluate its results. Twenty-five lower extremity procedures were performed that included nine soft tissue releases about the hip (i.e., seven hip adductor tenotomies and obturator neurectomy) and two posterior muscle releases; six soft tissue procedures about the knee (i.e., release of knee flexion contractures and hamstrings); seven soft tissue procedures about the foot and ankle (i.e., heel cord lengthenings); and three bony foot surgeries. Five soft tissue releases in combination with bony surgery (wrist fusions) were performed on the wrist and hand. (Specific surgical procedures including those mentioned here are discussed in Section II.) The objectives of surgery were improvement in sitting posture, care, and comfort. Independent evaluation of active function, passive function, cosmetic, self-esteem, limb posture, ease of dressing, and hygiene were assessed by school staff. Significant improvement generally was noted in these areas and no student was made worse. It was concluded that selected surgical procedures, performed upon persons who are severely multiply handicapped, have a definite place in their physical management.

Chapters 5, 6, and 7 focus on orthopaedic treatment of specific joint deformities of the spine, lower extremities, and upper extremities that commonly occur among persons with multiple handicaps. Deformities and their development and relationships to various joints are discussed, and prevention, control/support, and surgical techniques appropriate to the unique needs of persons with multiple handicaps are described.

Neurosurgical Considerations

Until the late 1980s, persons with severe multiple handicaps were considered to be mainly patients of the realm of orthopaedists, pediatricians, neurologists, physiatirists, and therapists. The addition of a neurosurgical procedure—selective posterior rhizotomy—to treatment alternatives has caught the attention of parents, therapists, and physicians. Emphasis now is placed on the contributions of neurosurgeons (Oppenheim, Beauchamp, Dias, Sussman, & Gage, 1987). Selective posterior rhizotomy involves dividing certain posterior (i.e., sensory) rootlets of spinal nerves. The nerve rootlets to be divided are identified by intraoperative nerve stimulation and peripheral EMG recordings (Peacock & Ariens, 1982). The purpose of the selective posterior rhizotomy is to reduce spasticity. Patient selection involves the input of neurosurgeons, orthopaedics, therapists, and other specialists in pediatrics and is vital to the success of the surgery. Although selective posterior rhizotomy may improve function and mobility in children with mild to moderate cerebral palsy, the objectives of this procedure for persons with severe multiple handicaps are to facilitate positioning and reduce the deforming influence of spasticity. Selective posterior rhizotomy was introduced to the United States in 1986 and now is performed at several major medical centers throughout the United States (Staudt & Peacock, 1989). Additional references regarding selective posterior rhizotomy are listed in Appendix E for readers who wish more information on the subject.

CLOSING THOUGHTS

Orthopaedic/therapeutic coordination has proven effective in facilitating understanding and management of the complex abnormalities that are exhibited by persons with multiple impairments. Steps leading to an individual management plan include observation, assessment, and examination. Observation identifies potential or existing orthopaedic abnormalities and permits a subjective overall image of the person's motoric and social functioning level. Team assessment establishes objective baseline data needed for equipment prescription and examination. Examination includes diagnostic testing with specific attention directed to joints that generally are at risk of developing deformities or that have existing deformities. Following examination, approaches to treatment, hospitalization, and surgery must be tailored to meet the unique needs exhibited by persons with multiple handicaps.

REFERENCES

Bleck, E.E. (1987). *Orthopaedic management of cerebral palsy*. Philadelphia: J.B. Lippincott.

Cassidy-Conway, M., & Zawacki, R.M. (1983). Physical therapy. In G.H.

Thompson, I.L. Rubin, & R.M. Bilenker (Eds.), *Comprehensive management of cerebral palsy* (pp. 193–204). New York: Grune & Stratton.

Fraser, B.A., Galka, G., & Hensinger, R.N. (1980). *Gross motor management of multiply impaired students: Vol. I. Evaluation guide.* Austin, TX: PRO-ED.

Fraser, B.A., & Hensinger, R.N. (1983). *Managing physical handicaps: A practical guide for parents, care providers, and educators.* Baltimore: Paul H. Brookes Publishing Co.

Fraser, B.A., Marchello, J.L., Hensinger, R.N., & Louis, D.S. (1989). Photographic documentation of abnormal body posture. *Developmental Medicine & Child Neurology, 31*(5), 59. 43rd Annual Meeting of the American Academy of Cerebral Palsy and Developmental Medicine, San Francisco.

Goldberg, K. (1975). The high risk infant. *Physical Therapy, 55,* 1092–1096.

Lawlor, M.C., & Zielinski, A. (1983). Occupational therapy. In G.H. Thompson, I.L. Rubin, & R.M. Bilenker (Eds.), *Comprehensive management of cerebral palsy* (pp. 181–191). New York: Grune & Stratton.

Louis, D.S., Hensinger, R.N., Fraser, B.A., Phelps, J.A., & Jacques, K. (1989). Surgical management of the severely multiply handicapped individual. *Journal of Pediatric Orthopaedics, 9,* 15–18.

Oppenheim, W.L., Beauchamp, R.D., Dias, L., Sussman, M.D., & Gage, J.R. (1987). *Selective posterior rhizotomy for cerebral palsy.* Committee on Rhizotomy, Pediatric Orthopedic Society of North America, Los Angeles.

Peacock, W.J., & Ariens, L.J. (1982). Selective posterior rhizotomy for the relief of spasticity in cerebral palsy. *South African Medical Journal, 62,* 119–124.

Satterfield, J. (1981). *How the physical therapist can help in the educational environment.* White Hall: Pediatric Special Interest Group of Maryland.

Staudt, L.A., & Peacock, W.J. (1989, Spring). Selective posterior rhizotomy for treatment of spastic cerebral palsy. *Pediatric Physical Therapy, 1*(1), 3–9.

SECTION

II

Management
through Orthopaedics

Chapter
5

Orthopaedic Examination
and Treatment
of Spinal Curvatures

This chapter describes orthopaedic evaluation and examination techniques and treatment recommendations for those spinal curvatures common among persons with multiple handicaps. Curvatures include scoliosis (i.e., lateral curvature), hyperlordosis (i.e., abnormal anterior curvature in the lower portion of the spine), and hyperkyphosis (i.e., abnormal posterior curvature in the upper chest, thoracic, and dorsal portion of the spine). A discussion of examination techniques emphasizes variations to usual testing methods to adapt them for most persons with multiple handicaps. Prevention, control/support, and surgical correction in spinal curvatures are described, with the emphasis on surgical considerations.

Spinal curvatures are named for the direction of the curve's convexity or apex (e.g., right or left; front—lordosis; back—kyphosis) and area(s) of spinal involvement (e.g., chest or thoracic, lumbar). Curvatures may be functional (i.e., flexible) or structural (i.e., fixed, with permanent changes in joints, vertebrae, and ligaments). Abnormal spinal curvatures may appear in combination (e.g., scoliosis with hyperkyphosis and/or hyperlordosis) and are often accompanied by deformities of the pelvis and hips.

SCOLIOSIS

Scoliosis is an appreciable lateral deviation in the normally straight vertical line of the spine. The scoliotic spine also has some rotation that causes a portion of the spine to turn, pulling the rib cage along with it and creating a rib hump.

57

All persons with multiple handicaps should be considered at risk of developing scoliosis serious enough to require surgery. Incidence rates as high as 64% have been reported in studies that reviewed persons with severe disabilities who were institutionalized (Bonnett et al., 1975; Mital, Beklin, & Sullivan, 1976). A 1972 study by Samilson, Tsov, Aamoth, and Green demonstrated that the incidence of scoliosis is considerably greater in bed-care or quadriplegic patients (39%), less common in those able to sit (24%), and least common in ambulatory or hemiplegic and diplegic persons (7%). (It may be assumed that bed-care quadriplegic patients were the most severely handicapped, those capable of sitting had moderate involvement, and ambulatory persons had mild pathology.)

This research was conducted prior to the advent of specialized seating systems that allow many formerly bed-bound patients to sit in a supported manner at least a portion of the day. Regardless, studies continue to substantiate that the frequency of scoliosis is directly related to the severity of neurological involvement (Lonstein, 1981; Lonstein & Akbarnia, 1981; Samilson, 1981).

Similarly, persons with total body involvement combined with spasticity and athetosis have a high incidence of spinal deformity and severe curves (Malloy & Kuhlmann, 1981; Samilson & Richard, 1973). The more severely involved persons experience the worst curves. However, even persons with mild hemiplegia should be monitored for scoliosis during the growth years.

Much like persons with neuromuscular diseases such as polio, many persons with multiple handicaps tend to develop a collapsing long C-shaped curve (Fraser, Galka, & Hensinger, 1980) (Figure 5.1). S-shaped curves (Figure 5.2) and thoracolumbar or lumbar curves (Figure 5.3) are more typical of persons with mild to moderate cerebral palsy (Nash, 1983). The C-shaped curve is common with hypotonia and develops earlier than S-shaped curves. In the C-shaped curve, the pelvis and sacrum often form a part of the curve. Some persons with multiple handicaps do develop S curves with the bottom part similar to C curves in the sense that the pelvis and lower lumbar spine form the lower part of the S.

A C-shaped scoliosis often is associated with hyperkyphosis and posterior pelvic tilt (Figure 5.4). In fact, a sitting kyphotic posture may provide the first clue to a developing C scoliosis. Long, collapsing C curvatures, if untreated, ultimately lead to the most severe deformities that may prevent upright posture (Samilson & Bechard, 1973).

Regardless of shape, scoliosis is functional at first and can be corrected passively by manipulation and positioning. Toward the end of growth and maturation, the deformity often becomes fixed and rigid. Scoliosis in persons with mild to moderate cerebral palsy typically progresses during the growth years and ceases further development with skeletal maturation. With persons with multiple handicaps, however, skeletal maturation and growth may continue well into the 20s (Akbarnia, 1984; Horstmann, 1985; Horstmann &

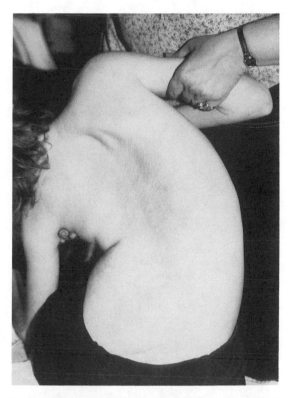

Figure 5.1. C-shaped scoliosis. Many persons with multiple handicaps tend to collapse into a long C-shaped scoliosis. Note that scoliotic spine rotation has caused a rib hump to appear on the right.

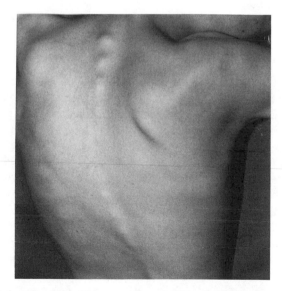

Figure 5.2. S-shaped scoliosis. This person has a double or S-shaped curve.

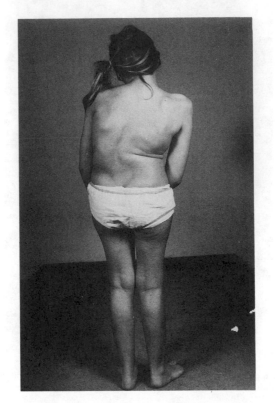

Figure 5.3. Thoracolumbar scoliosis. This S-shaped curve is typical of persons with mild to moderate cerebral palsy.

Boyer, 1984). Also, persons with severe scoliosis may experience progression of the deformity after skeletal maturation, but not as rapidly as during the growth years. Individuals with multiple handicaps should be followed clinically and radiographically for scoliosis throughout their lives. However, examinations and radiographs need not be as frequent as with a growing child.

Often it is assumed that scoliosis is painless. This is not entirely true. Pain increases as the deformity worsens (Nash, 1983). Bonnet, Brown, and Grow (1976) found that many patients with scoliosis have back pain. However, many persons with multiple handicaps have difficulty communicating pain or may not display typical signs of pain. Those who work with the person on a daily basis are best able to interpret an individual's pain signals.

Progression of a curvature presents serious problems for persons with multiple handicaps beyond the pain that may be present. Severe curvatures can compromise cardiopulmonary function and lead to frequent pulmonary infections and a shortened life span. Severe scoliosis usually involves asym-

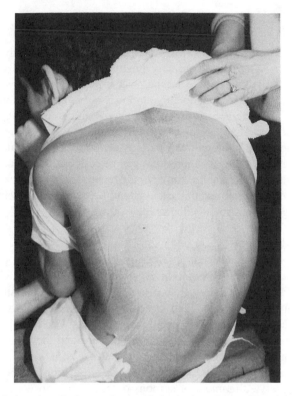

Figure 5.4. C-shaped scoliosis associated with kyphosis and posterior pelvic tilt. A sitting kyphotic posture, such as this, may be the first clue to a developing C-shaped scoliosis.

metrical hip alignment and pelvic obliquity. The spinopelvic deformity may be associated with windswept hip deformity or bilaterally tight hip adductors. Either may pose significant difficulties for caregivers in providing adequate perineal hygiene.

Pelvic obliquity also causes seated persons to bear weight only on one ischial tuberosity or greater trochanter. Most persons with multiple handicaps are not capable of independent weight shifts (i.e., transfers). As a result, they are susceptible to pressure ulcers.

Scoliosis Examination Considerations

All who work with persons with multiple handicaps should be alert to the following signs of scoliosis:

Shoulders appear uneven.
One scapula appears more prominent.

Waist on one side appears more prominent.
Pelvis and hip appear higher on one side.

Detection of a developing scoliosis should be brought promptly to a physician's attention. Therapists routinely monitor scoliotic development. Some therapists find it helpful to take annual posture picture of persons with scoliosis. While such photographic documentation is not as accurate a measurement of a curve as a radiograph, it provides a simple and noninvasive method for recording visible change or lack of change in spinal posture. The person with handicaps should be photographed in anterior, posterior, and lateral poses in standard sitting/standing positions that can be replicated at later dates. Any substantial changes in spinal posture should be brought to a physician's attention and a more detailed examination should be conducted, including a forward bending test and roentgenographic evaluation.

Forward Bending Test

The forward bending test that is used to identify curvature in persons with idiopathic scoliosis must be modified for use with persons with multiple handicaps. This test requires that a person stand independently and bend forward with arms extended and hands approximated while the examiner visually inspects the spine. However, many persons with multiple handicaps are not capable of maintaining a standing posture and lack the balance and understanding to bend upon command. In the case of a young individual, it may be necessary to support the child in a sitting position and bend the trunk forward to observe alignment of spinous processes in a forward flexed position. For older persons, it may be necessary to observe spinal flexibility with the person bending forward while seated in a chair.

Radiographic Measurement

Radiographic studies of the spine should include anterior, posterior, and lateral views to provide initial documentation of the degree of curvature and its pattern. Ideally, radiograph rays are taken with the person in a standing position. However, most persons with multiple impairments cannot assume and maintain a standing position. A seated position is often used for this population. Recumbent positions should be avoided if possible. In such a position, the spine tends to relax and roll, and a curve appears to be less severe than it would in a weight-bearing upright posture. It is important that a person be placed in a position that can be duplicated on subsequent testing occasions to obtain accurate comparative radiographs.

Radiographs are evaluated using the Cobb method, which has largely replaced the older Ferguson method (Bradford & Hensinger, 1985). The last vertebrae above and below the curvature are identified. Two lines, perpendicular to those vertebrae, are drawn on the X-ray, usually through the distal end plate of the vertebrae (although the facets or pedicles may be used). These lines are referred to as the end-plate lines. Next, a line is drawn at a right angle to each of the end-plate lines. The vertical angle formed where these lines intersect is the degree of scoliosis curvature (Figure 5.5). A mild curve measures approximately 20 degrees to 40 degrees (Figure 5.6a), a moderate curve 40 degrees to 60 degrees, and a severe curve 60 degrees and above (Figure 5.6b).

Scoliosis/Hip Abnormality Relationships

The majority of persons who are multiply handicapped with scoliosis also have soft tissue contractures around the hip and pelvis, with subluxation and dislocation occurring in 59% (Samilson & Bechard, 1973). A 1988 study by

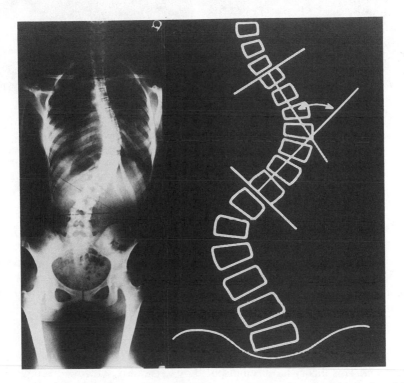

Figure 5.5. Cobb method of curve measurement. The radiograph on the left reveals a right thoracic, left lumbar S-shaped scoliosis. The illustration on the right shows the Cobb method of measuring the thoracic position of the curve. The last vertebrae above and below the curvature are identified. Two lines (i.e., end-plate lines) are drawn perpendicularly through the ends of the vertebrae. Next, a line is drawn at right angles to each of the end-plate lines. The vertical angle formed where these lines intersect is indicated by the arrows. This angle indicates the degree of scoliosis curvature.

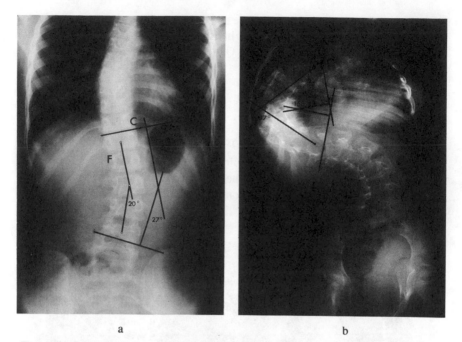

a   b

Figure 5.6. a) Mild lumbar curve. A 27-degree lumbar scoliosis is indicated by the letter C representing the Cobb method of measurement on this radiograph. The F designates the Ferguson technique of curve measurement that is not widely used, but may be helpful in measuring patients with congenital curves with multiple anomalies. b) Severe thoracic curve. This radiograph shows a severe thoracic scoliosis of 158 degrees.

Stegbauer and Lyne was conducted on 287 patients with severe cerebral palsy to determine the interrelationship of hip dislocation, pelvic obliquity and scoliosis. Results indicated that 85 had Cobb angles of more than 15 degrees (35%) and were divided into 23 persons with thoracic curves, 47 persons with thoraco-lumbar curves, 8 persons with double-major curves, and 7 persons with lumbar curves. Nineteen persons had bilaterally dislocated hips (23%), 33 had one hip dislocated (39%) and 33 had adequately located hips (39%).

It is commonly assumed that scoliosis leads to pelvic obliquity (i.e., unbalanced pelvis), which places the hip in jeopardy of subluxation or dislocation. This theory has been disputed by Cristofaro, Koffman, Woodward, and Baxter (1977), Letts, Turenka, and Klasser (1980), and Lonstein and Beck (1986). Letts et al. (1980) found that 62% of patients in their study first experienced hip subluxation or dislocation. In the patients who did develop scoliosis first, the presence of the primitive Galant reflex was a constant finding. Therefore, routine testing for potential scoliosis in persons with multiple handicaps should include testing for the Galant reflex (see Chapter 3) and examination for tight hip adductors (see Chapter 6).

Treatment Consideration

As discussed in Chapter 4, treatment of scoliosis in persons with multiple handicaps requires a continuum of interventions corresponding to expected deformity development.

Prevention

With a young child, physical therapy encourages normal development and establishes muscle balance to prevent, or at least delay, changes in soft tissue and joints. Positioning that emphasizes symmetrical body alignment is especially helpful in maintaining gains made with therapy (see Chapter 13). With a young child, positioning usually is accomplished by use of a wheelchair equipped with postural control devices such as scoliosis pads and hip abductors (see Chapter 8).

Early management of spinal curvatures stresses positioning to control the pelvis and lower extremities. Lower extremities should be kept balanced either through positioning (see Chapters 8 and 13) or surgery to maintain normal femoral head/acetabular relationships (see Chapter 6).

The authors have found the use of soft canvas-type corsets to be helpful in delaying spinal deformity in persons with flexible curves of less than 20 degrees (Fraser & Hensinger, 1983) (Figure 5.7). In a few cases, corsets have even prevented functional curvatures from becoming structural. Corsets are prescribed for children with trunk hypotonia, for those who show a positive asymmetrical Galant reflex, and for those who display asymmetrical supine, prone, or sitting postures. The corset is worn over the child's undershirt and under a blouse or shirt. While fairly soft, it does provide effective support. Skin irritations are rare and, if properly applied, the corset does not restrict respiration. In the authors' experience, use of corsets can help to delay the onset of structural scoliosis from age 7, when it might otherwise be anticipated, until the early teen years. However, this is difficult to document.

Control/Support

Once a structural curve develops, control is necessary and is provided through orthotic management. Generally, a total contact plastic thoraco-lumbo-sacral orthosis (TLSO) (see Chapter 9) is used to arrest progression of mild to moderate curvatures ranging from 20 degrees to 45 degrees (Figure 5.8). The goal of positioning via an orthosis must be to balance the pelvis in a neutral position, align the trunk, and improve spinal posture. While an orthosis should help to improve posture and retard progression, it does not correct a structural deformity (Figure 5.9).

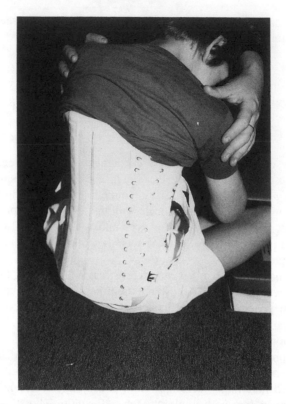

Figure 5.7. Canvas-type corset. This 5-year-old boy has a functional scoliosis. Corsets such as the one shown here may be prescribed for children with trunk hypotonia, for those who show a positive asymmetrical Galant reflex, and for those who display asymmetrical supine, prone, and sitting postures.

The cervico-thoraco-lumbo-spinal orthosis (CTLSO) or Milwaukee-type brace is not appropriate for use with persons with multiple handicaps. It is recommended only for ambulatory patients with mild spasticity. A TLSO, however, often is appropriate for persons with multiple handicaps with thoracolumbar, lumbar, and most collapsing curves (Bunnell & MacEwen, 1977). The TLSO, if properly fitted, is a comfortable brace that can be used in a variety of situations and for long periods of time.

The TLSO is also available as a wheelchair insert. Usually made of rigid plastic, it becomes a permanent part of the wheelchair. A major disadvantage of a TLSO wheelchair insert is that the person is unsupported when not in the chair. Also, TLSO wheelchair inserts limit sitting to that one chair or chair complex, when a variety of alternative sitting positions may be desirable. Some persons with multiple handicaps may even be unable to tolerate the rigidity of this support device.

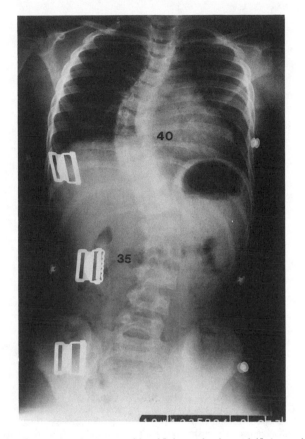

Figure 5.8. Radiograph ray of a person with a 35-degree lumbar and 40-degree thoracic curve wearing a TLSO.

In curves beyond 45 degrees to 50 degrees, bracing is no longer effective and surgical correction should be considered. For severe curves in persons for whom surgery is contraindicated, supportive techniques are necessary, such as comfortable seating in the form of foam inserts or bed-type wheelchairs.

Surgery

Improved surgical techniques and anesthesia advances developed during the last two decades give surgeons the technical ability to improve and stabilize spinal deformities in even more severely involved persons with cerebral palsy (Bonnett et al., 1976). Surgery is the only method of permanently improving a scoliosis and is reserved for moderate-to-severe curves (e.g., 50 degrees or greater). The best results from spinal surgery are achieved in those whose scoliosis is still in a moderate range and flexible. Spinal surgery is physically

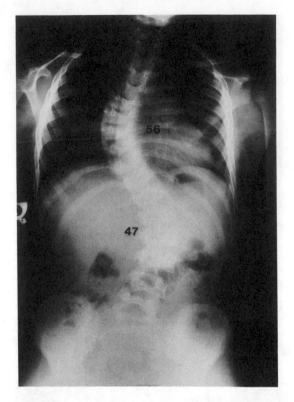

Figure 5.9. TLSO improves posture. This is a radiograph of the same person pictured in Figure 5.8 without a TLSO. Note that the TLSO helps improve posture by supporting the spine in an as straight as possible alignment. Compare the curve measurements between the two radiographs.

and emotionally demanding for persons with normal intellect. For those with multiple handicaps—many of whom are unable to cooperate with pre- and postoperative care—the decision for surgery is more difficult.

   Benefits, Potential Problems, and Complications   The pros and cons of surgery need to be discussed with parents, caregivers, therapists, and educators. Positive benefits should be weighed against potential problems of the procedure and postoperative care requirements. Similarly, the problems of an untreated scoliosis, risk of progression, and later complications should be considered.

   For persons with multiple handicaps, the decision for surgery is based primarily on anticipated functional gain, the presence of pain, and the difficulty of providing care. Added benefits of surgery are freedom from bracing (especially important in lessening care requirements), avoiding pressure ulcers, and improved appearance. While prevention of cardiopulmonary dysfunction is a legitimate indication for surgery, spinal surgery does not reverse existing cardiopulmonary deficits to any great extent (Mital et al., 1976). Self-abusive behavior, chronic respiratory disease, and decreased pulmonary function may be contraindications to surgery.

Complications that arise from spinal surgery performed on patients with multiple handicaps include neurological injury (e.g., paraplegia), instrument failure, pseudoarthrosis (e.g., false joint), infection, and death. Pressure ulcerations previously occurred in up to 30% of patients, usually being related to postoperative cast immobilization. Over time, however, use of well-padded casts have come to minimize this risk. More recent surgical advances (discussed later in the chapter) have greatly reduced, and in many cases, largely eliminated, the need for post operative casts.

Instrument failure and loss of bone fixation have been reported in as high as 25% of patients, due to such factors as asymmetrical muscle forces, rigidity, severe deformity, and poor bone stock. This failure rate has been improved by better fixation techniques, especially those involving intersegmental systems.

A pseudoarthrosis rate of 15%–25% can be anticipated (Nash, 1983). However, not all pseudoarthroses need to be fixed. Only those that lead to increased angulation or pain will require a second procedure. Infection occurs in about 5% of patients. Lonstein and Akbarnia (1981) report a death rate of 3%.

Preoperative Care Preoperative traction was popular for many years (Hensinger & MacEwen, 1974). Immobilization in casts also was used as a means for obtaining correction of the spine prior to surgery. Traction is difficult for persons with multiple handicaps to tolerate due to the long periods of bed rest and immobilization that are required. These increase the risk of aspiration pneumonia, produce pain and discomfort, and compromise cardiopulmonary and gastrointestinal function.

Present approaches to scoliosis management reduce the need for traction. Curves are not allowed to progress to a severe degree; most surgery is done before a severe 80-degree to 90-degree curve develops. Surgery also is done at an earlier age. When children are younger, the spine is also more supple, thus, fewer curves require traction.

Surgical Techniques and Instrumentation Spinal fusions have been used for 60 years. In the 1920s, Dr. Russell Hibbs of New York pioneered surgery for scoliosis, particularly in polio patients. However, such surgery was a considerable risk because of less reliable anesthesia and inability to replace blood loss. Surgical techniques for spine surgery really blossomed after World War II as anesthesia for long procedures became more predictable and transfusion of blood and blood products became more available.

Harrington Rod After World War II, Dr. Paul R. Harrington took a leadership role in the development of spine implants. He developed, in consort with the Texas Rehabilitation Institute, a method of spinal fixation that not only held the spine immobilized internally, but also allowed surgeons to achieve internal correction for the first time. (Previously, surgeons had to rely on external devices such as casts and/or traction to maintain the correction during the healing phase.) Dr. Harrington's device incorporated a notched rod and two hooks that could be ratcheted along the rod. The hooks were inserted at two sites: one in the facet (i.e., vertebral joint) above the curvature and one beneath the lamina of the vertebrae below the curvature. The spine was elongated using action much like that of an auto bumper jack (Figure 5.10).

The Harrington rod has been used in combination with spinal fusion and bone-grafting techniques for many years. These techniques produce a fusion of the spinal segments, thereby stabilizing the deformity. The idea of fusing the spine via bone grafts often gets overlooked and/or neglected in discussion of equipment and instrumentation used to straighten and stabilize the spine while fusion is occurring. The primary purpose of surgery is to achieve a fusion of the spine. The implant corrects and stabilizes the spine during the healing phase while this fusion is occurring.

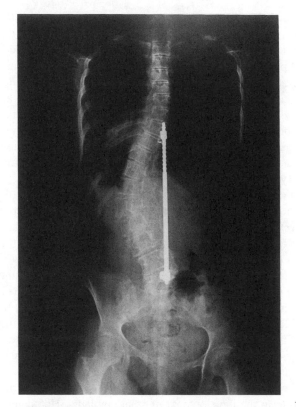

Figure 5.10.   Harrington rod implant. The Harrington rod is secured to two fixation sites, one above and one below the curve. It works on the same principle as an auto bumper jack. Surgeons use a rachet-type mechanism to elongate the spine into an improved alignment.

Dr. Harrington's invention was an excellent advance in spinal surgery since it permitted surgeons to both correct and stabilize the spine internally. However, it depends on only two fixation sites, one above and one below the curve. Initially, Dr. Harrington did not use any form of external support after insertion of his rod. However, he quickly realized that this was not sufficient. Due to increased demands, stress, and two fixation points, the bone could fracture or the equipment could loosen. Consequently, it was necessary to protect the spine externally with a cast. This procedure was standard for many years.

Luque Instrumentation In 1977, Dr. Eduardo Luque of Mexico City, in search of a better way to control the collapsing curves in young polio patients, developed a technique using multiple fixation points (i.e., intersegmental instrumentation) (Figures 5.11a, 5.11b, 5.11c) (Luque & Cardoso, 1977). This method employs a wire that is passed beneath the lamina of each vertebra and is secured to a rod. Thus, points of fixation are spread over the entire expanse of the curvature, resulting in a much more stable construct that does not need to be as rigidly protected (Luque, 1982).

For persons with multiple handicaps, the Luque procedure has been a significant improvement. Surgeons now have an internal construct that is strong enough to require very little and, in many cases, no postoperative immobilization. While casts are rarely required postoperatively, some surgeons do elect to control the spine after surgery for a few months by use of a simple TLSO. This may be required in cases where extreme spasticity or athetosis puts high demands on the fixation sites. A TLSO also may be needed to control the pelvis when it is part of the curve. As surgeons become more experienced with the Luque procedure, the use of postoperative immobilization will likely be reduced even further or perhaps eliminated.

Combinations and Variations of Harrington and Luque Procedures Today, many spine surgeons use variations or combinations of the Harrington and Luque procedures. For example, during surgery on a long C curve, the Harrington instrumentation may be used to stretch out the spine in conjunction with a Luque rod using intersegmental wiring attached to the spine. This uses both principles (i.e., distraction, multiple fixation points) to correct the spine by: 1) distracting the top and bottom of the curve, 2) providing horizontal corrective forces that pull the spine to the rods, and 3) spreading the force loads over many sites so that if one or two sites fails, a stable construct remains.

Surgical Procedure The patient is anesthetized using a general anesthetic technique with an endotracheal tube. The patient is then turned onto a frame that allows the abdomen to be free in order to decrease venous pressure and to position the spine as straight as possible. This helps to decrease the force needed to achieve correction. The surgical incision is straight and the posterior elements (e.g., lamina, facet joints) of the vertebrae are exposed

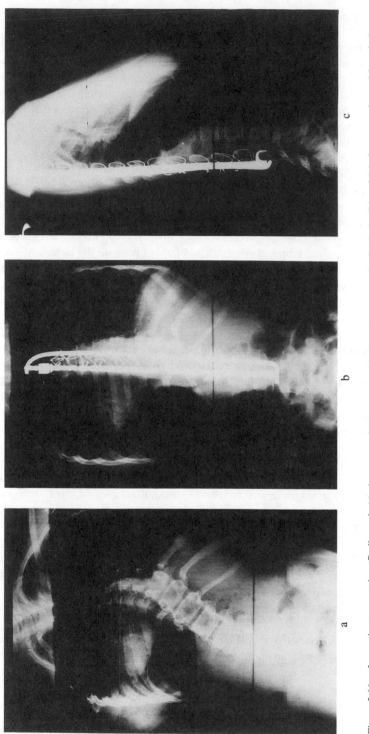

Figure 5.11. Luque instrumentation. Radiograph (a) shows a moderate-to-severe S-shaped curvature. Radiographs (b) and (c) show posterior and lateral views, respectively, of the correction of the curvature shown in (a), achieved using a Luque instrumentation.

over the entire length to be fused. The instrumentation is inserted. The facet joints are excised to promote fusion, and bone graft is added. Usually, the patient's own bone from the back of the pelvis is used for graft material. Small children may require supplemental bone from the bone bank. Surgery using the Harrington procedure usually requires 4–5 hours including anesthetic time of about 1 1/2 hours, with blood loss averaging 800 cc.–1200 cc. The Luque procedure and other segmental techniques usually add another hour to operating time, and additional blood loss.

There is extensive monitoring during the operation. In addition to the routine observation of all cardiopulmonary functions (e.g., heart rate, blood pressure, level of oxygen and carbon dioxide), spinal cord function is closely watched to avoid potential complications of nerve injury or paraplegia.

Anterior Approaches   Anterior approaches have limited applications as the surgeon cannot expose as many vertebrae from the front as from the back. Thus, this type of surgery is directed to the apex (worst part) of a curve. Anterior approaches are used with patients who have severe and contracted curvatures where the intent is to achieve a more extensive release than is possible posteriorly, and therapy to improve correction. The anterior procedure is done at a separate time, usually a week or 10 days prior to the posterior surgery. An anterolateral incision is made that permits a retroperitoneal approach to the vertebral bodies. If the curve is in the chest, the approach is through the chest cavity and often involves the diaphragm. The vertebral bodies are exposed and the vertebral discs excised along with the contracted soft tissue. Bone graft is usually added as well.

Some surgeons do use anterior instrumentation, such as the Dwyer or the Zielke, to achieve correction—especially with short curvatures and few spinal segments involved. However, surgeons generally do not depend on anterior instrumentation alone with persons who are severely involved because of their asymmetrical muscle forces, pelvic obliquity, rigidity, severe deformity, and poor bone stock. Anterior instrumentation is especially helpful for children who have defective bone posteriorly and may need anterior support over the involved area of the spine. This is more likely to involve persons with myelodysplasia or those who have had a surgical removal of the posterior structures than those with cerebral palsy.

Surgery for Scoliosis with Pelvic Obliquity   Many persons with multiple handicaps have scoliosis in which the pelvis and sacrum are integral portions of the curve (Figure 5.12). In these cases, it is necessary to relieve pelvic obliquity and to balance the trunk over the pelvis (Figure 5.13). A variety of instrumentations and techniques may be used, such as the Harrington instrumentation with sacral fixation or the Luque with the Galveston technique. The Galveston technique was popularized by Dr. Ben Allen and Dr. Ron Ferguson. It uses the Luque rod instrumentation that is contoured appropriately and inserted into the pelvis. Similarly, the Harrington instru-

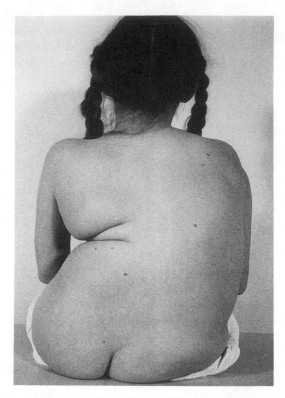

Figure 5.12.   C-shaped curve with pelvic obliquity. This scoliosis includes the pelvis and sacrum as an integral position of the curve. Note that the person is bearing weight mostly on the right buttock.

mentation has a variety of hooks and bars that fit on the sacrum. However, balancing a pelvic obliquity or controlling the pelvis continues to pose a significant surgical problem. Sometimes casts have to be employed postoperatively to control the pelvis and trunk until the spine is stabilized by the fusion. Presently, investigation is being proposed to develop techniques that will improve correction and control the pelvis and sacrum.

ABNORMAL LORDOSIS AND KYPHOSIS

Hyperlordosis and hyperkyphosis (often referred to simply as lordosis and kyphosis) are commonly found in persons with multiple handicaps. Although they compromise body posture and function, these curves are less of a problem to persons with handicaps and their caregivers than scoliosis.

Hyperlordosis is associated with an anterior pelvic tilt that usually involves hip flexion contractures and abdominal muscle weakness (i.e., low

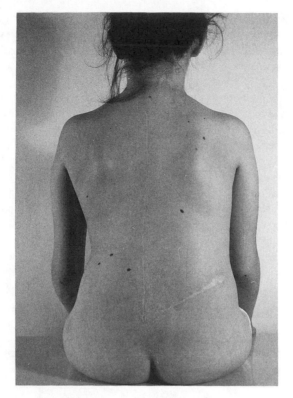

Figure 5.13.   Postoperative correction. This is the same person pictured in Figure 5.12. Spinal fusion straightened the spine, relieved pelvic obliquity, and balanced the trunk over the pelvis. Note that the scar, running the length of the spine, is barely noticeable.

muscle tone). With time, the extensor muscles of the low back also become contracted. Such contractures make neutral positioning of the pelvis difficult. In standing, a person with hyperlordosis usually compensates by flexing the hips, knees, and ankles (e.g., jump position) to maintain standing balance. In sitting, that individual may strive to maintain balance by hyperextending the neck and retracting the shoulder girdle.

Hyperkyphosis is an accentuation of the normal convexity of the thoracic spine (beyond the normal 20-degree to 40-degree curve). It is accompanied by a forward head and protracted shoulder girdle. While severe hyperkyphosis rarely becomes life threatening, it can, unlike scoliosis, lead to paraplegia.

Examination Considerations

Interest in anterior/posterior curves of the spine has increased throughout the past 10–20 years. A moderate amount of lumbar lordosis is normal and important both in sitting and standing. If a person is unable to compensate for hip flexion contractures using the lumbar lordosis, the entire trunk will be tilted forward and unbalanced. Similarly, lumbar lordosis in sitting keeps the center of gravity of the trunk more in line with the thighs and less over the ischium. This sitting posture provides better sitting balance and lessens the chance of decubiti.

Hip flexion contractures are usually the primary cause of increased lumbar lordosis in standing persons with cerebral palsy. These contractures often develop in children who have hyperextension of the knees. This is a common occurrence in persons with myelodysplasia.

Thoracic kyphosis is normal, and concern should be shown only when the curve is greater than 40 degrees. Severe long C-type hyperkyphosis (see Figure 5.4) can lead to difficulty with sitting balance and upright head posture. Similarly, severe hyperkyphosis can unbalance those persons who are marginal walkers. Hyperkyphosis does not cause pulmonary compromise, and, in fact, many persons with hyperkyphosis have barrel-like chests. Hyperkyphosis and hyperlordosis are measured in much the same manner as scoliosis. Radiographs are taken and measured using a variation of the Cobb technique.

Treatment

The treatment of hyperlordosis and hyperkyphosis parallels that of scoliosis. Prevention consists of therapy and positioning (described in Chapters 3, 8, and 13). Discussion here focuses on control/support and surgical treatment.

Control/Support

Control/support is an important phase in the treatment of hyperlordosis and hyperkyphosis. Hyperlordosis is most effectively controlled in a sitting position by a seat belt that holds the pelvis in a neutral position. For standing, a lumbar orthosis may be used to flatten the spine, along with exercises to stretch out the hip flexors.

In the young child, hyperkyphosis initially may be controlled by a canvas-type corset with dorsal extensions. The corset may be used as an adjunct to sitting or standing positioning. Severe hyperkyphosis may require a chest support (see Figure 8.4) or a plastic orthosis to maintain an upright sitting position. Hyperkyphosis may be accompanied by severe forward thrust of the head due to the exaggerated thoracic curve and weak cervical extensor muscles. A modified cervical collar may be used to improve head position (Figure 5.14); however, the collar does little to improve hyperkyphosis.

Surgical Considerations

It is difficult to control hyperkyphosis of greater than 60 degrees by posterior surgical techniques alone. As a consequence, correction of the hyperkyphosis for most patients means anterior/posterior surgical procedures. This necessi-

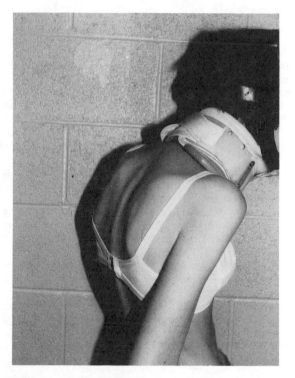

Figure 5.14.   Modified cervical collar. This collar is used to support a severe forward head. However, the collar does little to improve the hyperkyphosis.

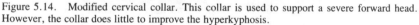

tates an anterior release over the affected area followed in a week to 10 days later with a posterior stabilization using compressions rather than distraction instrumentation. Generally, surgical corrections of hyperkyphosis are quite good. However, this surgery is not often considered for persons with multiple handicaps because it requires two extensive procedures with significant risks.

CLOSING THOUGHTS

Surgical advances in the 1980s offer a variety of innovative instrumentations emphasizing multiple fixation points on the spine. These intersegmental techniques allow greater strength of fixation in the immediate postoperative period. These greatly reduce, and in some cases, eliminate, the need for external postoperative support, allowing relatively quick return to preoperative functional status. As such, they are particularly attractive when contemplating surgery on an individual with multiple handicaps who is unable to understand or cooperate in related care.

REFERENCES

Akbarnia, B.A. (1984). Spinal deformity in patients with cerebral palsy. *Orthopaedic Transcripts, 8,* 116.

Bonnett, C., Brown, J.C., & Grow, T. (1976). Thoracolumbar scoliosis in cerebral palsy. *Journal of Bone and Joint Surgery, 58A,* 328–336.

Bonnett, C., Brown, J.C., Perry, J., Nickel, V.L., Walinski, T., Brooks, L., Hoffer, M., Stiles, C., & Brooks, R. (1975). The evolution of treatment of paralytic scoliosis at Rancho Los Amigo Hospital. *Journal of Bone and Joint Surgery, 58A,* 206.

Bradford, D.S., & Hensinger, R.N. (1985). *The pediatric spine.* New York: Thieme, Inc.

Bunnell, W.P., & MacEwen, G.C. (1977). Non-operative treatment of scoliosis in cerebral palsy (Preliminary report on the use of plastic jacket). *Developmental Medicine and Child Neurology, 19,* 45–49.

Cristofaro, R., Koffman, M., Woodward, R., & Baxter, S. (1977, October). *Treatment of the totally involved cerebral palsy problem sitter.* Paper presented at the Annual Meeting of the American Academy for Cerebral Palsy and Developmental Medicine, Atlanta.

Fraser, B.A., Galka, G., & Hensinger, R.N. (1980). *Gross motor management of severely multiply impaired students: Vol. I. Evaluation guide.* Austin, TX: PRO-ED.

Fraser, B.A., & Hensinger, R.N. (1983). *Managing physical handicaps: A practical guide for parents, care providers, and educators.* Baltimore: Paul H. Brookes Publishing Co.

Hensinger, R.N., & MacEwen, G.D. (1974). Evaluation of the cotrel dynamic spine traction in the treatment of scoliosis: A preliminary report. *Orthopaedic Review, III*(5), 27–34.

Hortsmann, H.M. (1985, October). *Skeletal maturation in cerebral palsy.* Paper presented at the 39th annual meeting of the American Academy for Cerebral Palsy and Developmental Medicine, Seattle.

Horstmann, H.M., & Boyer, B. (1984). Progression of scoliosis in cerebral palsy patients after skeletal maturity. *Orthopaedic Transcripts, 8,* 116.

Letts, R.M., Turenka, S., & Klasser, O. (1980, September). *Windswept hip phenomenon and scoliosis in cerebral palsy.* Paper presented at the 15th annual meeting of the Scoliosis Research Society, Chicago.

Lonstein, J.E. (1981). Deformities of the spine in children with cerebral palsy. *Orthopaedic Review, 10,* 33.

Lonstein, J.E., & Akbarnia, B.A. (1981, September). *Operative treatment of spine deformities in patients with cerebral palsy and mental retardation.* Paper presented at the 16th annual meeting of the Scoliosis Research Society, Montreal, Canada.

Longstein, J.E., & Beck, K. (1986). Hip dislocation and subluxation in cerebral palsy. *Journal of Pediatric Orthopedics, 6,* 521–526.

Luque, E.R. (1982). Segmental spinal instrumentation for correction of scoliosis. *Clinical Orthopaedics and Related Research, 163,* 192–198.

Luque, E.R., & Cardoso, A. (1977). Segmental correction of scoliosis with rigid fixation: Preliminary report. *Orthopaedic Transactions, 1,* 136–137.

Malloy, M.K., & Kuhlmann, R.F. (1981, September). *Severe mental retardation, scoliosis, and spinal fusion.* Paper presented at the 16th annual meeting of the Scoliosis Research Society, Montreal, Canada.

Mital, M.A., Beklin, S.C., & Sullivan, R.A. (1976). An approach to head, neck and trunk stabilization and control in cerebral palsy by use of the Milwaukee brace. *Developmental Medicine and Child Neurology, 18,* 198.

Nash, C.L. (1983). Spinal deformities. In G.H. Thompson, I.L. Rubin, & R.M. Bilenker (Eds.), *Comprehensive management of cerebral palsy* (pp. 257–272). New York: Grune & Stratton.

Samilson, R.L. (1981). Orthopaedic surgery of the hips and spine in retarded cerebral palsy patients. *Orthopaedic Clinics of North America, 12,* 183.

Samilson, R.L., & Bechard, R. (1973). Scoliosis in cerebral palsy: Incidence, distribution of curve patterns, natural history and thoughts on etiology. *Current Practice in Orthopaedic Surgery, 5,* 183–205.

Samilson, R.L., Tsov, P., Aamoth, G., & Green, W.M. (1972). Dislocation and subluxation of the hip in cerebral palsy: Pathogenesis, natural history, and management. *Journal of Bone and Joint Surgery, 54*(A), 863–873.

Stegbauer, S.A., & Lyne, E.D. (1988, October). The etiology of scoliosis in the severely involved cerebral-palsy patient. *Developmental Medicine and Child Neurology, Supplement No. 57, 30*(5), 4.

Chapter

6

Orthopaedic Treatment of Lower Extremity Deformities

This chapter identifies deformities of the lower extremities and discusses examination and treatment techniques that are appropriate for use with persons with multiple handicaps. Postural abnormalities that lead to bony deformities, along with therapeutic means for their prevention and control, are discussed in Chapters 3 and 11. This chapter deals with fixed deformities that involve soft tissue and bony changes. Lower extremity deformities and their examination and treatment (both nonoperative and operative alternatives) are presented on a joint-by-joint basis.

DEFORMITIES

Deformities of the lower extremities pose serious problems to persons with multiple handicaps. These deformities affect a person's ability to ambulate, bear standing weight, and maintain an upright sitting posture. In later life, persistent bony deformities of the lower extremities may lead to osteoarthritis of major weight-bearing joints that may cause pain upon limb movement and sitting discomfort. Hip deformities are particularly serious because they disturb the balance of the pelvis, contribute to development of scoliosis, prevent good perineal hygiene, and may cause pain. Hip deformities have a profound effect on seating posture. While knee and foot deformities have less impact on seating, they often interfere with standing, transfers, and wearing shoes.

Deformities of the lower extremities are seldom isolated, generally involving several joints (Bleck, 1987). Proximal deformities pose more complex and serious problems than distal deformities. Also, there is a close relationship between hip and spinal deformities (e.g., pelvic obliquity and scoliosis). This relationship is discussed in Chapter 5. The following discussion focuses on bony deformities of the pelvis and hip, the knee, and the foot.

Deformities of Pelvis and Hip

Pelvis and hip deformities include positional types (e.g., hip adduction, abduction, flexion, extension) and joint abnormalities (e.g., subluxation and dislocation). Pain should be searched for and evaluated if deformities are present.

Hip Adduction Deformity

Adduction is the deformity most commonly experienced by persons with multiple handicaps. In a young child, it often leads to hip subluxation and dislocation, especially when it occurs in combination with hip flexion contractures. Bilateral hip adduction deformity is characterized by scissoring legs. Hip adduction may be accompanied by hip extension and internal rotation and knee extension (Figure 6.1). This combination renders perineal care difficult and interferes with sitting and standing balance.

Hip Abduction Deformity

Hip abduction deformity produces a "frog leg" position with hip flexion and external rotation and knee flexion (Figure 6.2). This deformity poses less

Figure 6.1. Bilateral hip adduction deformity. This deformity is characterized by scissoring lower extremities. In this case, the deformity is accompanied by hip extension and internal rotation and knee extension. This combination renders perineal care difficult and interferes with sitting and standing balance.

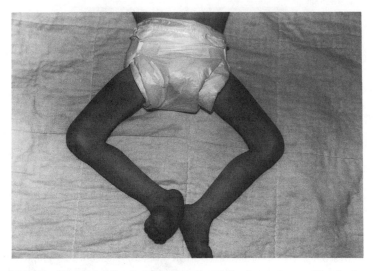

Figure 6.2. Hip abduction deformity. Hip abduction deformity produces a "frog leg" position with hip flexion and external rotation and knee flexion.

difficulties for persons with multiple handicaps and their caregivers than the adduction deformity. It does not interfere with perineal hygiene and rarely causes pain. However, in a severe state, abduction deformity may interfere with sitting and recumbent (i.e., sidelying) positioning.

Hip Flexion Deformity

Hip flexion deformity is a contracture of the hip flexors that is usually associated with a crouched standing posture (i.e., knee and ankle flexion). It may occur in conjunction with either hip abduction or adduction in nonambulators. In a young child, hip flexion and adduction often result in hip subluxation and dislocation. When hip flexion is combined with hip abduction/external rotation, a "frog leg" position results. In general, hip flexion deformities present few barriers to positioning wheelchair- or bed-bound persons.

Windswept Deformity

A windswept deformity (see Figure 11.9) combines flexion with abduction/external rotation of one hip and adduction/internal rotation of the opposite hip. Both knees are flexed. Therapeutic positioning for a windswept deformity is presented in Chapter 13.

Hip Extension Deformity

Hip extension deformity is associated with an extended leg position (i.e., hip and knee extension) and may be accompanied by lower extremity adduction

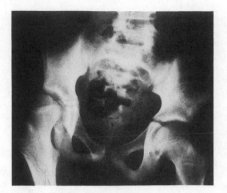

Figure 6.3.   Subluxation of the right hip. A radiograph of a 5-year-old shows evidence of a right hip subluxation. Note that the head of the femur has migrated upward in the acetabulum, caused by the unbalanced pull of the spastic hip adductor muscles on the right thigh.

(see Figure 6.1). Hip extension deformity usually is caused by spasticity of the hip extensor muscles and hamstrings. It poses significant difficulty for wheelchair patients since it prevents satisfactory flexed sitting posture. In a severe state, hip extension deformity may lead to anterior hip dislocation and confine a young patient to a bed existence.

Hip Subluxation and Dislocation

Subluxation is an incomplete or partial separation of the head of the femur from the acetabulum (Figure 6.3). Subluxation differs from dislocation in that the two surfaces of the joint still touch. Clinically, bilateral subluxation appears similar to adduction deformity (i.e., scissoring legs due to adductor muscle tightness), and the limb lengths appear equal. If one hip is subluxed, that limb may appear shorter than the other.

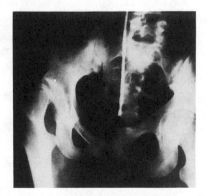

Figure 6.4.   Dislocated right hip. This is a radiograph of the same child pictured in Figure 6.3, taken at age 13. Note that the head of the right femur is now almost completely out of the acetabulum, which is misshapen (i.e., dysplastic).

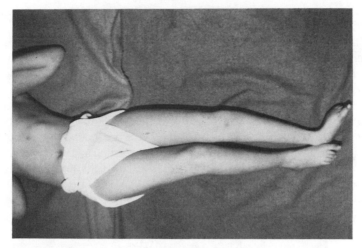

Figure 6.5. External appearance of a dislocated hip. The right hip is dislocated as evidenced by shortening of an entire extremity, different knee levels, pelvic obliquity, and adduction of the right thigh.

When the hip is dislocated, the femoral head is no longer in contact with the acetabulum (Figure 6.4). Externally, a dislocation on one side is detected by shortening of an entire extremity, different knee levels, pelvic obliquity, and persistent adduction of the thigh (Figure 6.5). Hip dislocations usually occur in either a posterosuperior or posterior direction depending upon the degree of flexion deformity. Occasionally, an extension deformity will produce an anterior hip dislocation (Figure 6.6). Anterior hip dislocations present

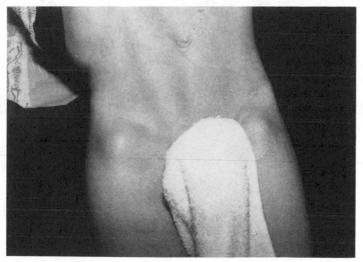

Figure 6.6. Bilateral anterior hip dislocations. In this case, the femoral heads are clearly visible. Anterior hip dislocations prevent this individual from sitting.

more difficulty to persons with multiple handicaps because they prevent sitting if untreated.

The incidence of hip subluxation or dislocation is high among persons with multiple handicaps. Those at greatest risk are the most severely neurologically involved and developmentally immature. Severely disabled nonambulatory persons with cerebral palsy experience an incidence of hip subluxation or dislocation of approximately 28% (Samilson, Tsov, Aamoth, & Green, 1972). Samilson's review of institutionalized patients revealed that of those having hip subluxation or dislocation, 62% were bed-bound, 27% could sit, and 11% were ambulatory. The distribution of unilateral and bilateral subluxation or dislocation was nearly equal. In a study of institutionalized cerebral palsy patients with dislocation of the hip, pain was present in about half of the patients (Moreau, Drummond, Rogala, Asworth, & Porter, 1978). Fortunately, in most cases, the pain was mild, with only 10% having severe pain.

Knee Deformities

Knee deformities involve either flexion or hyperextension.

Knee Flexion Deformity

Knee flexion deformity involves a bent knee and usually is associated with hip abduction/flexion deformity in nonambulatory persons. These deformities of-

Figure 6.7.   Knee flexion deformity. Knee flexion deformities often are seen in conjunction with hip flexion contractures and heel cord tightness causing a crouched gait. This individual is able to maintain standing and walking balance despite such a severe deformity.

ten are seen in conjunction with hip flexion contractures and heel cord tightness in persons who walk with a crouched gait (Figure 6.7). Knee flexion deformities seldom pose a serious problem for bed bound patients. Occasionally, severe knee flexion prevents comfortable sitting, with the tight hamstrings rubbing against the edge of a seat.

Knee Hyperextension Deformity

Knee hyperextension or limited flexion (i.e., genu recurvatum) deformity is identified by the knee being in extension with the patella positioned higher than normal (i.e., patella alta). Most persons with this deformity are ambulators, but it may occur in nonambulators as well. Knee hyperextension deformity permits standing transfers, but prevents knee flexion during the stance phase of walking (Seymour & Sharrard, 1968). For nonambulatory persons, knee hyperextension deformity limits wheelchair positioning. Knee hyperextension may be due to several causes. Surgical overcorrection of knee flexion deformities is a common cause, along with insufficient calf muscle activity and quadriceps spasticity (Cottrell, 1963).

Foot Deformities

Three basic kinds of foot deformities found among persons with multiple handicaps are equinus, equinovarus, and equinovalgus (Fraser, Galka, & Hensinger, 1980). In young children, these deformities can be corrected passively. With growth, the musculotendinous units and soft tissue become contracted, joints remodel, and a deformity becomes fixed and rigid. In fixed foot deformities, such as equinovarus and equinovalgus, bony prominences and decreased weight-bearing surface combine to produce significant discomfort, stiffness, and poor fit.

Equinus Deformity

An equinus deformity positions the foot in plantar flexion. Equinus is caused by tightness of the heel cord. Ambulatory persons with equinus deformity walk on the forefoot and toes (see Figure 6.7).

Equinovarus Deformity

Equinovarus deformity positions the foot in plantar flexion with inward angulation of the forefoot, causing ambulatory patients to walk on the lateral border of the foot. Equinovarus is caused by a tight heel cord and tight structures on the medial side of the foot, predominantly the posterior tibial tendon.

Equinovalgus Deformity

Equinovalgus (i.e., rocker-bottom foot) positions the hindfoot in equinus and the forefoot in outward angulation, with collapse of the arch (Figure 6.8). This gives the foot a "bottom-of-a-rocking-chair" appearance. Equinovalgus is caused by a tight heel cord (i.e., equinus of the hindfoot) combined with

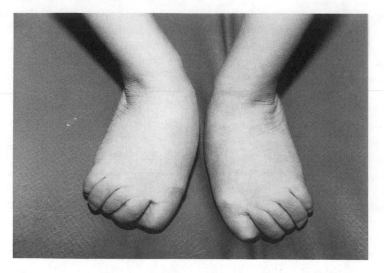

Figure 6.8. Equinovalgus deformity. This deformity is often called rocker-bottom foot. Equinovalgus deformity positions the hindfoot in equinus and the forefoot in outward angulation, and collapses the arch, giving the appearance of the bottom of a rocking chair.

tight structures on the lateral side of the foot, usually the peroneal tendons. The talonavicular joint is likely to be subluxed, and the majority of weight is borne on the medial side of the foot.

Toe Deformities

Troublesome toe deformities include clawed (i.e., flexed) toes and hallux valgus (i.e., outward angulation of the big toe). Flexed toes may appear in combination with a cavus foot deformity (i.e., abnormally high longitudinal foot arch) (Figure 6.9). These deformities may make it difficult to fit shoes. Furthermore, the pressure of the shoes on the toes may cause painful calluses and corns.

EXAMINATION TECHNIQUES

Simple clinical techniques usually are most helpful in examining lower extremity deformities of persons with multiple handicaps. Invasive techniques or complex procedures, such as dynamic electromyography and local nerve blocks, are not tolerated well by persons who lack the ability to cooperate. Similarly, tests requiring patient cooperation, understanding, and assistance—such as manual muscle testing—are of limited benefit. Instead, a functional assessment is far more revealing.

Observation of the person performing such motor activities as standing, creeping, and sitting provides information about the coordination and strength of muscle groups. Videotapes of a person's functional use and movement of

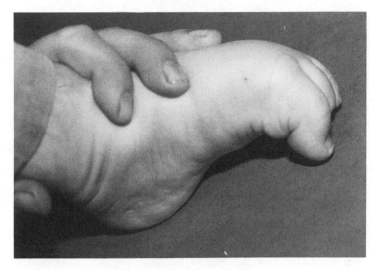

Figure 6.9. Cavus foot deformity. A cavus foot deformity is characterized by an abnormally high longitudinal foot arch and is often associated with flexed toes.

the lower extremities can be reviewed and compared for long-term documentation. Lower extremity joint movement should be measured using passive range-of-motion techniques and recorded periodically to provide continuing documentation. Usually, standard range-of-motion procedures, as described by the American Academy of Orthopaedic Surgeons (1965) and Norkin and White (1985), need little modification for use with persons with multiple handicaps. Roentgenographic studies should be ordered to determine the integrity of the joint in question and as a baseline for long-term evaluation. Tests designed to measure contractures of individual muscles should be performed. In many cases, such tests may need to be modified for this population. Modifications are discussed in the following paragraphs.

Examination of Hips

Scissoring legs and hip adductor tightness are early clinical signs of hip adductor deformity and potential hip subluxation. Adduction contractures alone usually do not produce a spastic hip dislocation (Thompson, 1983); however, tight hip adductors combined with tight hip flexors are especially conducive to hip subluxation or dislocation. Hip subluxation and dislocation are common among persons with multiple handicaps (Fraser & Hensinger, 1983; Samilson et al., 1972). Risk is especially high in children who are handicapped, ages 3 through 7 (Samilson et al., 1972). Every child with retardation or cerebral palsy should have a hip examination at least yearly (Thompson, 1983). This examination is performed by placing a child in supine and abducting the hips with the knee extended and flexed. The hip adductors are tight if each hip does not abduct to 45 degrees (90 degrees combined) (Figure 6.10). In such a

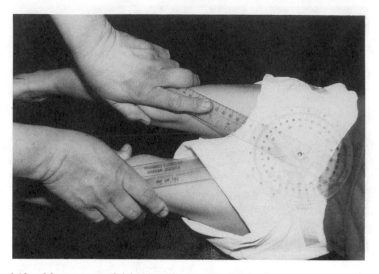

Figure 6.10.   Measurement of tight hip adductors. Total abduction measures only 35 degrees with this individual. Normal combined range of motion for hip abduction should be 90 degrees.

case, radiological examination should be conducted to determine if hip sub-luxation or dislocation is present.

Radiographic Studies

If hip subluxation or dislocation is suspected, radiographic anterior and pos-terior views of the pelvis and hips should be taken. Positioning is important. Standing controls hip rotation and is preferable to recumbent positioning. In cases where supine and prone positioning are necessary, the hips should be extended and the lower limbs supported in as neutral alignment as possible.

Radiographic studies indicate that acetabular dysplasia (i.e., abnormal acetabular development), femoral anteversion (i.e., forward rotation of the femur), and coxa valga (i.e., increased angle of the femoral head and neck and the femoral shaft) precede hip dislocation (Drummond, Rogala, & Cruess, 1979). Every person with multiple handicaps should have periodic (usually yearly) radiographs of the hip to detect such secondary osseous changes. If the radiographs remain normal through 7–10 years of age, the hip problems probably will not occur.

Hip Contracture Measurement Tests

Examination of the hips also should include measuring hip flexion contrac-tures. If the person tolerates a prone position, hip flexion contracture tests may be used (Staheli, 1977). The person is placed in a prone position with the torso from waist up supported on the table. One examiner steadies the body by placing a hand over the buttocks. Another examiner lifts one limb into extension. A contracture exists when the pelvis begins to roll anteriorly. At this point, a goniometer is used to measure the angle formed by the femoral shaft and the horizontal plane (Figure 6.11).

An examinee's inability to tolerate this prone position may necessitate using the Thomas test to examine for hip flexion contracture (Bleck, 1987). This test is conducted with the person supine. The opposite limb is supported in a flexed knee-to-chest position so the spine and pelvis are flat against the table. The limb under examination is held in maximum extension. The angle of the femoral shaft to the horizontal plane indicates the degree of contracture (Figure 6.12). In cases of severe contractures, hip flexion contractures may have to be measured with the patient in a sidelying position. This is least desirable, since it is difficult for one examiner to stabilize the spine and pelvis.

Examination of Knee

Examination of the knee includes tests for hamstring and quadriceps contractures, observation of lower extremity function, and radiographic studies.

Test for Hamstring and Quadriceps Contractures

Hamstring contractures are responsible for knee flexion deformity, and quadriceps contractures are responsible for knee extension deformity. The test for

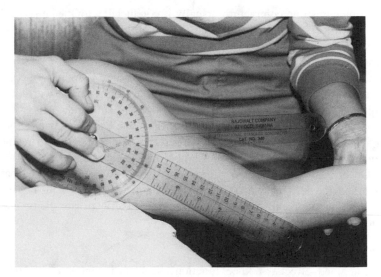

Figure 6.11.   Staheli's hip flexion contracture test. The person is placed in a prone position with the torso from waist up supported on a table. The extremity being tested is lifted into extension. A contracture exists when the pelvis begins to roll anteriorly. A measurement is taken at this point. The individual pictured has a 30-degree hip flexion contracture.

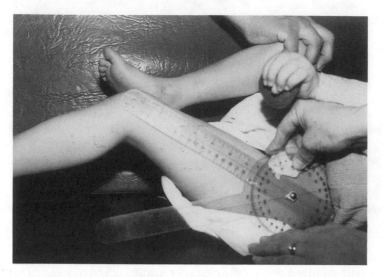

Figure 6.12. Thomas test for hip flexion contracture. This test is conducted with a person in a supine position. The opposite extremity is supported in a flexed knee-to-chest position so the spine and pelvis are flat against the table. The extremity under examination is held in maximum extension. The angle of the femoral shaft to the horizontal plane indicates the degree of contracture. This individual's contracture measures about 40 degrees.

measuring hamstring contractures usually is conducted with the person supine with both lower extremities extended. The limb being tested is flexed to 90 degrees at the hip. The knee is initially flexed and then extended to the point of contracture. The popliteal angle (i.e., angle formed by the tibia with the extended knee position equaling 0 degrees) is measured to indicate the degree of hamstring contracture (Figure 6.13). When testing a person with multiple handicaps, two examiners often are needed: one to stabilize the pelvis and the other to raise the limb to be measured. If only one examiner is present, the individual may be tested sitting with the hip flexed to 90 degrees. The knee is extended to the limit possible and the popliteal angle is measured.

Quadriceps spasticity and contracture should be tested with the patient supine and the legs extended. The examiner gently flexes both knees and measures the popliteal angles. Persons with quadriceps spasticity usually cannot flex their knees past 90 degrees.

Function

The combined effects of knee function, heel cord contractures, and foot position should be observed during a variety of activities. The degree of voluntary quadriceps control and strength should be assessed during weight

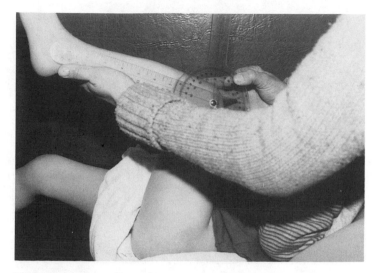

Figure 6.13. Measurement of hamstring contractures. This measurement is conducted with the person supine with both extremities extended. The limb being tested is flexed to 90 degrees at the hip, and the knee is extended to the point of contracture. The popliteal angle is measured to indicate the degree of hamstring contracture. This individual has an 80-degree hamstring contracture.

bearing. An individual may have standing or ambulation potential if the quadriceps are strong enough to straighten the knee against gravity and the pull of the hamstrings.

Persons who crawl often experience prepatellar bursitis (i.e., housemaid's knee). This condition thickens the skin and forms a heavy callus over the knee (Figure 6.14). Fluid accumulates within the bursa in front of the patella. While there is no joint damage, there is danger of infection caused by foreign bodies such as pins and needles that may enter the knee during crawling. Persons with prepatellar bursitis should wear sports knee pads or the rubber pads used by cement workers and gardeners.

Knee Pain

Occasionally, pain is experienced in the region of the knee. The pain may indicate a stress reaction in the patella and patella tendon caused by muscle imbalance between the quadriceps and hamstrings. In such cases, radiologically, the patella appears to be elongated (i.e., stretched like taffy), fragmented, and patella alta is present (Rosenthal & Levine, 1977). The bent knee gait makes the patella particularly susceptible to stress fractures. In addition, problems about the hip can cause pain referred to the region of the knee.

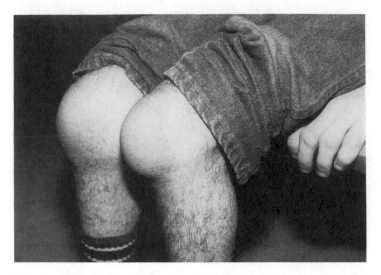

Figure 6.14.   Prepatella bursitis. This condition thickens the skin and forms a callus over the knee.

Examination of Feet

Examination of equinus deformity should include the Silverskoild (1924) test for heel cord tightness to determine whether the gastrocnemius is the main site of contracture or whether the soleus also is involved. Usually, this test is conducted with the person seated and knees flexed to 90 degrees over the edge of a table. The foot should be supported at the heel, with the hindfoot in varus to lock the midfoot and prevent midfoot dorsiflexion. The foot is dorsiflexed with the knee in both flexion and extension. If dorsiflexion of the foot is greater with the knee extended, only the gastrocnemius is likely to be involved. If there is little difference in the degree of dorsiflexion with the knee extended and flexed, both gastrocnemius and soleous muscles are involved in the contracture (Bleck, 1987). If the patient is able to stand, the distance of the heel from the floor may be measured to provide a functional indication of heel cord tightness.

Valgus and varus foot deformities and toe deformities are difficult to measure. Photographs provide a more accurate record of the extent of deformity and its effects on foot weight bearing.

TREATMENT

Treatment of lower extremity deformities includes therapy, bracing and footwear, and surgery. Therapy is discussed in Chapters 3 and 13. This section focuses on bracing and footwear, and surgery that is appropriate for persons with multiple handicaps.

Bracing and Footwear

Long-term bracing usually is not satisfactory for persons with multiple handicaps. Such persons are seldom able to apply their own braces, and often lose, break, or misplace them. Long leg braces are particularly inappropriate. They are cumbersome, difficult to fit, and have not proven successful in preventing or lessening contractures of the knees. Occasionally, a knee support is necessary to assist a person during early attempts at standing. A temporary soft knee splint may be used for this purpose.

Bracing for the feet is fairly common. Corrective and tone-reducing casts, used over a short duration, may help some persons with multiple handicaps by decreasing heel cord spasticity or tightness (Hinderer et al., 1988; Watt et al., 1986). A short leg brace attached to a high-top orthopedic shoe or an ankle-foot orthosis may be used as an interim measure to maintain a plantargrade foot position or to stabilize a foot during early phases of ambulation.

Footwear for persons with multiple handicaps usually consists of inexpensive shoes such as soft shoes or tennis shoes. Tennis shoes are better than "running" shoes, especially for children with equinus. The rubber that is extended over the toes of running shoes tends to catch and cause tripping. A high-top orthopaedic shoe or tennis shoe may help to provide ankle support for persons who are learning to stand or ambulate. High-top shoes also may be used by very young children to hold their feet in proper position as they grow. Complex shoe corrections, such as navicular pads, arch supports, and wedges may be appropriate for a few young ambulating individuals, but generally are not recommended for persons with multiple handicaps because they are uncomfortable, cumbersome, and have not been documented to be beneficial. Regardless of the type of shoes worn, heels and soles should produce good friction. Friction may be improved by adding a nonskid surface to the sole of the shoe. Nonambulatory patients need only use socks or slippers for warmth and protection.

Surgical Treatment

Surgery usually is indicated to prevent the development of deformity in a young child, to reverse deformity, and to halt further progression of deformity. For the standing child, surgery may be necessary to maintain the weight-bearing joints that are appropriate for standing and ambulation. For the sitting child, surgery is indicated to maintain a level pelvis and sitting balance. This is an important consideration in avoiding continuing hip and spine problems.

Other reasons for surgery are aiding perineal hygiene and relieving pain. Perineal hygiene is difficult for all persons with multiple handicaps, particularly those who are incontinent. Surgery can provide improved access to the perineum, thus, improving hygiene. Maintaining adequate hip motion is especially important for females who are experiencing menses.

Surgical procedures are not complex; they involve simple surgical lengthening or shortening of tendons or repositioning of joints. These procedures cannot duplicate complex muscle functioning, movement, control, and coordination that result from central nervous system control. Surgery should not be expected to change a recumbent or sitting person into someone who is capable of standing or walking. However, surgery can improve existing skills and facilitate gross motor activities (e.g., sitting, standing, walking).

Hip Surgery

There are two different types of hip surgery generally performed on persons with multiple handicaps. They include surgery for hip subluxation, for hip dislocations, and for hip hyperextension.

Surgery for Hip Subluxation Early identification of hip adductor tightness and hip subluxation makes a significant difference in preventing hip dislocation. As mentioned previously, routine clinical and roentgenographic evaluation should be done at least yearly with young children with multiple handicaps. Those who have increased adductor tightness on radiographs show signs of subluxation, and should be considered for soft tissue procedures. In many young children, early subluxation can be reversed using these procedures. For simple deformities, an adductor tenotomy may be used that lengthens the long adductor and partially lengthens the adductor magnus and brevis. This can be done in combination with an anterior obturator neurectomy if further weakening of the adductor musculature is needed. For children who have an internal rotation deformity in addition to tight adductors, it is a simple measure to lengthen the medial hamstrings at the hip through the same incision. This procedure does not alter knee extension, but can decrease internal rotation and posturing. For children who demonstrate subluxation radiographically, an iliopsoas recession is added, detaching the iliopsoas from the lesser trochanter and moving it back to the hip capsule. It should be noted that there are many variations of this procedure that can accomplish the same goal—to balance the forces across the hip joint. These variations have been described by a variety of authors (see Appendix E).

Following surgery, children are placed in a simple abduction brace or cast for 3 weeks. Adolescents or young adults usually have a great deal of joint stiffness and limitation. In such cases, range-of-motion exercises are used following surgery instead of casts and braces that often are too cumbersome.

Surgery for Hip Dislocations Persons with dislocated hips pose a very difficult problem. Surgical procedures necessary to reduce the hip are extensive, often requiring bone realignment of the proximal femur and restoration of the architecture of the acetabulum as well. Procedures may require prolonged cast immobilization until the bony structures heal. It is often difficult to decide when surgery of this magnitude is indicated, especially for persons who are nonambulatory. Many persons with dislocated hips do not experience sitting difficulties and only a few develop hip pain throughout the years. A decision for surgery of this type usually requires a great deal of time and discussion with parents, caregivers, and therapists. For many, professionals elect not to reduce the hip, preferring to wait until the person begins to experience difficulty with it. It should be noted that femoral head and neck resection is not always effective in relieving pain associated with degenerative osteoarthritis. Other procedures considered for nonhandicapped persons, such as hip arthrodesis and joint replacement, present added problems for persons with multiple handicaps.

There is no easy answer to surgical intervention for hip dislocations. The best approach is early identification of a subluxing hip and treatment by soft tissue procedures to either reverse the process or at least halt progression of the deformity.

Surgery for Hip Hyperextension   Persons with impending anterior subluxation of the hip (characterized by hip hyperextension) require careful examination preoperatively to determine the offending muscles. In most cases, a proximal hamstring release with a partial release of the hip extensors (i.e., gluteus maximus) is chosen to achieve more hip flexion.

Knee Surgery

Knee surgery that may be performed includes surgery for knee flexion contractures and for patella alta, both of which are discussed below.

Surgery for Knee Flexion Contractures   Surgical release of knee flexion contractures and hamstrings (modified Egger's procedure) may be necessary for persons who are ambulatory or capable of a standing transfer. This procedure is seldom necessary for persons who are wheelchair users. An extensive hamstring release may be harmful since persons with over-lengthened hamstrings may develop a reversal of the knee flexion deformity, creating a complete knee extension. Deciding the degree of lengthening of the hamstrings for an individual patient is a problem because it is difficult to assess the strength of the quadriceps. Occasionally, one side of the hamstrings is tight. In these cases, partial lengthening can be helpful. For example, if the lateral hamstrings are very tight causing an external rotation of the tibia, lengthening of the biceps femoris and iliotibial band may be indicated.

Surgery for Patella Alta   Ambulatory persons with spastic diplegia commonly develop knee pain. The quadriceps are very strong and through time, the patella can be stretched out or elongated. In such cases, stress fractures are likely to occur in the substance of the patella. Patella alta not only causes pain, but also makes the quadriceps less effective, elongating the attachment of the patella tendon to the tibia. Once this muscle complex is stretched, it is difficult to tighten it again and restore its effectiveness. Individuals with patella alta should be identified early in order to begin hamstring stretching and positioning. Once pain develops, a hamstring lengthening often is the only way to resolve the problem.

Foot Surgery

Surgical procedures, such as heel cord lengthening, are usually not considered until a child has attained gross balance and coordination skills needed for standing. Occasionally, surgery is done to allow wearing of appropriate footwear or to improve appearance in nonambulators. Initially, soft tissue procedures (e.g., tendon lengthening or release) are sufficient to achieve these objectives. With growth, the deformities, if uncorrected, become rigid and less amenable to soft tissue procedures. Thus, in older persons, bone procedures are required, such as triple arthrodesis, to achieve a satisfactory position and to stabilize the foot (see Figures 4.4 and 4.5).

FRACTURES

Fractures frequently occur with persons who are severely multiply impaired. Persons who have multiple contractures are prone to simple fractures during routine care (e.g., turning, positioning, perineal cleaning). Some therapeutic procedures, particularly stretching and range-of-motion exercises of the hips and knees, have been associated with increased fractures. This does not mean that there has been excessive force, but rather, that these individuals often have fragile bones secondary to poor mineralization (i.e., osteoporosis). Lee and Lyne (1988) evaluated a group of children who were treated for this type of fracture. They found that most fractures occur in the lower extremities and that the vitamin D blood levels in approximately one-third of the children were consistent with rickets. Radiography of all the children demonstrated osteoporosis (i.e., demineralization) of the bone in comparison to normal children.

The cause of osteoporosis in this population is related to problems with feeding and absorption of vitamin D. Also, seizure medications such as Dilantin and Phenobarbital have been associated with vitamin D deficiency. The fact that may persons with multiple handicaps spend a considerable amount of time recumbent contributes to osteopenia. Other causes of injury should be investigated and the question of abuse should be kept in mind and searched for when a specific history or clinical study indicates neither trauma nor rickets.

Most fractures resulting from osteopenia are low energy fractures and treatment consists of simple splinting and immobilization for a short period. However, when a fracture involves the hip, surgical stabilization may be necessary.

CLOSING THOUGHTS

Many of the 1970 studies referenced in this chapter are classics because they represent the last untreated population of persons with multiple deformities found in the United States. The surgical procedures discussed in this chapter have been well outlined in standard surgical textbooks. Selection of the proper procedures and timing for the individual is key to having a surgical procedure meet that person's needs. Surgery must be carefully coordinated with those who are most knowledgeable about the individual (e.g., parents, caregivers, therapists, educators). Similarly, postoperative management is essential for optimal results. Monitoring also helps guard against overcorrection. If there is an indication that overcorrection is developing, braces, positioning, and range-of-motion exercises may be employed to avoid complication.

REFERENCES

American Academy of Orthopaedic Surgeons. (1965). *Joint motion method of measuring and recording.* Chicago: Author. (American Academy of Orthopaedic Surgeons, 5430 North Michigan Avenue, Chicago, IL 60611)

Bleck, E.E. (1987). *Orthopaedic management in cerebral palsy.* Philadelphia: J.B. Lippincott.

Cottrell, G.W. (1963). Role of the rectus femoris in spastic children. *Journal of Bone and Joint Surgery, 45,* 1556.

Drummond, D.S., Rogala, E.J., & Cruess, R. (1979). *The paralytic hip and pelvic obliquity in cerebral palsy and myelomeningocele. (American Academy of Orthopaedic Surgeons Instructional Course Lectures, Vol. 28.)* St. Louis: C.V. Mosby.

Fraser, B.A., Galka, G., & Hensinger, R.N. (1980). *Gross motor management of severely multiply impaired students.* Austin, TX: PRO-ED.

Fraser, B.A., & Hensinger, R.N. (1983). *Managing physical handicaps: A practical guide for parents, care providers, and educators.* Baltimore: Paul H. Brookes Publishing Co.

Hinderer, K.A., Harris, S.R., Purdy, A.H., Chew, D.E., Staheli, L.T., McLaughlin, J.F., & Jaffee, K.M. (1988). Effects of "tone-reducing" vs. standard plaster-casts on gait improvement of children with cerebral palsy. *Developmental Medicine and Child Neurology, 30,* 370–377.

Lee, J.K., & Lyne, E.D. (1988, November). *Pathological fractures in severely handicapped children.* Paper presented at the annual meeting of the American Academy of Pediatrics, San Francisco.

Moreau, M., Drummond, D., Rogala, G., Asworth, T., & Porter, T. (1978, October). *The natural history of hip dislocation in adult cerebral palsy patients.* Paper presented at the annual meeting of the American Academy for Cerebral Palsy, Toronto.

Norkin, C.C., & White, D.J. (1985). *Measurement of joint motion: A guide to goniometry.* Philadelphia: F.A. Davis.

Rosenthal, R.K., & Levine, D.B. (1977). Fragmentation of the distal pole of the patella in spastic cerebral palsy. *Journal of Bone and Joint Surgery, 59*(A), 934.

Samilson, R.L., Tsov, P., Aamoth, G., & Green, W.M. (1972). Dislocation and subluxation of the hip in cerebral palsy. *Journal of Bone and Joint Surgery, 5,* 183–205.

Seymour, N., & Sharrard, W.J.W. (1968). Bilateral proximal release of the hamstrings in cerebral palsy. *Journal of Bone and Joint Surgery, 50B,* 274.

Silverskoild, N. (1924). Reduction of the uncrossed two joint muscles of the one-to-one muscle in spastic conditions. *Acta Chirurgica Scandinavia, 56,* 313–330.

Staheli, L. (1977). The prone hip extension test. *Clinical Orthopaedics, 123,* 1215.

Thompson, G.H. (1983). Hip and knee deformities. In G.H. Thompson, I.L. Rubin, & R.M. Bilenker (Eds.), *Comprehensive management of cerebral palsy* (pp.231–244). New York: Grune & Stratton.

Watt, J., Sims, D., Harckham, F., Schmidt, L., McMilan, A., & Hamilton, J. (1986). A prospective study of inhibitive casting as an adjunct to physiotherapy for cerebral-palsied children. *Developmental Medicine and Child Neurology, 28,* 480–488.

Chapter

7

Orthopaedic Treatment of Upper Extremity Deformities

Dean S. Louis

The central denominator in individuals with multiple handicaps is an alteration in central nervous system function. The problem may be of congenital onset, or it may be of the acquired variety following central nervous system trauma, infection, or vascular accident. Peripheral physical manifestations may be classified according to the observed and demonstrable physical abnormalities. Zancolli, Goldner, and Swanson (1983), in their report for the International Federation of Societies for Surgery of the Hand, stated that there are six principal factors that influence surgical treatment: 1) the type of neuromuscular disorder, 2) general neurological disorders, 3) topographic involvement, 4) hand sensibility impairment, 5) severity of the hand's deformity, and 6) voluntary ability to grasp and release. They further pointed out, as have others, that of the three main types of neuromuscular disorder (i.e., spastic or pyramidal, dystonic or extrapyramidal, and mixed), the spastic variety is the most amenable to surgical treatment. Their comments, however, were directed at the universe of individuals with cerebral palsy, and not specifically to that population who has not only severe physical, but also mental impairments.

Dean S. Louis, M.D., is Professor of Surgery at the University of Michigan Medical School and Chief of Orthopaedic Hand Service at the University of Michigan Hospitals in Ann Arbor.

This chapter is devoted to that group of individuals whose involvement is so severe that there is little hope for improvement in their functional status. Functional status is such a broad term that it is pertinent to be more specific. To pick up a pin off a table is a fine, discreet function, representative of the ultimate integration of the central nervous system with the peripheral upper extremity and its components. The present state-of-the-art surgery has no possibility of translating these higher functions to an individual who is severely impaired, and thus, the goals of surgery are extremely limited when dealing with the individual with multiple impairments.

DEFORMITIES

Deformities of the upper extremities are generally more severe distally than proximally. This is one of the classical paradoxes of cerebral palsy, in that fine distal hand function is more important for independence than more proximal control, and yet the manifestations of this disease are much more evident distally than proximally. It is unusual to see a child affected with both severe shoulder and elbow problems, and also severe involvement of the fingers, thumb, and wrist.

Shoulder Deformities

Severe deformities of the shoulder are infrequent, yet they may range from the extremes of adduction/internal rotation contractures that severely limit usefulness of the hand, to subluxation and even frank dislocation of the shoulder, secondary to extreme muscle imbalance (Keats, 1965).

Elbow Deformities

Deformities of the elbow may be of several varieties. When one considers that the elbow is a link between the arm and the forearm, it becomes apparent that multiple possibilities exist. For example, flexion and extension, and pronation and supination all are possible at the elbow joint. Therefore, the deformities that exist there can be extension-supination-pronation deformities, as well as flexion-supination-pronation deformities. The more common complex seen, however, is that of elbow flexion and pronation of the forearm in combination with wrist and digital flexion posturing (Figure 7.1) (Bleck, 1987).

Wrist and Hand Deformities

The wrist is most commonly seen in an attitude of severe flexion. This may be so severe that the wrist may assume flexion of more than 90 degrees (Figures 7.2 and 7.3). Extension postures may also be seen, but they are distinctly less common. The deformities that are seen in the hand are multiple, but most commonly, they are those of dominating flexion of the fingers and adduction

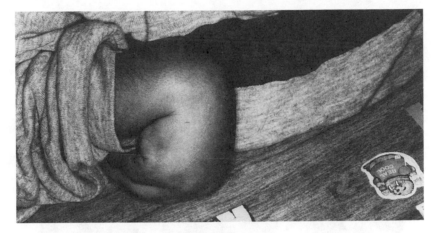

Figure 7.1. Severe pronation of the forearm combined with severe spasticity of the wrist prevents any useful function of this child's extremity.

and flexion of the thumb. At times, these deformities may be so severe that maceration of the skin may occur.

Splinting and passive stretching exercises may be necessary to prevent the development of fixed contractures and hygiene problems. Such methods, however, may prevent any independent use of the digits where that is, in fact, at all possible.

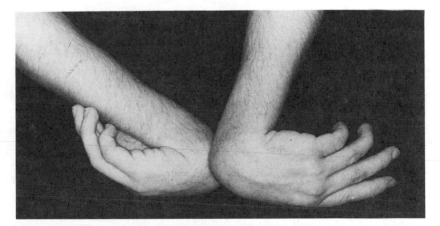

Figure 7.2. Although the fingers are relatively free of the spasticity that is often seen, severe spastic deformity of the wrist has made this individual's hands totally nonfunctional.

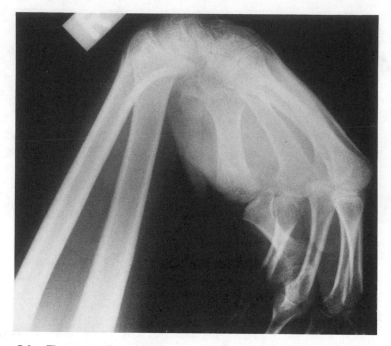

Figure 7.3.   The severe radiocarpal and intercarpal flexion demonstrated here and as seen in the individual in Figure 7.2 has resulted in a totally nonfunctional posture of the distal upper extremity.

SURGICAL GOALS

Multiple surgical procedures have been advocated to correct the deformities found in the cerebral palsied upper extremity. These procedures (Chait, Kaplan, Stewart-Lord, & Goodman, 1980; Goldner, 1974, 1979; Green & Banks, 1962; House, Gwathmey, & Fidler, 1981; Inglis & Cooper, 1966; Manske, 1985; Matev, 1970; Sakellarides, Mital, & Lenzi, 1981; Swanson, 1964, 1966; Zancolli et al., 1983; Zancolli & Zancolli, 1981) involving tendon transfers, small joint arthrodeses, and muscle releases have their most beneficial effects when the deformities are less severe than those usually seen in individuals with multiple handicaps. The severe deformities seen in these individuals are most commonly observed as a combination of severe spasticity involving wrist flexors, digital flexors, and flexion and adduction of the thumb. The isolated procedures listed above usually have no place in the management of these severe deformities, inasmuch as they may be a combination of pyramidal as well as extrapyramidal involvement, combining not only spasticity but athetoid motions. There is currently no available technique to satisfactorily correct or alleviate the central cause of these problems. Isolated distal surgical procedures tend to cause a shift of the abnormal posture into another dynamically unacceptable attitude. Therefore, the goals in managing upper extremity posturing of an individual with multiple handicaps are directed at a more limited focus (i.e., not directly aimed at causing an individual functional improvement). For example, in patients with mild spastic cerebral palsy, releasing a thumb-in-palm deformity may be specifically directed toward improving pinching or grasping. Likewise, step-cut lengthening of flexor tendons or muscle origin slides may lead to improvement in the same two functions.

Limited goals are directed primarily toward three areas:

1. Cosmesis that may have the benefit of allowing the individual to appreciate more normal posture. This is not a measurable end result when severe mental retardation and lack of ability to communicate are present. It is cited only because it has been cited before as one of the stated aims.
2. Facilitation of the use of a communication board. This has been effectively accomplished where the wrist was placed in an attitude that would allow the fingers to come in better contact with the communication board.
3. Gaining wrist extension and digital extension to the extent that hygiene problems are eliminated and dressing can be facilitated. This is a distinctly achievable and desirable aim in these individuals, so as to facilitate their management by family and/or other caregivers. It has been found (Louis, Hankin, & Bowers, 1984) that arthrodesis of the wrist, even when no attempt is made to change the digital posture, may be singularly successful (Figures 7.4–7.7). This has been achieved by

Figure 7.4.   This individual has undergone capitate radius fusion and has sufficiently decreased the severity of her spasticity so that the observed handshaking is now possible.

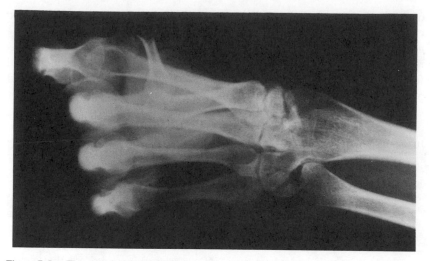

Figure 7.5. The capitate has been fused to the radius and it will also be noted that the hamate has been incorporated into the fusion. This has placed the hand in a much more acceptable position, especially for the donning of apparel.

means of fusion of the capitate to the radius, which accomplishes several aims. It will take the wrist out of the extreme flexed position, and will, in addition, diminish the severity of the spasticity by placing the musculotendinous units at less than the resting length. A retrospective review of the authors' experience in this area has proven, to the satisfaction of all,

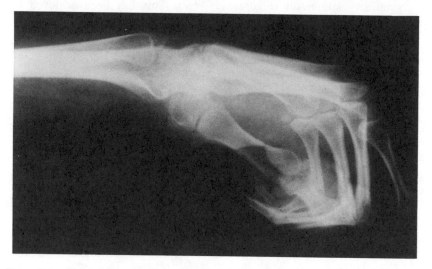

Figure 7.6. This is a lateral radiographic view of the same patient as seen in Figure 7.5. The obvious improvement from the posture demonstrated in Figure 7.3 is apparent.

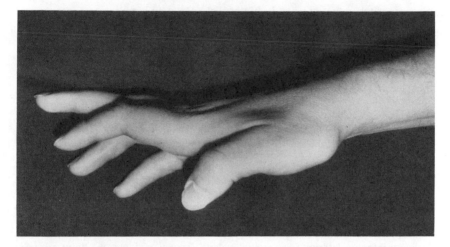

Figure 7.7.   The capitate radius fusion performed on this individual allowed significant relief of the spasticity and an overall improvement in the ability to actively extend and voluntarily flex the digits. The residual flexion and adduction of the thumb were later managed by the means indicated in this chapter.

that this procedure has a definite place in the treatment of persons with severe multiple handicaps (Louis, Hensinger, Fraser, Phelps, & Jacques, 1989).

CLOSING THOUGHTS

Surgery of the upper extremity in individuals with multiple handicaps is very limited in its scope. The most gratifying of these procedures to date have been properly performed wrist arthrodeses that result in a cosmetically more acceptable distal upper extremity and facilitate clothing changes. Most procedures that are effective in the management of spastic cerebral palsy, such as tendon lengthenings, tendon releases, tendon transfers, and small joint arthrodeses, have a very limited place in the management of the individual with multiple handicaps.

Individuals with multiple handicaps exist in a world that is foreign to others. The contents of their intellects and the frustrations that they may perceive can only be partially appreciated on the one hand, and occasionally observed on the other. Do persons who are manifestly limited in so many ways appreciate the contrast between their limits and others' abilities? Perhaps it will never be known.

It is known, however, that there are some endeavors that may be pursued that will make their lives easier. Limited as objectives may be, they have a place in such situations, and, hopefully, serve to ameliorate these severe afflictions.

REFERENCES

Bleck, E.E. (1987). *Orthopaedic management in cerebral palsy.* Philadelphia: J.B. Lippincott.

Chait, L.A., Kaplan, I., Stewart-Lord, B., & Goodman, M. (1980). Early surgical correction in the cerebral palsied hand. *Journal of Hand Surgery, 5,* 122–126.

Goldner, J.L., (1974). Upper extremity tendon transfers in cerebral palsy. *Orthopedic Clinics in North America, 5,* 389–414.

Goldner, J.L. (1979). Upper extremity surgical procedures for patients with cerebral palsy. *American Academy of Orthopaedic Surgeons Instructional Course Lectures* (Vol. 28, pp. 37–66). St. Louis: C.V. Mosby.

Green, W.T., & Banks, H.H. (1962). Flexor carpi ulnaris transplant and its uses in cerebral palsy. *Journal of Bone and Joint Surgery, 44A,* 1443–1452.

House, J.H., Gwathmey, F.W., & Fidler, M.O. (1981). A dynamic approach to the thumb-in-palm deformity in cerebral palsy. *Journal of Bone and Joint Surgery, 63A,* 216–225.

Inglis, A.E., & Cooper, W. (1966). Release of the flexor-pronator origin for flexion deformities of the hand and wrist in spastic paralysis: A study of eighteen cases. *Journal of Bone and Joint Surgery, 48A,* 847–857.

Keats, S. (1965). Surgical treatment of the hand in cerebral palsy: Correction of thumb-in-palm and other deformities. *Journal of Bone and Joint Surgery, 47A,* 274–284.

Louis, D.S., Hankin, F.M., & Bowers, W.H. (1984). Capitate radius fusion in the spastic upper extremity—an alternative to wrist arthrodesis. *Journal of Hand Surgery, 9,* 365–369.

Louis, D.S., Hensinger, R.N., Fraser, B.A., Phelps, J.A., & Jacques, K. (1989). Surgical management of the severely multiply handicapped individual. *Journal of Pediatric Orthopaedics, 9,* 15–18.

Manske, P.R. (1985). Redirection of extensor pollicis longus in the treatment of spastic thumb-in-palm deformity. *Journal of Hand Surgery, 10A,* 553–560.

Matev, I.B. (1970). Surgical treatment of flexion-adduction contracture of the thumb in cerebral palsy. *Acta Orthop. Scandinavica, 41,* 439–445.

Sakellarides, H.T., Mital, M.A., & Lenzi, W.D. (1981). Treatment of pronation contractures of the forearm in cerebral palsy by changing the insertion of the pronator radii teres. *Journal of Bone and Joint Surgery, 63A,* 645–652.

Swanson, A.B. (1964). Surgery of the hand in cerebral palsy. *Surgical Clinics of North America, 44,* 1061–1070.

Swanson, A.B. (1966). Treatment of swan-neck deformity in cerebral palsied hand. *Clinical Orthopaedics, 48,* 167–171.

Zancolli, E.A., Goldner, J.L., & Swanson, A.B. (1983). Surgery of the spastic hand in cerebral palsy: Report of the committee on spastic hand evaluation. *Journal of Hand Surgery, 8,* 766–772.

Zancolli, E.A., & Zancolli, E.A., Jr. (1981). Surgical management of the hemiplegic spastic hand in cerebral palsy. *Surgical Clinics of North America, 61,* 395–406.

Management through Seating Systems, Orthotic Devices, and Transportation Safety

Chapter
8

Seating Systems

with Glenda Atkinson

This chapter is the first of three in a section that addresses physical management through seating, orthotics, and transportation safety. It presents an overview of mobile and stationary seating systems (including wheelchairs, classroom chairs, and other seats). Chapter 9 introduces orthotics and orthotic devices (including seating orthoses).

In this chapter, general principles of seating and positioning are reviewed, and seating products that meet the needs of persons with multiple handicaps are discussed, along with special adaptation and photographic evaluation documentation that the authors have found to be helpful. Prescription processes also are discussed. Pictures are provided to demonstrate seating principles and concepts. Readers are advised to obtain manufacturer's catalogs for specific product information (see Appendix B). Power wheelchairs are not included since independent mobility is an unrealistic goal (due to cognitive limitation) for the population described in this text. However, individuals who demonstrate the skill and judgment necessary to learn to operate a power wheelchair should be given the opportunity to use one.

IMPORTANCE OF SUPPORTED SITTING POSTURE

Less than two decades ago, many persons with multiple handicaps were confined to recumbent positions. Even considering recent advances in seating, it still is a formidable task to support such persons in an upright sitting posture. However, the work, time, and expense involved in providing appro-

Glenda Atkinson, P.T., is a faculty member at The University of Central Arkansas and seating consultant to several facilities in the Central Arkansas area.

priate seating systems are well worthwhile since the benefits of upright posture are numerous. Social and environmental stimulation, health considerations, and therapeutic management all are facilitated. Nonhandicapped people tend to respond positively to handicapped persons who are in an upright (e.g., sitting, standing) posture; whereas persons functioning on a horizontal plane are likely to be perceived as being ill, sleeping, or infantile. Upright posture gives persons with multiple handicaps an appearance of self-control. An individual who can sit upright is able to take advantage of the mobility offered by wheeled seating systems, and, thereby, receive the benefits of environmental stimulation. He or she can be transported from home to school and community functions. Persons who are confined to carts or bed-type wheelchairs have substantially less mobility, since many vehicles cannot accommodate such large, awkward pieces of equipment.

Upright posture also facilitates cardiopulmonary and gastrointestinal functions and provides a base for therapeutic management. Seating systems with head supports can enhance an individual's cognitive and communication skills. For many persons with multiple handicaps, seating systems may be their total living environment and only mode of transportation.

The goal of adapted seating is to provide "maximum function with minimum pathology" so that a seating system does the most for a person and causes the least problems (Bergan & Colangelo, 1985). Therapeutically, the effects of a good seating system normalizes muscle tone, decreases influence of primitive reflexes, minimizes deformities, maintains range of motion, increases postural stability, and may improve function.

PRINCIPLES OF SEATING

The optimal sitting position for all persons, including those with mild to moderate involvement, is with the hips, knees, and ankles flexed to about 90 degrees. Weight should be evenly distributed over the buttocks and thighs, with feet plantigrade on a footplate or the floor. Forearms should rest at elbow height on armrests. The entire body should be maintained in an upright midline posture.

The following paragraphs summarize positioning techniques that are used with persons who have cerebral palsy and other central nervous system deficits to achieve proper positioning of the pelvis, thighs and knees, feet, and trunk. The comments reflect the work of authors who are experienced in seating persons who have these conditions (Atkinson, 1988, 1989; Bergan & Colangelo, 1985; Fraser, 1989; Phelps, 1989; Trefler, 1984). In achieving proper positioning, attention should be directed first to total body considerations followed by a detailed look at the pelvis; trunk; buttocks, thighs, and knees; feet; head; and upper extremities.

Total Body Positioning

There are two angles of primary concern in seating—the seat-to-back angle (Figure 8.1) and tilt-in-space angle. Seat-to-back angle is indicated by the degrees the seat is angled from the back of the chair. Usually, a 90 degree seat-to-back angle is recommended. However, there are instances where the seat-to-back angle may be opened (increasing the angle) or closed (decreasing the angle). For example, a person with less than 90 degrees of hip flexion may require a seat-to-back angle of more than 90 degrees to accommodate a hip extension deformity (Figure 8.2). Conversely, a person with hip flexion contractures may require an 85-degree seat-to-back angle. Tilt-in-space is the angle to which the entire seating system (keeping the seat-to-back angle at a fixed point) is tilted backwards from a 0 degree (i.e., upright) position (see Figure 8.2). The combination of these two angles should be determined on an individual basis. Generally, a complete upright seating position (seat-to-back angle of 90 degrees) with no (0 degrees) tilt-in space requires an active sitting posture and facilitates standing transfers in and out of a seat (Pedotti & Andrich, 1986). It is often necessary to create a passive resting posture for persons with multiple handicaps. This is accomplished by reclining the tilt-in-space to between 15–20 degrees and/or opening the seat-to-back angle to

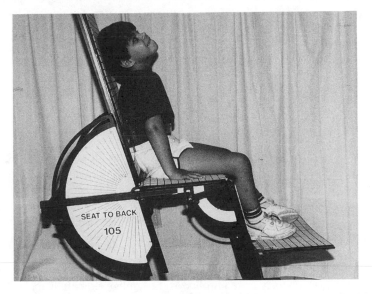

Figure 8.1. Seat-to-back angle. This Posture Evaluation Chair allows an unrestricted lateral view of sitting posture. In this case, a seat-to-back angle (i.e., degree the seat is angled from the chair back) of 105 degrees was set and marked for this photograph. The development of the Posture Evaluation Chair was supported by ERIA Chapter 2 Mini Grant No. 982, under the direction of Wayne County Intermediate School District.

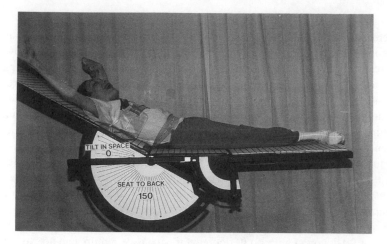

Figure 8.2.   Open seat-to-back angle. This individual has extension contractures of the hips allowing only about 30 degrees of flexion. Therefore, his seat-to-back angle is established at 150 degrees, as shown on the Posture Evaluation Chair. Note that there is no tilt-in-space because the seat is horizontal to the floor. In this case, tilt-in-space is indicated by 0 degrees.

between 95–110 degrees. Both the seat-to-back and the tilt-in-space angles of a seating system depend upon an individual's needs. Seating positions as close to upright as possible lessen the chance of aspiration and allow for improved body function.

A seating system should provide only as much support as needed. Every effort should be made to encourage active motion for muscular strength, function, and pressure relief. Total support and relief from pressure areas should be provided for those who have no active or functional movement.

Positioning of Pelvis

The pelvis should be stabilized in a neutral position on a firm padded rather than sling-type seat. Usually, this is accomplished by maintaining a 90–105 degree seat-to-back angle and using a positioning belt mounted as close as practicable to the point of intersection between the seat and back (Figure 8.3). (In addition, a separate "auto-type" seat belt attached to the chair's frame is recommended for safety.)

Posterior Pelvic Tilt

Posterior pelvic tilt may be controlled by a lumbar support if the pelvis is passively mobile. In such cases, the lumbar support positions the pelvis anteriorly. Hips guides (Figure 8.4) may be added to the seat portion of the chair to promote pelvic symmetry and to keep the buttocks centered in the chair. Occasionally, a preischial block may be used to prevent sliding forward, but usually is not effective in the case of a strong thrusting movement.

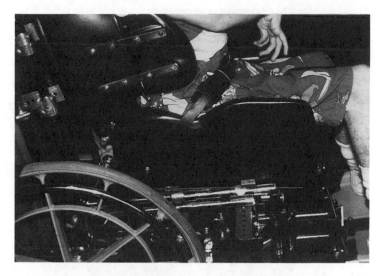

Figure 8.3. Lap belt. This lap belt is mounted from the point of intersection between the chair's seat and back to help stabilize the pelvis in a neutral position. Note the flat lateral support that provides trunk stability.

In some cases, a sacral pad and a knee block may be used to control a person who tends to slide forward. A thorough evaluation of the person's hip joints should be completed before using a knee block (Monahan, Taylor, & Shaw, 1989).

Anterior Pelvic Tilt

The pelvis may tilt anteriorly as a result of low trunk muscle tone, tight hip flexors, or tight trunk extensors. Flexible anterior pelvic tilts may require an adjustment of the seat belt angle in order for it to come across the top of the pelvis. This alignment helps pull the top of the pelvis back against the seat, bringing the pelvis into a more neutral position. A second belt may be placed across the anterior superior iliac crests to pull an anteriorly tilted pelvis back into a neutral position. If the anterior pelvic tilt is rigid, the space in the lumbar region may be filled with foam to distribute equal pressure against the back.

Hip Thrusting

Hip thrusting may be controlled (in some cases) by use of a fully wedged seat (i.e., high side of the wedge aligned with the front edge of the seat and sloping toward the rear) (Figure 8.5), half-wedged seat (i.e., high side of wedge aligned with the front edge of seat and sloping to the middle of the seat), and an antithrust seat (i.e., similar to a half-wedge with a contoured bucket for buttocks) designed to hold the hips in more than 90 degrees of

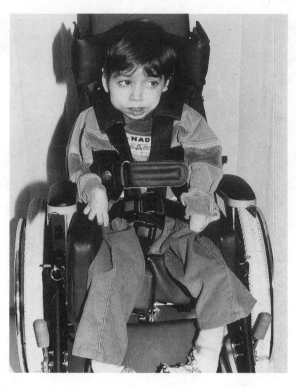

Figure 8.4. Hip guides on seating system. This child is sitting in a Kidster Chair available from Gunnell, Inc. This chair features curved lateral supports (e.g., scoliosis pads) and hip guides to hold the thighs in as adducted position as possible. The seat cushions are cut to accommodate a leg length discrepancy.

flexion. This position decreases extensor tone and helps hold the buttocks well back in the chair. Wedged seats, while useful in positioning, interfere with forward transfers. Rigid pelvic stabilizers sometimes are used to prevent undesirable pelvis positioning.

Pelvic Obliquity

Tilting of the pelvis in the sagittal plane (i.e., pelvic obliquity) may be caused by complex musculoskeletal deformities or may be triggered by something as simple as a too soft or hammock-type seat. Hammock-type seats tend to exaggerate asymmetry. A firm padded sitting surface should be used unless it is medically contraindicated. A pelvic obliquity may also be present from asymmetrical hip thrusting and should be blocked if possible. In the case of a severe rigid obliquity, a contoured cushion should be used to distribute the sitting pressure more equally across the pelvis.

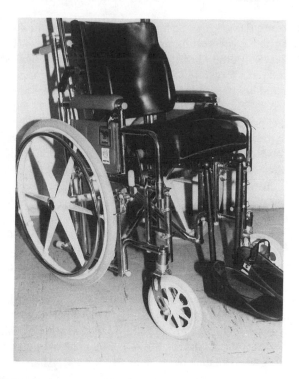

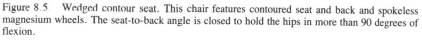

Figure 8.5. Wedged contour seat. This chair features contoured seat and back and spokeless magnesium wheels. The seat-to-back angle is closed to hold the hips in more than 90 degrees of flexion.

Positioning of Trunk

Ideally, the trunk should be held in a symmetrical, midline position. Generally, firm seat backs should be used. Most commonly encountered postural problems of the trunk are lateral and forward flexion.

Lateral Trunk Flexion

Persons with fair to good trunk control usually require lateral supports (either flat—Figure 8.3 or curved—Figure 8.4) to maintain a midline orientation. Those with mild to moderate scoliosis may benefit from a three-point control system. One support is placed at the apex of the curve on the convex side, the second support just under the axilla on the opposite side, and the third support on the concave side at the pelvis. Persons with multiple handicaps often require a four-point control system—similar to the three-point system, but including two hip supports to keep the pelvis aligned. (Use of only one hip support may result in the person shifting his or her hip away from the support.)

Lateral trunk flexion may be a postural response to gravity. If this is the case, reclining the entire seating unit (i.e., tilt-in-space) 5–10 degrees may offer a solution. Response to this recline should be noted. This should not be done if a person pulls forward in an attempt to regain upright posture. Clinical judgments should be used to decide the correct tilt-in-space angle for an individual.

A lateral support should be used in conjunction with pelvic stabilization to ensure a symmetrical base of support. Care should be taken to prevent lateral pads from cutting into the axillae and from limiting upper extremity movement. Most seating systems have lateral support pads available or the pads may be custom-made. Frequently, persons with severe spinal deformities contact a regular scoliosis pad at a small area that causes dramatic skin pressures. In this case, custom-molded scoliosis pads may be made of splinting material. These pads are molded directly on the person's body when he or she is in an upright sitting position. These pads distribute the pressure of the trunk over the entire surface of the pad to alleviate discomfort and skin pressure.

Persons with multiple impairments often experience significant fixed rotational components of the spine. Posteriorly rotated portions of the back may be relieved by removing some of the padding behind a back cushion. A back section may be cut out if the rotational component of the curve is severe (frame and cushion available from Gunnell, Inc.). It should be noted that attempts to correct a fixed deformity often result in pain and postural compensation at another area of the body.

Forward Trunk Flexion

Forward trunk flexion is another trunk asymmetry that is frequently encountered. A forward trunk may be caused by lack of adequate muscle tone in the trunk or may be due to active forward pulling. Forward flexion may be prevented by a number of options. The simplest way of providing trunk control is by using a chest strap. If control over the shoulders is needed, an H harness may be used. In either case, the chest strap or harness should be secured through a second lap belt to avoid pulling the positioning seat belt upwards. Shoulder straps or pommels may be added to a chest strap allowing individual alignment. Shoulder straps and pommels (see Figure 8.8) should be positioned away from the neck, over the humeral heads, to avoid cutting into the lateral aspects of the neck.

Forward flexion of the trunk also may be controlled with a tray or lap board. A person with fair trunk control may be able to stabilize the trunk by resting his or her arms on a tray. A molded trunk support may be placed on the inner cutout of the tray if anterior and lateral control is needed.

Added control of the flexion of the trunk and rounding of the shoulders may be provided by use of a vest. Careful fitting and application of a vest is necessary to keep pressure off the side of the neck and to allow for upper extremity movements.

Positioning of the Buttocks, Thighs, and Knees

Positioning of the thighs and knees can affect the pelvis and trunk. Weight should be distributed as evenly as possible over both buttocks and along the length of the thighs. The seat should be long enough to support the thigh almost to the knee. Contact with the popliteal fossa should be avoided to prevent circulatory difficulties. Caution should be used to avoid a seat length that is too long. A long seat length places the pelvis in a posterior tilt, encourages pelvic and spinal rotation, and causes knee extension. Frequently, an apparent thigh length difference may be present. This situation is easily accommodated by cutting each side of a seat to match each thigh length (Figure 8.6).

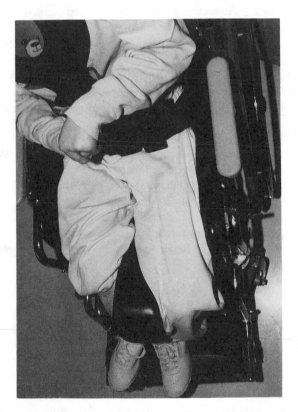

Figure 8.6.   Seat accommodates apparent thigh length difference. This person has unequal thigh lengths. The right side of the seat is cut to the correct length for the shorter thigh. Note the abductor wedge that controls hip adduction.

Thigh Alignment

In sitting, thigh alignment may assume either an abducted position requiring an adductor or may adduct requiring an abductor for positioning.

Abductors An abductor wedge is frequently used to control hip adduction (see Figure 8.6). An abductor wedge should make contact with medial aspects of the thigh and knee and should be proportional to the amount of abduction desired. A person with strong extensor internal rotation muscle tone may benefit from having a wide abductor that holds the thighs in the maximum comfortable abducted position as possible. This position helps prevent the adductor muscles from getting a strong mechanical advantage and assists in controlling a posterior pelvic tilt. Abductors may be stationary, removable, or drop-away. If an abductor is removable, it may be attached to the chair with a chain to ensure that it is not lost. Generally, abductors that do not release to an under-the-seat position should be avoided since they may interfere with transfers and other activities of daily living.

Adductors Adductors are a support placed against the lateral thigh and knee areas to hold an abducted leg in a more neutrally aligned position. Excessive hip abduction makes lower extremity position difficult. Adding lateral knee and thigh pads (i.e., adductors) or extending the hip pads along the lateral thigh helps hold the thighs in a more neutral position (Figure 8.7). If hip abduction is rigid, an extra wide seat may be designed, but this often creates a problem when the chair is wheeled through doorways.

Knee Alignment

Contractures at the knee can have a serious effect on a seating system. Knee flexion contractures up to 90 degrees do not create a problem since the person is able to sit in the chair. Past 90 degrees, however, the legs pull back into the seat edge, often causing the feet to get caught under the chair. Attempts to extend the knee cause a posterior pelvic tilt that compounds seating problems. One solution is to let the knees flex into a soft support to prevent the feet from coming in contact with wheelchair casters or other metal parts. Extension contractures of the knees may require elevated legrests.

Positioning of Feet

Positioning the feet in a plantigrade position or in slight dorsiflexion is recommended to reduce clonus and extensor tone. In a wheelchair, this may be accomplished by securing each foot to a footplate, using heel loops and a strap that cross the ankle diagonally. (Use of heel loops or shoe holders is recommended to prevent the feet from slipping off the back of footplates.) Angle-adjustable hardware may be used to mount footplates. This allows various foot positioning, often needed to accommodate deformities. Toe loops generally are not recommended. They do not help hold a foot on a footplate and may elicit a positive support reaction or plantar grasp reflex. A solid footboard may be indicated for persons with athetosis because of the larger area provided for foot support.

Positioning of Head

The simplest method of head support is a high seat back. For persons with good head control, this may be enough to help keep the head in alignment and prevent hyperextension without unnecessary restriction. An area on the seat back, behind the occiput, may be recessed to avoid excessive head flexion. High seat backs should have a removable headrest section to facilitate transfers and placement of the seating system in cars or vans.

Many headrests that are available are designed for persons with fair to good head control. These headrests usually provide posterior and partial lateral support. They act as a guide or "reminder" for head placement. Lateral head supports may be used if lateral head and neck flexion occurs. Lateral head supports should be positioned in order to not block sound from the ears or restrict the individual's visual field. Commercially available neck rings and collars often provide control for lateral movements (see Figure 8.7). The Hen-

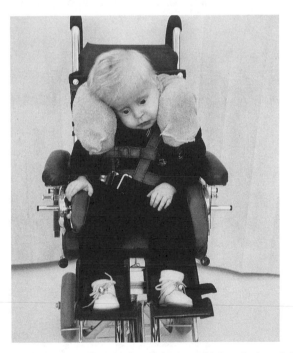

Figure 8.7.   Adductor pads control abduction. Pads were added to the lateral thigh and knee areas to hold the thighs in as neutral position as possible. The headrest (a modified Hensinger head positioner) may serve as a collar and a head support. In this photograph the positioner is open allowing lateral movement of the head. During transportation, the positioner is fastened under the chin to provide posterior, lateral, and anterior support.

singer head support (available from Danmar Products, Inc.) provides posterior, lateral, and anterior support (Fraser, Hensinger, Marchello, & Taylor, 1985). This works well for many persons, but should not be used for someone who forcibly flexes the head forward or bites the collar. Halo headrests (Figure 8.8) may be used to prevent mild forward head movement, but may not be safe for persons with strong forward head thrust. In select cases, custom-made headrests have been constructed for persons with severe head control deficiencies using a trial-and-error approach (Bergan & Colangelo, 1985). Such custom-made headrests are expensive and, in the authors' experience, not completely satisfactory, but may be a last resort option.

Positioning of Upper Extremities

The upper extremities should be placed in a comfortable position with no extremes of range of motion. The shoulder girdle should be in a stable neutral position that allows for as much mobility of the arms as possible. The shoulders may be slightly flexed and abducted with neutral humeral rotation. Elbows should be flexed between 40–100 degrees with the forearms in a neutral (i.e., neither supinated or pronated) position. The wrists should be

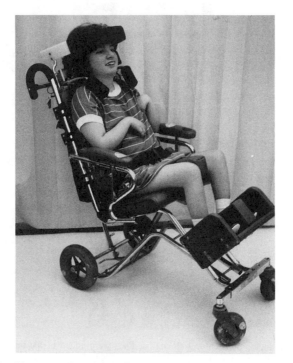

Figure 8.8. Shoulder pommels and halo head support. This chair demonstrates a "mix-and-match" approach to seating. The base chair is from Ortho-Kinetics, Inc. with shoulder pommels, neckrest, and halo head support from Mobility Plus, Inc. and a custom-made footrest.

slightly extended with the hands loosely open. This ideal upper extremity positioning is often difficult to achieve. Upper extremity positioning is discussed in detail in Chapter 13.

PRODUCTS FOR PERSONS WITH MULTIPLE HANDICAPS

Advancements in seating systems, in most cases, has made it possible to select, prescribe, and design an appropriate seating system for an individual. Many persons with multiple handicaps require more than one seating system to accommodate their life-styles and positioning needs. An individual may use a travel chair for transportation and general use, but need a floor feeder chair for feeding, positioning, and relaxation. Or, a person who uses a standard wheelchair may need to transfer to a large stable classroom-type chair for table or group activities. Optimal positioning (see "Principles of Seating," p. 112) remains the goal with persons with multiple handicaps even though its achievement is rarely possible. To even approximate this goal, seating systems need to be adapted to provide comfort and security, maximize function, minimize or delay contractures and deformities, inhibit abnormal reflex activity, and facilitate movement. The following suggestions reflect the authors' experience in prescribing, designing, and modifying seating systems and seating positioning aids for persons with multiple handicaps. (Trays are discussed in Chapters 11 and 13.)

Standard Wheelchairs

Standard (sometimes called traditional) wheelchairs usually feature large rear wheels, caster-type front wheels, and a soft (e.g., sling-type hammock) back and seat. In recent years, this basic design has been expanded to include many light weight wheelchairs. Most can be folded for easy storage and transportation, and may be ordered with reclining backs. Originally, standard wheelchairs were designed for persons with good or normal trunk and head control who were capable of independent self-propelled transportation (e.g., paraplegics). Persons with multiple handicaps are most likely to use this type of chair (with appropriate adaptations such as a padded firm seat and back) if they have fair to good trunk and head control, have the ability for assisted standing transfers, and do not have severe fixed deformities. Standard-type chairs (or at least their frames) also serve as the foundation for many individually designed orthotic seating systems. Manufacturers and distributors of standard type wheelchairs include Everest & Jennings; Invacare Corp.; Motion Designs, Inc.; Quadra Wheelchairs, Inc.; Stainless Medical Products; and Scandinavian Mobility Products.

Wheelchair Stability

Persons with multiple handicaps who are capable of using a standard-type wheelchair often need special features and/or modifications to accommodate behavioral and muscle tone abnormalities. Persons who demonstrate rocking behavior or athetoid movements often need a heavy-duty wheelchair frame and need to specify that at the time of the original order. An indoor-style frame with the large wheels in the front also can provide stability for someone with strong extraneous movements. In addition, a one-piece fiberglass bucket-type seat provides extra seat strength (available from Gunnell, Inc.). Semireclining wheelchairs should be permanently secured at the desired angle. This prevents loss of wheelchair parts and maladjustments, especially if several caregivers are handling an individual.

Backs and Seats

Persons who do not need to have a wheel that folds the chair (e.g., those who are transported in their wheelchairs in specially designed buses or vans) should have a hard back, permanently installed, for improved postural control as well as increased stability. The hard back should be attached to the front of the chair's metal uprights for stability. Seat depth is reduced by such an installation. This needs to be taken into account when measuring to provide adequate support for the thighs. Hard backs and seats also may be installed in folding wheelchairs. (Use of sling-type seats and backs is not recommended because they facilitate asymmetrical sitting posture.) Also, hard seats and backs are needed to provide a strong base of support for persons who wear bracing for scoliosis (see Chapter 9). Hard backs and seats may be attached to the wheelchair frame via angle-adjustable hardware (e.g., clip-on brackets) for easy removal and depth adjustments. Such hardware should be used with wedged seats to accommodate changes in the wedge's angle. (It should be noted that angle-adjustable hardware requires extra chair width.) Companies that provide hardware include Adaptive Engineering Lab., Inc.; Consumer Care Products; Creative Rehabilitation Equipment; Jay Medical, Ltd.; Miller's; Otto Bock Orthopedic Industry; and Variety Village.

An alternative solution involves strapping a solid seat and back over existing seat and back upholstery. Incontinent persons need a water-proof seat. (Urine seeps through the seams of stitched vinyl fabric and rots underlying foam and wood.) Solutions include the use of hard plastic seats (available from Gunnell Inc.; Theradyne Corporation), vacuum sealed vinyl (available from Pin Dot Products), and vinyl coating (available from Danmar Products, Inc.). An inexpensive solution is to wrap the foam and wood in plastic before covering it with vinyl.

Wheelchair Armrests

In some cases, wheelchair armrests should be permanently attached. Many persons with multiple handicaps are not capable of side transfers and do not need removable arms. Permanently attached armrests add to the stability of the chair. Since severe deformities often prevent persons with multiple handicaps from resting their arms on an armrest, adjustability of armrest height often is unnecessary. Desk arms should be considered if the wheelchair is to be placed under a table. Durastat armrest covers or pads may be used instead of plastic or wooden ones (available from Theradyne Corporation). Wood has a tendency to split and plastic to crack under the strain of a tray that is supported by the armrest. Durastat armpad covers hold up quite well to daily stress. However, they are hard, and prolonged arm resting may become uncomfortable. Also, tray brackets may have to be adjusted to fit over these armrest pads.

Wheels, Tires, Rims, and Wheel Locks

Spokeless wheels (see Figure 8.5), often constructed of magnesium, are recommended. Magnesium wheels are strong and weigh about the same as standard-type spoked wheels. Spoked wheels do not hold up well when used with tie-down systems on buses and need frequent repairs. Special wheel weight, placement, and rims should be considered for persons capable of maneuvering their own wheelchairs. Standard wheels with toggle locks (i.e., single brake position) generally are sufficient for this population. However, quick release axles and wheel weight may be considerations for parents or caregivers who fold and lift a wheelchair into a car. Nonpneumatic or polyurethane tires are recommended to reduce maintenance requirements. (Pneumatic tires are subject to leakage and puncture.) If a wide tire is needed, a flat-free tube should be used (e.g., No-More Flats tube from Cyclo).

Legrests, Footplates, Footboards, and Calf Panels

Elevating legrests usually are not recommended unless needed for orthopaedic reasons (e.g., to accommodate knee extension deformities). Swing-away legrests are helpful to clear space for front-of-chair transfers. However, they should be permanently attached to the wheelchair to prevent removal and loss. For persons whose equipment is handled by several caregivers, additions to a chair, such as abductor pommels, should be permanently attached. Large-size individual footplates are useful for many persons with multiple handicaps. Some even require the extra room and stability provided by a one-piece footboard. Generally, such footboards should not be used in cases of rigid knee flexion contractures because the contractures interfere with raising and lowering the footboard. Calf panels often are used to prevent the legs and feet from slipping off or being caught behind a footplate or footboard. In cases of behavioral kicking, the calf panel can extend from the seat to the footplate or footboard to prevent the person's feet from being caught in the wheels.

Lap Belts

Car-type lap belts with a button release mechanism are recommended in most instances. They prevent persons with multiple handicaps from accidentally or behaviorally unbuckling the belt. (It is more difficult for such persons to release a push-button mechanism than a flip-up-type buckle.) Buckle size should be appropriate to the individual. Padding may be added to the underside of the metal buckle to prevent abrasion and the transfer of hot and cold sensations to the user. Also, the buckle should be positioned to the side of the person to avoid extra pressure over the abdomen. It has been common practice to place the buckle at the rear of the wheelchair if inappropriate unbuckling is a concern. However, certain advocacy groups have taken the position that this constitutes a restraint and, therefore, is not allowable.

Specialized Wheelchairs and Strollers

Specialized wheelchairs are usually derived from standard wheelchairs or wheelchair frames onto which adjustable features have been mounted (Hobson, 1984; Shaw, 1984). They came into being because seating/wheelchair systems were needed that provided individualized full body support, yet allowed for change when necessary without destroying the system. For example, one manufacturer offers reclining fiberglass bucket seats that are attached to a standard wheelchair frame (available from Gunnell Inc.). Other examples include a car seat that may be inserted into wheelchairs equipped with removable armrests (available from American Sunroof Corporation) and growth guidance chairs that feature portability for automobile travel.

Lightweight strollers provide temporary transportation for persons with handicaps. Some strollers are similar in appearance to those used by young nonhandicapped children and feature optional postural control devices (available from Andrews Macaren Ltd; Theradyne Corporation). Other stroller features available include a push-type wheelchair design with postural controls (available from Ortho-Kinetics, Inc.; Safety Rehab.) One seating system for infants and small children is the Snug Seat (available from Snug Seat, Inc.). It is an extremely adjustable system using multiple pads velcroed together in a car seat. It can be used in a stroller or a trolley or as a car seat. The Carrie Seat, also for use with infants and small children (available from J. A. Preston), can be used in a stroller frame or as a positioning/car seat as well. Another system, the CP seat (available from Pin Dot Products), is mounted in a stroller or wheelchair frame and fits infant sizes.

Specialized wheelchair and stroller concepts have stimulated a "mix-and-match" approach to seating (see Figure 8.8). Thanks to new advances that feature product compatibility, it is now possible to mix and match features of various seating systems. For example, thoracic support pads may be purchased from one company (e.g., Medical Equipment Distributors, Inc.; Otto Bock Orthotic Industry, Inc.) and added to another manufacturer's wheelchair frame; or a modular chest support may be added to a sports-type wheelchair. Some manufacturers offer entire positioning systems that may be added to standard wheelchairs (e.g., Mobility Plus, Inc.; Scott Therapeutic Designs).

Custom Contour Seating

Another innovation in wheelchair seating involves the use of contour backs and seats. Contour seating provides a firm surface (as opposed to soft cushions) that conforms to the shape of an individual's back and/or buttocks and thighs. Contour backs and seats may be fashioned by hand carving foam—a process that is accomplished by trial and error (Figure 8.9). Once the desired result is obtained, the foam is covered with a vinyl fabric or dip. Hand-carved polyurethane foam seats may be used for positioning, such as an anteriorally wedged seat or raised seat, where a precise body mold is not required. Foam-in-Place seating allows the formation of a contoured system of Sun-Mate foam (available from Dynamic Systems, Inc.). A liquid mixture is used that expands around the patient's body forming a contoured mold or foam that is covered with terry cloth and silicone or is vinyl dipped. Pin Dot Systems offers a similar system.

A more sophisticated process uses atmospheric pressure to consolidate small particles, such as plastic beads, thereby transferring a body shape or creating a definite body support (Hobson, 1984). With this process, a mold is created of an individual's back, buttocks, and thighs by having the person sit in a sealed plastic bean-bag–type apparatus while air is extracted. A plaster cast is then made of the impressions in the bean bag, and the hardened plaster is used as a guide for carving foam to match the body's contours. Once the foam is dipped in a vinyl coating, the seating system may be placed in a standard wheelchair frame.

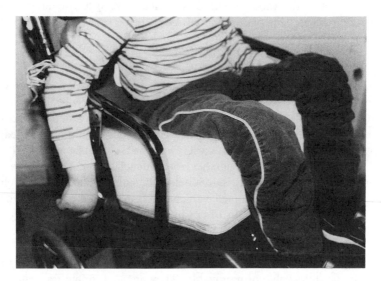

Figure 8.9.   Hand-carved foam seat. The foam is carved from a block by trail and error until a desired configuration is obtained.

This concept has found many applications in industry. One manufacturer (e.g., Pin Dot Products) has combined prefabricated and/or custom-molded cushion and multi-adjustable hardware to produce tailor-made shapes and a variety of positioning options for use in a standard wheelchair base (see Figure 8.5). This is commonly known as the Contour U seat. This type of system does not require separate pieces such as scoliosis and abductor pads, thus, minimizing adjustment and eliminating replacement of lost parts.

Orthotic Seating

Seating orthoses are constructed using a casting process. An orthotist casts the back, buttocks, and thighs of an individual who is prone over the edge of a table. This position allows for elongation of the spine and, in most cases, improved positioning of a spinal deformity. Also, casting may be made with the person in a sitting position by using a process that extracts air from a bean bag on which the individual is seated. A cast is taken of the impression left in the bean bag once the person is removed.

This method takes into account the force of gravity acting on the hips and thighs during sitting—a realistic approach that results in added seating comfort. The cast (i.e., a negative mold) is removed once the plaster hardens. Plaster is poured into the mold cavity to form a positive likeness of the person's body. The positive likeness is secured to a vacuum pump by a hollow (i.e., mandrell) pipe. Heated polypropylene is then draped over the model. The valve of the vacuum pump is opened and air is extracted through the hollow pipe. This process adheres the polypropylene to the model. The polypropylene retains the model's shape unless it is reheated to at least 400 degrees Fahrenheit. This plastic impression is then inserted into a wheelchair frame or stroller as a seating orthosis (Figure 8.10).

Travel and Care Chairs

Originally, travel or transport chairs were designed for small children. They could double as a car seat because of their retractable rear wheels (available from Ortho-Kinetics, Inc.). Presently, travel chairs are available in several sizes and, therefore, can accommodate larger persons. Some models feature removable rear wheels (from Safety Travel Chairs, Inc.) or an added fifth wheel that is used as a pivot (available from Gunnell, Inc.). Travel chairs are a popular means of transporting individuals with multiple handicaps on school buses and other handicap-adapted vehicles. Their designs have changed in recent years to reflect the results of crashworthiness tests. However, because they have grown in size as the passenger compartments of most automobiles have shrunk, their use as car seats has diminished.

Care chairs are similar in design to travel chairs, except that their rear wheels are not retractable or removable. They are appropriate for many ado-

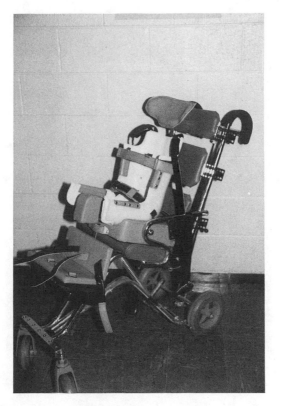

Figure 8.10. Seating orthosis. This orthosis is inserted into an Orthokinetic Travel Chair. Liners may be removed to accommodate growth.

lescent- and adult-size persons with multiple handicaps, especially those residing in nursing homes or institutions.

Travel and care chairs offer a wide range of postural controls, including adductor and abductor pommels, lateral supports, headrests, and lap belts. Y-shaped harness trunk supports that posed possible neck injury and strangulation risks to persons with poor head control have been replaced by "H" or butterfly harnesses.

Modifications

Modification may be inexpensively made in existing seating system. For example, wedged and antithrust seats may be substituted for standard ones in order to position the hips in more than 90 degrees of flexion. Covers may be placed over existing scoliosis supports to broaden and soften contact with the chest wall. The use of a 1-inch-wide H harness with a separate lap belt and a

Figure 8.11. Wayne County Intermediate School District chair prototype. This sturdy chair features seat adjustability, lateral torso supports, and flip-up footplates (available from Danmar Products, Inc.).

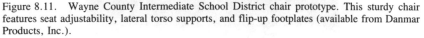

2-inch-wide pelvic belt helps caregivers distinguish between the two and avoids confusion in securing an individual into the chair. In addition, the pelvic belt helps stabilize the pelvis and hips.

Classroom Seating

The mid–1970 developments involving special education programs brought awareness of classroom seating needs. Equipment designed for positioning severely deformed students in a classroom was almost nonexistent (Fraser & Hensinger, 1983). At that time, classrooms were equipped with small "kindergarten chairs," unpadded wooden chairs, and regular classroom-type chairs—rarely appropriate for students with multiple handicaps. Generally, wooden chairs were easier to adapt than plastic or metal classroom ones. At present, several types of classroom seats (e.g., bolster chairs, adjustable chairs, corner chairs, chair/desk sets) are commercially available (from Equipment Shop; Kaye Products; Motor Development Corporation). In addition, floor feeder seats provide a major supplement to wheelchair seating and a means for classroom, recreational, and therapeutic positioning (available

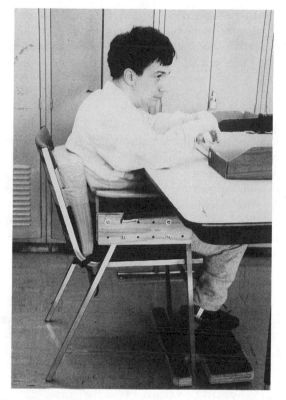

Figure 8.12.   Custom adaptations to a classroom chair. A back wedge and side supports offer security and help maintain good sitting posture. A footrest is placed under the front legs of the chair to accommodate leg length (available from Danmar Products, Inc.).

from Tumble Forms, Inc.). A large, sturdy classroom chair with seat adjustability, lateral supports, and a flip-up height-adjustable footplates is commercially available for adolescents and adults (Figure 8.11) (from Danmar Products, Inc.) In addition, custom-built adaptation may be added to a classroom chair for postural control and safety (Figure 8.12) (available from Danmar Products, Inc.)

Protective Coverings

Persons with multiple handicaps often have bony prominences due to deformities, and soft parts of their seating systems, such as belts and ankle straps, need extra padding as a result. Metal parts, such as footplates, also can be padded to prevent skin abrasions. Trays often are padded to prevent injury from head banging or loss of head control in a forward direction during seizure.

Persons in bed-type wheelchairs or carts (many of whom have a severe scoliosis) need a safety restraint to protect them in the event of sudden stops, bumps, or other unusual occurrences. A soft vinyl-covered foam pad that covers the trunk and hips is used instead of a safety strap to prevent localized pressure on the trunk and abdomen that could lead to internal injuries.

Foams

Open cell foams allow air exchange and have effective pressure-relief qualities, but tend to absorb fluids and odors (e.g., polyurethane foams, temperature-respondent foams). Foams such as Sun-Mate and Temper Foam soften under body heat to obtain better pressure distribution, but also get hard when exposed to cold and tend to readily bottom out (from Dynamic Systems, Inc.; AliMed, Inc., Relyan Medical Products). A wide range of densities and conforming capabilities are available. An overly soft system enhances any postural abnormalities that may be present; therefore, the foam should be firm enough to support the body well.

Closed cell foams are impermeable to fluids and can be sculpted to create a contour seat or back. These range from very course-cell foams, such as Adaptafoam, Constructafoam, or styrofoam (available from Modular Medical Corp.; AliMed, Inc.; floral supply warehouses), to fine-cell foams, such as super constructafoam and Formafoam (available from AliMed, Inc.; Danmar Products, Inc.). These foams can bear heavy weights for long periods of time and do not tend to bottom out easily.

Seating System Prescription

Seating systems are sophisticated and expensive pieces of equipment. It is important that they meet the present and anticipated medical, therapeutic, educational, home, and transportation needs of their users as fully as practicable. This goal is best achieved through a prescription process (a necessity in third-party pay situations) that involves the coordinated efforts of a physician or physicians, physical and occupational therapists, parents and caregivers, and the person with the handicap. In addition, teacher, social worker, speech-language pathologist, and orthotist contributions should be solicited. In this way, a balanced view of the person's need may be obtained. Often, compromise is required of all concerned.

Wheelchair or seating clinics for wheelchair-bound patients of various medical diagnostic categories have been conducted at several rehabilitation centers and hospital (Jones, Margolis, & Brown, 1983; Riani & McNeny, 1981; Shaw, 1984). Also, school-based equipment clinics have been established specifically for students with multiple handicaps (Fraser & Hensinger, 1983). This is particularly feasible in special school programs where large numbers of students with handicaps are located in one building and seating equipment is available for trial purposes. Professionals prescribing seating equipment should remember that one system will not meet all persons' needs. There is no one "global" seating approach satisfactory for persons with multiple handicaps.

Coordinated prescription of seating systems includes assessment of the person's needs; equipment trials, modifications, and selection; equipment provision; and follow-up.

Assessment of Person's Needs

Medical, therapeutic, and parental/caregiver assessments of an individual's needs should be given before looking at equipment. The physician's assessment establishes a diagnosis and prognosis, provides a medical history, and describes past or planned surgeries. Therapeutic (e.g., physical, occupational, possible speech-language) assessment usually follows and entails a description of developmental motor skills, joint limitations, abnormal muscle tone, pathological reflexes that affect posture, strength, coordination, sensation, functional activities, and gross and fine motor skills. Speech-language contributions include information about the type of communication system the person is using if it is to be incorporated into the seating system.

Parental and caregiver assessment includes a description of the home environment, method of transportation, and life-style of the family and the person who is handicapped. Family needs should receive careful consideration. A social worker well-versed in financial or funding arrangements for seating systems should be available for consultation. In the case of a school-age person, teacher input is recommended as seating systems often become the foundation upon which an educational program is built.

Coordination of assessments should be handled by a health professional. Depending upon the situation, this may be a physical or occupational therapist, social worker, or physician. Coordinated assessments may be shared during a wheelchair or seating clinic, or reports may be circulated.

Equipment Trials, Modification, and Selection

A review of commercially available equipment is the second step in the prescription process. Aid should be obtained from equipment specialists or vendors who are familiar with the needs of persons with multiple handicaps and knowledgeable about the availability of seating products. Commercially available seating systems should be considered first in order to contain costs. Custom-made systems should be considered only as a last resort. Before making decisions regarding the purchase of equipment, the handicapped person should be evaluated using the seating systems. This can be particularly useful if a multistage prescription process is used (i.e., physician or therapists see the handicapped persons at different times).

Ideally, equipment selection should take place at a seating, wheelchair, or school equipment clinic. In the event such a clinic is not available, assessment and recommendation reports, along with photographs, may be sent to the referring physician for prescription consideration.

Equipment Provision

A protocol for specifying seating system via prescriptions should be established to avoid the appearance of favoritism. Riani and McNeny (1981) suggest that attempts not be made to allocate orders equitably among vendors since that practice contradicts the goals of selecting the most appropriate equipment for each individual. They recommend giving priority to the vendor that assures quickest delivery of a particular seating system. Rapid delivery is appropriate for persons who require no or little seating adaptations. However, specialized seating systems that require extra care in fitting will inevitably take longer to deliver, a process that is often more important in the long run than speed. Considerations especially important for persons with multiple handicaps are a vendor's ability to provide adaptations, repair service, and loaner seats.

Follow-Up

Follow-up consists of reviewing the assessments and the prescription, observing the individual using the seating system, and receiving feedback from parents, caregivers, and others regarding everyday use of the equipment. Follow-up should be performed by the same persons involved in the original assessment, if possible. If necessary, revisions are provided or prescribed at this time. Follow-up should occur routinely every 6 months to 1 year, and more frequently during growth spurts.

Future Directions

Contributions to seating for persons with multiple handicaps have come from many sources: industry, rehabilitation engineers, physicians, therapists, orthotists, and educators. Even so, these groups have worked largely in isolation. Until the late 1980s, there has been little communication either within groups or among groups about new developments. Information reaching users has been haphazard and incomplete. There has been a tendency to focus on "pet" seating concepts while ignoring other systems, and reliance on trial-and-error approaches to customized seating.

In the past, few attempts have been made to develop a common nomenclature. For example, trunk supports are called lateral pads, scoliosis pads, thoracic supports, or chest supports at the discretion of the manufacturer or researchers. Many times, a general type of seating system is identified only by a manufacturer's name (e.g., Ortho-Kinetic chair, Gunnell wheelchair, Maclaren Buggy). This is confusing to persons who may not be familiar with the particular manufacturer. Also, it is not fair to manufacturers who produce a wide range of products.

There is also a need to define the population for whom specific seating systems are intended, especially in the case of persons with multiple handicaps. These persons demonstrate a wide range of abilities and disabilities. Descriptions such as good, fair, and poor trunk or head control need quantitative definition. Combinations of deformities need analysis to establish classification by shapes, sizes, and body contours common to persons with multiple handicaps. Such information will help researchers and manufacturers to design and mass produce seating products for these persons. It also will help to take the guesswork out of the seating prescription process by establishing guides for matching physical impairments with appropriate seating equipment.

CLOSING THOUGHTS

Seating systems and positioning techniques for persons with mild to moderate handicaps are well established. However, only more recently has attention been given to seating that meets the unique and complex needs of persons with multiple handicaps. Much progress has been made in providing a variety of seating systems (e.g., standard wheelchairs, specialized wheelchairs and strollers, contour seats, travel and care chairs, classroom chairs). Major contributions have come from industry and health and educational professionals. Even so, on-site modifications usually are required to seat an individual with multiple handicaps correctly and safely. Future efforts (including application of space-related technology) may be expected to produce further advances in seating systems that will improve the quality of life for persons with multiple handicaps.

REFERENCES

Atkinson, G. (1988, February). *Seating for geriatric and pediatric clients*. Lecture presented at the Annual Combined Sections Meeting of the American Physical Therapy Association, Washington, DC.

Atkinson, G. (1989, March). *Commercially available seating products and do-it-yourself seating*. Lecture presented at the Fifth Annual Conference on Developmental Disabilities, Southfield, MI.

Bergan, A.F., & Colangelo, C. (1985). *Positioning the client with central nervous system deficits: The wheelchair and other adapted equipment* (2nd. ed.). Valhalla, NY: Valhalla Rehabilitation Publications.

Fraser, B.A. (1989, March). *Principles and protocol of seating*. Lecture presented at the Fifth Annual Conference on Developmental Disabilities, Southfield, MI.

Fraser, B.A., & Hensinger, R.N. (1983). *Managing physical handicaps: A practical guide for parents, care providers, and educators*. Baltimore: Paul H. Brookes Publishing Co.

Fraser, B.A., Hensinger, R.N., Marchello, J.L., & Taylor, S.R. (1985, October). *Headrest development project*. Paper presented at the annual meeting of the American Academy for Cerebral Palsy and Developmental Medicine, Seattle, WA.

Hobson, D.A. (1984). Matching client needs with specialized seating option. In E. Trefler (Ed.), *Seating for children with cerebral palsy: A resource manual* (pp. 93–101). Memphis: The University of Tennessee Center for the Health Sciences, Rehabilitation Engineering Program.

Jones, R.M., Margolis, S.A., & Brown, B.E. (1983, October). *Meeting the seated positioning needs of the cerebral palsied population.* Paper presented at the 37th annual meeting of the American Academy for Cerebral Palsy and Developmental Medicine, Chicago.

Monahan, L.C., Taylor, S.J., Shaw, C.G. (1989, February). *Pelvic positioning: Another option.* Paper presented at the fifth International Seating Symposium, Memphis, TN.

Pedotti, A. & Andrich, R. (1986). *Evaluation and information in the field of technical aids for disabled persons: A European perspective* (Monograph No. 35). New York: International Exchange of Experts and Information in Rehabilitation, World Rehabilitation Fund, Inc.

Phelps, J.A. (1989). *Functional therapeutic positioning.* Lecture presented at the Fifth Annual Conference on Developmental Disabilities, Southfield, MI.

Riani, R.M., & McNeny, R. (1981). Wheelchair clinic: A better way to prescribe. *Clinical Management in Physical Therapy, 1*(2), 18–19.

Shaw, C.G. (1984). The service delivery process. In E. Trefler (Ed.), *Seating for children with cerebral palsy: A resource manual* (pp. 163–179). Memphis: The University of Tennessee Center for the Health Sciences, Rehabilitation Engineering Program.

Trefler, E. (Ed.). (1984). *Seating for children with cerebral palsy: A resource manual.* Memphis: The University of Tennessee Center for the Health Sciences, Rehabilitation Engineering Program.

Chapter
9

— . —

Overview of Orthotics

with Steven R. Taylor
and Carol L. Topper

The word orthotics is relatively new. Orthotics, taken from the Greek word orthostatic, meaning to straighten and cause to stand, was introduced in 1953 (Licht, 1966). At that time, orthotics meant straightening of deformities by external support. Presently, orthotics refers to external support devices and the art and science of applying such devices to external surfaces of the body. An orthosis is an assistive, substitutive, or corrective external device designed to improve the quality of a patient's functioning (Drennan & Gage, 1983).

While the term orthotics is relatively new, use of orthoses (i.e., braces) has occurred since the Egyptian dynasty (2750–2625 B.C.) (Smith, 1908). Well into the 20th century, physicians (especially orthopaedists) served as the brace makers. Winthrop Phelps was one of the first physicians to develop a system of bracing for persons with cerebral palsy (Phelps, 1952). In 1963, orthotics became a paramedical profession. Its direction and control were assumed by the American Orthotic and Prosthetic Association.

Today, an orthotist is a nonphysician practitioner who designs, fabricates, and fits orthoses to persons with disabling conditions of the limbs and spine. An orthotist may assist physicians in evaluating an individual's functional loss and needs and in formulating orthotic prescriptions. Responsibility for orthotic design, measurements, casts, fittings, modifications, and static and dynamic alignments lies with the orthotist.

Steven R. Taylor, C.O., is an orthotist in private practice in Ann Arbor, Michigan.

Carol L. Topper, C.O., O.T.R. is an orthotist at Detroit Institute for Children in Detroit, Michigan.

PRACTICE SETTINGS

There are five principal areas of orthotic involvement: private practice, institutional practice, fabrication and supply laboratories, teaching, and research. Private practioners are independent providers of services and devices. They serve physicians and persons with handicaps in specific geographic locations. This type of practice setting is the most prevalent. Institutional practice (e.g., large hospitals, rehabilitation centers) involves orthotic services via an internal staff usually to inpatients. Orthoses may be fabricated and supplied by orthotists working in central fabrication laboratories. Such laboratories are separate from the sites where fitting and measurement take place. Private practitioners and institutional orthotists often send negative casts and measurements to fabrication laboratories to have an orthosis fabricated and returned to them for fitting. This arrangement is similar to central dental laboratories used by most dentists. Some orthotists provide instruction to students attending university-sponsored orthotic courses. Presently, there are 11 such programs in the United States that offer entry-level orthotic training (Donald & Shurr, 1984). A few orthotists devote their practice to research. However, funding for orthotic research is difficult to procure, and most research is conducted by orthotists working in university or institutional settings.

ORTHOTIC CATEGORIES AND NAMING SYSTEMS

Orthoses are divided into three categories: lower extremity, upper extremity, and spinal devices. An orthosis is described by the joint(s) it encompasses and influences and is commonly abbreviated using initials (Foster & Milani, 1979). For example, an ankle-foot orthosis (AFO), controlling joints of the ankle and foot, is a lower extremity device. A wrist-hand orthosis (WHO) is an upper extremity device. A thoraco-lumbo-sacral orthosis (TLSO) influences the thoracic, lumbar, and sacral areas of the spine.

ORTHOTIC MATERIALS

Until the early 1960s, almost all orthoses were made of metal and leather. The metal components gave structural support, with leather elements providing diffuse (i.e., circumferential) pressure over the skin contact areas. Metal and leather orthoses still are widely used today. However, metal is heavy and leather poses a hygiene problem. Leather is stained by perspiration buildup and is also difficult to clean.

Introduction of thermoplastics in the early 1960s had a marked impact on orthotics. Molded thermoplastic orthoses enhanced the function, fit, and cosmetic appearance of these devices (Drennan & Gage, 1983). Plastics are approximately one-fourth the weight of metal and are easily cleaned. Plastic orthoses may be removed, washed, and dried quickly and maintain a new-like appearance after periodic washings. Also, plastic orthoses provide better control of joint segments than metal and leather bracing. This is possible because thermoplastic bracing provides total joint contact; thus, forces can be applied directly to the joint to maintain a desired alignment. Most plastics used in orthotics are high-temperature molding plastic. In some cases, such as neonates or fast-growing children, low-temperature plastics that become malleable under hot tap water may be used (Figure 9.1). They are less expensive and may be fabricated easily as growth or change causes replacement needs. In many cases, low-temperature plastic orthoses are effective in improving spinal alignment (Figure 9.2).

The introduction of seating orthoses (see Chapter 8) focused orthotists' attention on a variety of materials, such as polyurethane and polyethylene foams, and styrene and other plastic composites, that are useful in maintain-

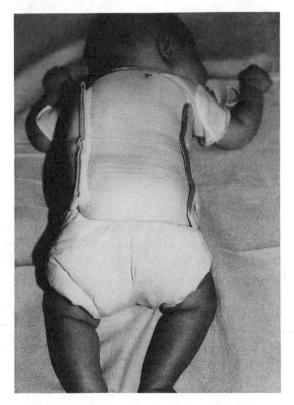

Figure 9.1.   Low-temperature plastic orthosis. Low-temperature plastic (i.e., orthoplast) may be used for interim bracing (e.g., when rapid growth is expected). The TLSO pictured consists of an orthoplast posterior shell and an elastic anterior segment.

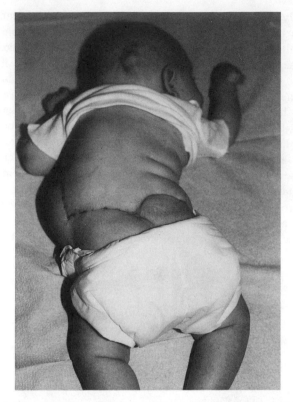

Figure 9.2.   Infant with scoliosis. This infant with myelodysplasia needs a TLSO to align the spine and prevent the scoliosis from progressing. Note the corrected position achieved by use of a low-thermal plastic and elastic TLSO by comparing this picture to that of the same infant pictured in Figure 9.1.

ing the body in a sitting position. Since orthotic research is limited, orthotists have tended to find new materials appropriate for orthotic applications in other industries. For example, Surlyn, a golf ball covering, is also used as an orthotic material.

ORTHOSES FOR PERSONS WITH MULTIPLE HANDICAPS

In general, orthoses are appropriate for persons with multiple handicaps if deformities are mild to moderate and the total contact provided by an orthosis can be tolerated. Poor physical condition (e.g., deteriorated cardiopulmonary function) and/or fixed severe deformities may contraindicate the use of orthoses (see Chapter 5).

Persons with multiple handicaps often require spinal orthoses, less frequently need lower extremity orthoses, and least often use upper extremity orthoses. The following discussion pertains to those spinal and lower extremity orthoses that are used most frequently by individuals with multiple handicaps. Upper extremity orthoses are not discussed; however, splinting is presented in Chapter 12.

Spinal Orthoses

There are generally two types of spinal orthoses: jacket (i.e., wraparound) (Figure 9.3) and clamshell (Figures 9.4 and 9.5). The jacket-type orthosis with an anterior opening is usually prescribed for persons with multiple handicaps to allow for quick removal of the orthosis by caregivers. (Persons with idiopathic scoliosis benefit from a jacket-type orthosis with a posterior opening that allows a more direct pull on the apex of the scoliotic curves.) Clear plastic or polyethylene is recommended rather than opaque. Clear plastic allows caregivers to observe the fit and undershirt beneath the orthosis. (The undershirt should be relatively free of wrinkles for wearing comfort.) The jacket-type orthosis provides total contact, is easy to fabricate, and doesn't pinch the skin. It probably offers more correction than the clamshell-type because the tightening of the straps over the posterior opening provides a dynamic assist in reducing a scoliotic curve.

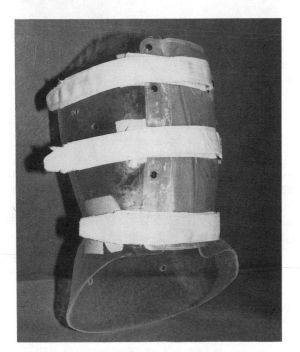

Figure 9.3. Jacket-type orthosis. This orthosis has an anterior opening for quick, easy removal. It is vented via drilled holes to increase air circulation for wearing comfort.

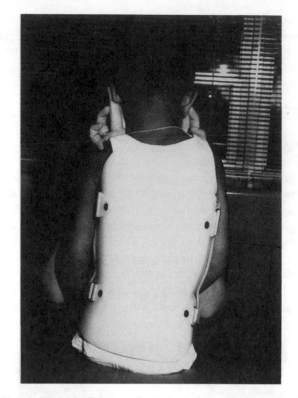

Figure 9.4. Clamshell orthosis. This type of orthosis also is known as a molded plastic bivalved TLSO. Bivalved indicates separate anterior and posterior plastic shells.

The clamshell orthosis is two-pieced with posterior and anterior segments that fit together much like a clam's shell when the two halves close. Clamshell orthoses usually are prescribed for paraplegic children who are capable of self-dressing in a prone position. Straps are conveniently located at the side of the orthosis instead of the back. Occasionally, clamshell orthoses are prescribed for persons with multiple handicaps. If so, a 3-inch overlap is recommended where the anterior and posterior sections join to avoid pinching the person's skin. The rigid side support doesn't compromise pulmonary function and avoids pressure over bony prominences.

Evaluation

An orthotist receives a prescription for a spinal orthosis from a referring physician or may develop a prescription in consultation with a physician. Considerations include the amount of correction expected, the amount of force the skin and bones can stand, the location and direction of the curve, the

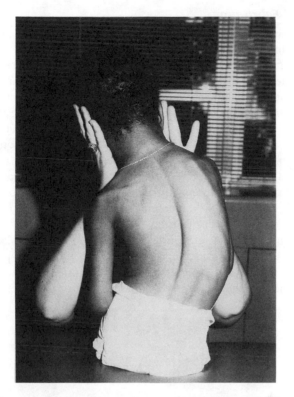

Figure 9.5. Rotoscoliosis. This is the same person shown in Figure 9.4 without the TLSO. A comparison of the pictures shows the support that the TLSO provides for a flexible curve. The TLSO also helps prevent progression of the curve.

presence of a rib hump, and the alignment of the trunk. A prescription includes the person's diagnosis and prognosis and indicates the type of orthosis desired. Generally, an X-ray is provided with the prescription to indicate curve measurements. After reviewing the prescription, the orthotist evaluates the person with the handicap, usually in the orthotist's office. In the case of persons with multiple handicaps, a combined evaluation by an orthotist and an attending physical therapist is recommended. Evaluation includes observing the spinal curve or curves and exploring respiratory and digestive problems. (Spinal orthoses may increase intraabdominal pressure, and, in some cases, an ill-fitting orthosis can restrict respiration and digestion.) Attention is paid to the handicapped person's life-style, activities, and tolerance to wearing the prescribed type of orthosis. Orthoses for persons with multiple handicaps should accommodate diapers and permit the cleaning of urine and feces stains.

Casting and Fabrication

After the evaluation is completed, a cast is taken of spinal areas that the orthosis should control. Plaster of Paris bandage strips are used in casting. A stocking is placed over the designated body surface, the plaster strips are soaked in water, and then wrapped over the stocking (see Figure 8.10). The spine is manipulated into the straightest achievable alignment during this process. Usually good results may be achieved by positioning the person's torso prone over the edge of a table with the hips flexed to about 90 degrees. This position reduces the natural lordosis and allows an orthotist to apply pelvic traction to elongate the spine and reduce scoliosis. Also, manual pressure is applied to the apex of the curve to obtain at least a partially corrected position. The plaster hardens quickly and is removed (Figure 9.6). The rest of the process is similar to that described for seating orthoses in Chapter 8. A trial fitting is conducted once the orthosis is fabricated. Revision may be made by heating the plastic and remolding a part of the orthosis. Also, pads are added at the curve's apexes and excess material is removed to prevent pressure from the inferior and superior borders of the orthosis. Detailed written wearing instructions should be given to parents and/or caregivers at the time

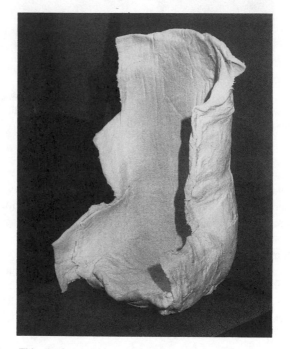

Figure 9.6. Cast. This cast is a negative mold of the back and buttocks of an individual with multiple handicaps.

of the final fitting. A period of adjustment to orthoses wearing is required. This usually consists of 1- to 2-hour wearing sessions in the morning and afternoon for the first week and then gradually increasing wearing time to tolerance.

Orthosis Modifications

Meeting the special needs of persons with multiple handicaps often requires that orthoses be modified. For example, an individual with temperature control difficulties may benefit from having a ventilated orthosis. This may be accomplished by drilling holes through the orthosis (see Figure 9.3). Or, a person with aerophagia may require a plastic posterior shell and an elastic anterior segment to accommodate varying degrees of abdominal protrusion (Figure 9.7). Riveted areas should be padded to prevent skin breakdown.

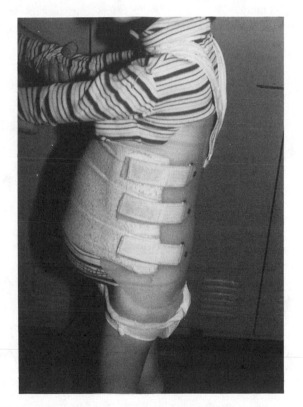

Figure 9.7. Modified thoraco-lumbo-sacral orthosis (TLSO). This TLSO was modified to accommodate a protruding abdomen that changes size due to aerophagia. It consists of a high-temperature plastic posterior shell and an elastic anterior segment.

Lower Extremity Orthoses

Generally, hip-knee-ankle-foot orthoses (HKAFO) or knee-ankle-foot orthoses (KAFO) are not indicated for persons with multiple handicaps (see Chapter 5); therefore, they are not discussed here. (AFOs) (Figure 9.8) may be used to maintain the ankle-foot complex in a straight or corrected alignment. Occasionally, AFOs with floor (sometimes called ground) reaction (Figure 9.9) are used in cases of gastrocnemius and quadriceps muscle weakness, assisting in extending the knee (Harrington, Lin, & Gage,1983). They hold the foot in slight plantar flexion and encourage an extended knee posture during standing or walking activities. During weight-bearing stance and heel-off phase of gait, the anterior portion of the orthosis presses against the front of the leg just below the knee, thus encouraging knee extension. In this way, floor reaction AFOs serve as a training device for standing and ambulation. In order to be effective, it is important that the orthosis is casted with the foot in a corrected alignment. The plastic AFO offers foot protection and avoids rubbing. It has the added advantage of fitting into a regular shoe.

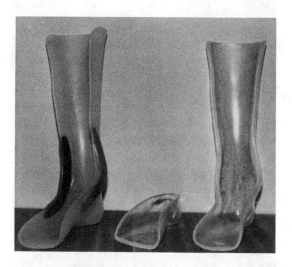

Figure 9.8.   Ankle-foot orthoses (AFOs). This photograph shows three types of AFOs. The one on the right is a solid molded plastic AFO. This type commonly is used to provide medial and lateral support to the ankle joint, to prevent malalignment or contracture of the foot-ankle complex, and to assist in dorsiflexion. The foot orthosis in the middle offers medial and lateral control of the ankle-foot complex by locking the subtalar joint in a neutral position. It is commonly referred to as a U.C.B.L. because it was developed at the University of California, Berkeley Laboratory. The solid plastic AFO on the left has carbon composite inserts that provide extra ankle stability during weight bearing.

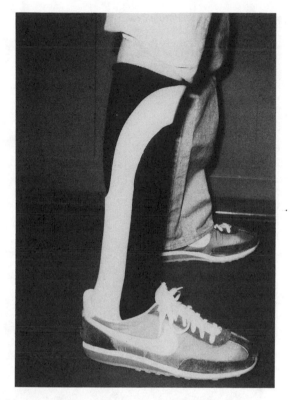

Figure 9.9. Ankle-foot orthosis (AFO) with floor reactor. The ground reactors are located on the front of the leg, just distal to the knees. During weight bearing, the ground reactors press against the front of the leg causing the knee to straighten.

Tone Reducing Ankle Foot Orthoses

Tone reducing ankle foot orthoses (TRAFOs) were originally designed to assist in maintaining a stable base of support for the feet (Jordan, Riesseque, & Cosack, 1983) (Figures 9.10 and 9.11). This is accomplished by locking the feet and ankles in neutral alignment. Once a stable base of support has been achieved, it is easier for the individual to control more proximal areas. It, also, is felt that this stable base of support results in a decrease in the amount of distal fixation used by an individual.

There are a number of reflexes that may be elicited by stimulating various areas of the plantar surface of the foot. Stimulating any of these reflexes may result in increased tone. TRAFOs distribute pressure evenly along the

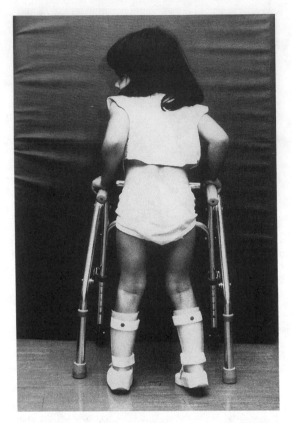

Figure 9.10.   Child wearing tone reducing ankle-foot orthoses (TRAFOs). A comparison with Figure 9.11 shows the postural improvement obtained when wearing TRAFOs.

weight-bearing surface of the foot and, thereby, prevent stimulation of any one of these reflexes. In addition, toe clawing, which may lead to an increase in tone, may be eliminated by providing a small lift under the toes to maintain them in neutral extension (Figure 9.12).

TRAFOs may be constructed of a fiberglass cast that is molded directly to the person and then bivalved, providing an anterior and posterior shell or they can be made from high temperature plastics.

CLOSING THOUGHTS

Orthotics, a relatively new paramedical profession, refers to external support devices and the art and science of applying such devices to external surfaces

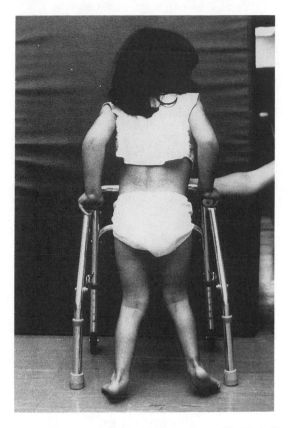

Figure 9.11. Child without tone reducing ankle-foot orthoses (TRAFOs). Note the crouched gait with flexion, the hips, the knees, and the valgus of the feet. The use of TRAFOs shown in Figure 9.10 increases lower extremity extension and decreases valgus of the feet.

of the body. Orthoses are divided into three categories: upper extremity, lower extremity, and spinal devices. The orthoses used most often by persons with multiple handicaps are those in the last two categories. An orthosis is described by the joint(s) it encompasses and influences. Specifically, thoraco-lumbo-sacral orthoses (TLSOs) are required to control C-shaped scoliosis, common to this population; ankle-foot orthoses (AFCs) may be used to align and support the ankle-foot complex. Presently, orthotic materials include thermoplastics and foams, as well as metal and leather. Orthosis modifications often are required to meet an individual's needs.

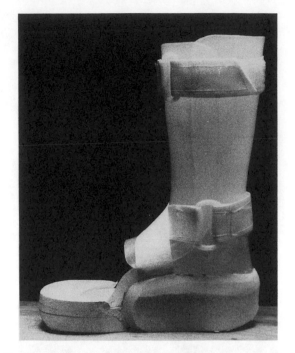

Figure 9.12. Tone reducing ankle-foot orthosis (TRAFO) with plastic bivalve ankle-foot orthosis and crepe sole. Note the slight elevation under the toes to help prevent toe clawing.

REFERENCES

Donald, G., & Shurr, M.A. (1984, Spring). The delivery of orthotic and prosthetic services in America. *Orthotics and Prosthetics, I,* 55–63.

Drennan, J.C., & Gage, J.R. (1983). Orthotics in cerebral palsy. In G.H. Thompson, I.L. Rubin, & R.M. Bilenker (Eds.), *Comprehensive management of cerebral palsy* (pp. 205–213). New York: Grune & Stratton.

Foster, F., & Milani, J. (1979). The genucentric knee orthosis—a new concept. *Orthotics and Prosthetics, 33,* 31.

Harrington, E.D., Lin, R.S., & Gage, M.D. (1983). Use of the anterior floor reaction orthosis in patients with cerebral palsy. *Journal of American Orthotic-Prosthetic Association, 37*(4), 34–42.

Jordan, P., Riesseque, D., & Cosack, J. (1983). *Biomechanics group workshop on TRAFOs.* Chicago: Langer.

Licht, S. (1966). *Orthotics ETC* (1st ed.). Baltimore: Williams & Wilkins.

Phelps, W.M. (1952). Bracing in the cerebral palsies. In J.W. Edwards (Ed.), *Orthopaedic appliances atlas* (Vol. 1, pp. 521–536). St. Louis: C.V. Mosby.

Smith, G.E. (1908, March). *British Medical Journal, I.*

Chapter
10
— • —

Transportation of Wheelchair-Seated Students

Lawrence W. Schneider

On a per vehicle mile basis, school bus transportation is one of the safest means of travel, with an accident rate of only one-fourth that of passenger automobiles. Transportation safety of the able-bodied student is further enhanced by Federal Motor Vehicle Safety Standard 222 (FMVSS 222) that requires that school buses be provided with high-backed, padded, forward-facing, closely spaced seats that provide protection in a vehicle frontal impact through "compartmentalization." For the student who is disabled, however, and especially those students who travel seated in wheelchairs and other mobile seating devices, the transportation situation is quite different. Not only do these students frequently travel over longer distances and in smaller buses and van-sized vehicles, thereby increasing their exposure and risk to vehicle accidents, but they are often transported without any effective provision for protection in the event of a vehicle crash or even an emergency maneuver or stop.

Thousands of students with severe disabilities travel to and from school each day and throughout the community in family passenger vans and buses, with the sole hope for safe transportation based on avoidance of an accident or emergency maneuver. This need not be the case if general principles of occupant protection are followed, if equipment used to secure and restrain the

Lawrence W. Schneider, Ph.D., is a research scientist and head of the Biosciences Division of The University of Michigan Transportation Research Institute in Ann Arbor.

wheelchair and its occupant is designed to withstand forces that can develop in a crash, and if restraint devices, wheelchairs, and securement procedures are properly evaluated using standard and well-established dynamic test procedures. In most cases, crashworthiness "packaging" of wheelchair-seated students can be greatly improved beyond what is generally offered in school buses today.

It must also be recognized that providing safe transportation for the student with severe disabilities is a *systems* problem that involves the wheelchair, the student with his or her unique disabilities and requirements, the wheelchair securement devices or tie-downs, the occupant restraint system, and finally, the vehicle—its structural design and the procedures used for installing occupant restraints and wheelchair tie-downs. Providing effective occupant protection requires consideration and resolution of each of these aspects of the total system. Failure to adequately deal with any one of these aspects can result in ineffective occupant protection. For example, if an otherwise effective wheelchair tie-down system is inadequately installed in a vehicle, the installation points may fail during crash loading, thereby releasing the wheelchair and occupant to become free projectiles in the vehicle. The discussion that follows deals primarily with the procedures and equipment used to provide wheelchair tie-down and occupant restraint.

GOALS OF OCCUPANT PROTECTION SYSTEMS

It is a well established fact that the primary cause of serious injury to motor vehicle occupants in a crash is the "human collision" or "second impact," where the occupant's body strikes components of the vehicle's interior after it has come to a stop as a result of the "first collision." The goal of any occupant protection system is, first of all, to prevent the traveler from being thrown out of the vehicle and, secondly, to prevent or minimize the human collision within the vehicle by allowing the occupant to "ride down" the vehicle crash in the space available between him- or herself and the vehicle interior.

For the wheelchair user who can transfer or be transferred out of the wheelchair, these goals are best accomplished by moving the occupant to the vehicle seat so the Original Equipment Manufacturer (OEM) restraint systems, or other properly evaluated restraint system, can be used. The wheelchair can then be stored and secured more easily with effective tie-down hardware and procedures.

There are, of course, many students for which transfer is not practical. In these cases, an effective occupant protection system must provide both *wheelchair securement* or *tie-down* and an integrated *occupant restraint system*. Both must be designed to deal with crash-level forces and with adherence to established crashworthiness design principles.

Restraining the Wheelchair
Effectively and Independent from Occupant

A basic rule of crashworthiness safety is not to allow the vehicle seat to add to the forces applied to the occupant during a crash. A simple way of estimating the magnitudes of required restraint forces is to multiply the average vehicle deceleration (i.e., rate of stopping) by the mass of the object being restrained. Thus, in a 48km/hr (30 mph) crash where the vehicle deceleration averages 20 g's (i.e., 20 times gravitational acceleration), the force required to restrain a 45 kg (100 lb) wheelchair would be 900 kg (2000 lb). The actual tension in two rear tie-down straps would be half of this divided by the cosine of the angle of the belts or about 640 kg (1400 lb) for each side, if the belts are angled at 45 degrees. This is a significant and undesirable amount of additional load to place on an occupant.

Adhering to this principle is particularly important for the person in a wheelchair or other special seating device where the chair mass can range from 10 to 90 kg (25 to 200 lb) and more, and where the occupant's tolerance to impact loading is likely to be less than that of an able-bodied person. Following this rule means that the wheelchair must be secured in place with minimal movement during a crash (e.g., 2 to 6 cm) and without tipping over, collapsing, or breaking apart in a manner that would be injurious to the user or other vehicle occupants. It also means that the wheelchair tie-down system should secure the wheelchair independent from the occupant. That is, the same belt should not be used to restrain both the wheelchair and the occupant so that the forces generated by the mass of the wheelchair are not applied to the occupant. Even if different belts are used to restrain the wheelchair and occupant, but both are secured to the vehicle, the wheelchair can add to the loading of the occupant if there is more stretch or "give" in the tie-down straps than in the occupant restraints.

Use of Both Upper and Lower Torso Restraints

Since the purpose of an occupant protection system is to prevent violent contact of the occupant's body with vehicle structures, both lower and upper torso restraints are needed to minimize knee, chest, and head excursions. While a properly positioned lap belt alone will prevent an occupant from being ejected from the vehicle or thrown about inside, it will not prevent the torso from "jackknifing" forward, which can allow the chest and head to impact with nearby vehicle structures and components or with other nearby occupants and wheelchairs.

Application of Force to Bony Regions of the Body

Another general principle that has often been ignored with the wheelchair-seated motor-vehicle occupant, but that must be followed in any good occupant protection system, is to apply restraint forces to the bony regions of the body and not to the soft tissues regions such as the abdomen. For a lap belt, this means keeping the angle of the belt reasonably steep (e.g., 45 degrees to the vertical or greater) so that it stays on the pelvic bone. For the shoulder belt, this means allowing it to cross over the shoulder (i.e., clavicle) as well as the chest and, if the shoulder belt is part of a three-point lap and shoulder belt system, the shoulder belt should merge with the lap belt near the hip of the occupant (i.e., not over the lap) so that it doesn't pull the lap belt up onto the soft abdominal tissues during impact loading.

Frequently, seat belts are used to provide postural support and seating stability for persons in wheelchairs. These are often wrapped around the seat back of the wheelchair at the level of the abdomen or chest. Such belts should not be intended for use as a crash restraint system and should, in fact, be designed so that high forces will not be applied by these belts (e.g., so that these belts will break away prior to inflicting injury-producing forces).

Because of the difficulty in fitting vehicle-anchored lap belts low on the pelvis of a person who is wheelchair-seated due to interference with wheelchair armrests, wheels, and other structures, it can be more desirable, in terms of fit, to provide lap-belt anchor points on the wheelchair. Thus, while it is generally necessary to attach the upper anchor point of a shoulder belt or harness to a vehicle structure (i.e., the structures of wheelchairs are usually neither strong enough, nor high enough), it is generally best to anchor the lower portion of the shoulder belt to the lap belt, as is done in a standard three-point belt system.

Orient Wheelchairs and
Occupants in Forward or Rearward Positions

The issue of whether it is safer to face wheelchairs and their occupants forward (or rearward) versus sideways is a statistical one. It is a well established fact that most motor vehicle accidents involving serious and fatal injuries have the primary component of impact from the front (i.e., more than 50%). While such statistics generally refer to personal licensed vehicles, similar percentages have been compiled from the Fatal Accident Reporting System (FARS) data base for school bus fatalities. These accident statistics, with regard to frequency of impact direction, have been taken into account in FMVSS 222 that requires all school buses to be manufactured with forward-facing, high-backed, padded seats, thereby providing impact protection during frontal crashes by compartmentalization, as mentioned earlier. Because of practical and economic considerations, however, the wheelchair passenger has generally been transported facing sideways, backed up to the side wall of the bus and facing the aisle, often with several wheelchairs, travel chairs, and/or stroller-type chairs aligned next to each other. From an occupant protection standpoint, this is probably the least safe way to travel, for anyone.

From a strictly crashworthiness perspective, the safest direction for an occupant to face is rearward, if a properly designed and padded seat back or structure is provided to absorb and distribute impact loads over the occupant's back during a frontal crash. In general, this may prove to be impractical and unacceptable for both the vehicle driver and the passengers.

A significant step toward improving occupant protection for the student who is wheelchair-seated can be made by facing the wheelchair forward, providing adequate spacing between chairs, and, as described below, using dynamically tested wheelchair tie-downs and occupant restraint systems. Comments from some transportation professionals who have made the change to forward-facing wheelchairs have indicated that the traveler may also arrive at the destination with less fatigue and in a more pleasant and attentive mood, apparently from not having to fight the lateral jerking movement as the vehicle changes speeds or from having to watch the scenery passing by through the opposite-side windows.

Padding of Vehicle Interior and Nearby Surfaces

In the previous section, mention was made of providing adequate space around the passengers to prevent the second impact with other occupants, their wheelchairs, or other vehicle structures. As specified in FMVSS 222 regarding school bus seats, consideration should be given to padding vehicle structures near wheelchair-seated travelers. This padding should be of sufficient thickness and density to prevent bottoming out during impact loading from vehicle occupants.

Use of Dynamically Tested Equipment and Procedures

Finally, and perhaps most importantly, any hardware and procedures for securing a wheelchair and restraining its occupant must be dynamically evaluated using an appropriate size anthropomorphic crash dummy and an impact pulse representative of expected real-life crash conditions. Such tests are typically conducted on an impact sled, such as shown in Figure 10.1, at the University of Michigan Transportation Research Institute (UMTRI). In these tests, the forces developed in the tie-down and restraint equipment depend on the impact velocity and deceleration, the size and weight of the anthropomorphic crash dummy, and the weight of the wheelchair and any add-on equipment.

The level of crash severity for which a wheelchair tie-down and occupant restraint system must perform (i.e., the impact velocities, decelerations, resulting restraint forces) will depend to a great extent on the vehicle size and its travel mode. Thus, for a large school bus that only travels on city streets, a crash pulse of 16 to 32 km/hr (10 to 20 mph) and eight to fifteen g's deceleration (1g = acceleration of gravity = $9.8 m/sec^2$) would be reasonable test

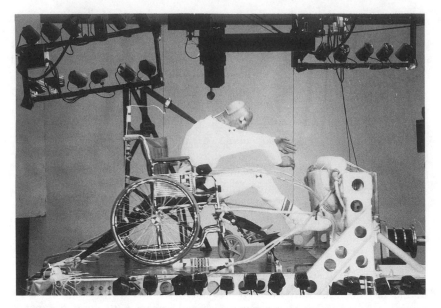

Figure 10.1. Impact sled. University of Michigan Transportation Research Institute (UMTRI) impact sled showing peak-of-action photo of a dynamic test of a wheelchair tie-down and restraint system.

conditions. However, for a van or van-sized school bus that travels on exressways, a 48 km/hr (30 mph) crash velocity may be more appropriate.

The deceleration level associated with a crash velocity depends on the vehicle structure, which determines the amount of "crush" developed during a frontal barrier crash (i.e., a crash into a flat, vertical, nonmoving structure). For a typical full-sized van with a relatively short front end (i.e., small crush distance), decelerations can average 30 g's and above for a 48 km/hr (30 mph) barrier crash. For a full-sized passenger vehicle with greater frontal crush, a typical 48 km/hr (30 mph) barrier crash will produce average decelerations of about 20 g's. As a consequence, the Federal standard for sled testing and performance of child restraint systems specifies a 48 km/hr (30 mph), 20 g crash pulse.

Since a large proportion of wheelchair-bound travelers are transported in vans or van-sized vehicles, a case could easily be made for using a crash pulse of 48 km/hr (30 mph) and 30 g's for testing most restraint system adaptive equipment. Recognizing the lower limits of human impact tolerance of persons with severe disabilities and the limitations in wheelchair designs and strengths, the UMTRI has suggested and uses 48 km/hr (30 mph), 20 g crash pulse conditions, similar to those specified in FMVSS 213, to evaluate wheelchair tie-down and occupant restraint equipment intended for general use.

EFFECTIVE TIE-DOWN/RESTRAINT SYSTEMS

Through the use of sled impact testing, several manufacturers of restraint equipment have made significant improvements with respect to occupant protection and safety for persons seated in wheelchairs. For school bus transportation, the most universal type of wheelchair tie-down that can adapt to different sizes and styles of wheelchairs utilizes four belts or straps to secure the wheelchair to the vehicle. There are currently three strap- or belt-type four-point tie-down systems available to the consumer that incorporate a three-point occupant restraint system and that have effectively restrained a power wheelchair weighing 68 kg and a 50th percentile test dummy (i.e., 77 kg) during 48km/hr (30 mph), 20 g impact tests.

"Q'Straint" by Giram, Inc.

A system by Giram, Inc., known as Q'Straint, is shown in Figure 10.2. Four 5 cm wide (i.e., 2″ wide) tie-down straps anchor to the vehicle floor by means of steel clips that attach into stainless steel pockets or brackets bolted to the vehicle floor structure at four points. Two of these points are in front of the wheelchair and two behind. Longer tie-down tracks with multiple anchor points are also available from Q'Straint if adjustability in tie-down locations is desired but are not traditionally used. The straps attach to the wheelchair frame by means of vinyl-coated steel hooks and are tightened by tensioning

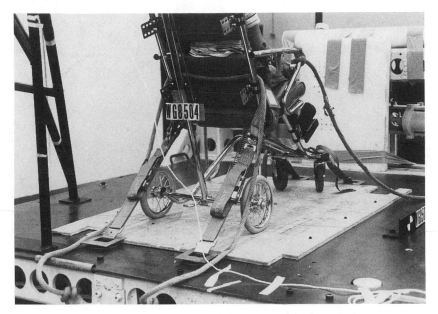

Figure 10.2. Q'Straint tie-down system. This is a rear view of the Q'Straint four-point system with integrated three-point restraint system that is attached to a travel wheelchair.

mechanisms in the rear tie-down belts. The left and right lap belt segments attach to metal snap-on fasteners that are sewn into the rear tie-down straps on each side. The lower end of the shoulder belt attaches to a similar snap-on fastener that is sewn into each part of the lap belt webbing. The upper end of the shoulder belt anchors to the vehicle structure on the vehicle side wall, above and behind the occupant's shoulders.

Both the hooks that attach to the wheelchair and the clips that insert into the floor brackets remain open for ease of installation and removal. Because of this, the system depends on maintaining a reasonable amount of tension in the tie-down straps during a crash, and care must be taken to attach the hooks to front and back wheelchair parts between which there will be little or no deformation during impact loading (e.g., opposite ends of a horizontal frame member). The primary concern is at the floor brackets, where overlap of the anchor clips with the steel lip of the floor brackets is less than 2 cm. A retrofit kit, to eliminate the possibility of disengagement, will be available in the early 1990s.

"Protector" by Ortho Safe Systems, Inc.

The system known as "Protector" (pictured in Figure 10.3) is manufactured by Ortho Safe Systems, Inc. of New Jersey. This system uses four 5-cm-wide tie-down belts and includes a three-point occupant restraint system integrated

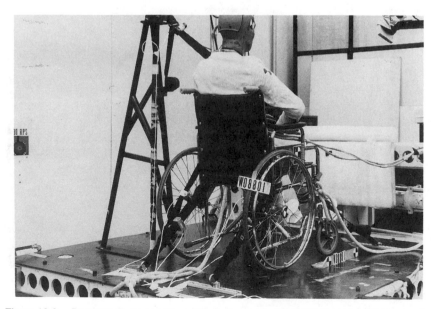

Figure 10.3.   Protector tie-down system. The Protector is a four-point tie-down and integrated three-point restraint system manufactured by Ortho Safe Systems, Inc.

into the rear tie-down straps. The system uses standard seat belt buckles to attach the occupant restraints to the tie-down straps as well as to secure each strap to the wheelchair after it is looped around the wheelchair frame and buckled back to itself. The tie-down straps are tensioned from the front to the back by means of hand-turned adjustment mechanisms on the front straps. The tie-down assemblies fasten to the vehicle by means of anchor plugs that insert into aluminum tracks bolted laterally (i.e., side to side) across the vehicle floor, in front and behind the wheelchair. This allows for lateral adjustment in tie-down locations for different sizes of wheelchairs. Both the anchor plugs and the attachments to the wheelchairs are positive-locking, thereby minimizing the possibility of a strap coming free, should it become slack during impact.

Aeroquip/Indiana Mills Tie-Down/Restraint System

Aeroquip tie-down straps, made of nylon webbing and having a width of 2.5 cm (e.g., 1″), have been utilized for many years to secure wheelchairs in motor vehicles. However, until the late 1980s, an occupant restraint system was not provided. Modifications to the original tie-down hardware have greatly improved this equipment as a protective system for persons who are wheelchair-seated, as pictured in Figure 10.4. The anchor plugs that insert into slots in the steel track have been strengthened and pivoting steel rings have replaced the slotted bracket to which the webbing attaches thereby

Figure 10.4.   Aeoroquip tie-down system. This is a rear view of an Aeroquip four-point tie-down system with three-point restraint system by Indiana Mills, Inc.

allowing the straps to align with the direction of impact loading. The Aero-quip tie-down straps have positive attachments to both the tie-down track and the wheelchair, and can be moved to different locations to accommodate different-size wheelchairs. Attachment to the wheelchair is accomplished by wrapping the webbing around a frame member (preferably at a welded junction of two frame members) and hooking the positive-locking steel hook onto a steel ring that is sewn into the tie-down-strap.

For the occupant restraint portion of the Aeroquip system, Indiana Mills, Inc. has modified a three-point belt so that it hooks to the steel rings on the Aeroquip anchor plugs. In a recent modification of the shoulder belt, a floor anchor plug is installed at the upper end of the webbing and a section of the tie-down track is bolted to the side structure of the vehicle. This provides an adjustable shoulder belt anchorage.

The Aeroquip/Indiana Mills tie-down/restraint system is currently marketed with instructions stating that the occupant restraint belts should be anchored to separate anchor plugs that insert into separate slots in the tie-down track from those to which the wheelchair tie-down straps are attached. Because the 2.5 cm-wide nylon tie-down straps, typically used with the Aeroquip tie-down system, will stretch more than the 5-cm-wide restraint belt material, Aeroquip changed to polyester belt material to minimize the possibility of providing partial restraint of the wheelchair through the vehicle-anchored occupant restraint belts.

"Strap-LOK" by Creative Controls, Inc. and "Sure-Lock" by Gresham Driving Aids, Inc.

Two additional tie-down/restraint systems that have been effective in 48km/hr (30 mph), 20 g frontal impact collisions are the "Strap-LOK," by Creative Controls, Inc., and the "Sure-Lock," by Gresham Driving Aids, Inc. These systems are pictured in Figures 10.5 and 10.6, respectively. The Strap-LOK system utilizes an Aeroquip tie-down track, fastened to the vehicle floor, running front to back, underneath the center of the wheelchair. Two rear tie-down belts hook onto the wheelchair axles and anchor to the rear tie-down assembly that plugs into slots in the Aeroquip track. A single front tie-down strap anchors to the same length of Aeroquip track extending in front of the wheelchair and attaches to the wheelchair by means of a steel bar that spans across the wheelchair side frames, resting on the curved risers just above the front casters and behind the front vertical posts of the side frames. Large steel washers, welded to the ends of this bar, capture the wheelchair. However, as with Q'Straint, the system depends on maintaining tension between front and rear straps to keep the front bar in place. The lap belt attaches to the ends of the rear tie-down bar and the shoulder belt anchors to the tie-down track separately.

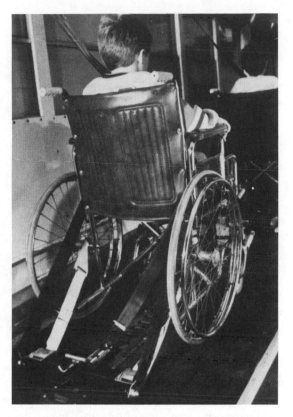

Figure 10.5. Strap-LOK manual tie-down system by Creative Controls, Inc. Lap belts attach to a tie-down structure and shoulder belt anchors to the tie-down track separately.

The "Sure-Lock" system utilizes front and back floor brackets into which tie-down anchor clips attach. These clips and floor brackets are similar in design to those of the Q'Straint system, but are much larger, thereby reducing the possibility of disengagement due to system slack. The back of the wheelchair is secured by two steel hooks that attach to the wheelchair axles on each side. These hooks are welded to an adjustable telescoping bar that connects to the floor bracket with an anchor clip and a heavy duty steel hinge. The lap belt ends anchor near the center of this bar and the shoulder belt attaches to the lap belt on one side. The front tie-down straps attach to a steel bar that fits across the width of the wheelchair, similar to that of the strap-LOK system. Flat plates, welded to the ends of this bar, keep it in place on the wheelchair as long as tension is maintained in the front tie-down strap.

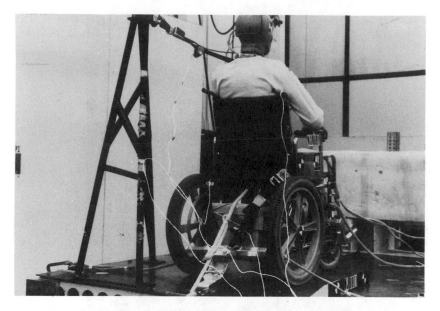

Figure 10.6. Sure-Lock tie-down system. This is a rear view of the Sure-Lock manual tie-down system by Gresham Driving Aids, Inc., with an integrated three-point restraint system.

WHEELCHAIR EVALUATION

As indicated previously, the problem of providing safe transportation for the wheelchair-seated passenger is a *systems* problem. Thus, a tie-down/restraint system that is effective for one type or size of wheelchair may not be equally effective with a different wheelchair. To date, all the systems described have been effective for 48 km/hr (30 mph) tests of standard manual and power wheelchairs with welded tubular steel frames weighing up to approximately 70 kg (150 pounds). Wheelchairs that differ significantly in design and materials should be subjected to dynamic testing to evaluate their crashworthiness potential with effective tie-down systems and to determine the optimal wheelchair attachment points. For example, the Q'Straint and Ortho Safe Systems have also been tested and shown to be effective in securing selected travel chairs such as those made by Orthokinetics, Inc. and Sunrise Medical, Inc.

At this time, no system has been found to be effective for 48 km/hr (30 mph) impacts with the three-wheel–type wheelchairs either due to the pedestal type seating system that cannot withstand crash forces or due to the large mass of the wheelchair that generates forces greater than the strength of current tie-down hardware. While tie-down systems mentioned above may be able to secure these chairs at lower g levels and, therefore, might provide suitable wheelchair and occupant restraint for larger vehicle transportation situations, it is recommended that persons using these types of chairs transfer to an OEM vehicle seat whenever possible.

CRASHWORTHINESS STANDARDS

While PL 94-142, enacted in 1976, requires that children with handicaps be provided an opportunity for public education including transportation to and from school, and while FMVSS 222 provides a high measure of safety for able-bodied children bused to and from school, there, as yet, are no federally established standards or even recommended guidelines for providing safe transportation of students who are severely disabled. In fact, while FMVSS 222 requires forward-facing seats for all able-bodied students, it specifically excludes the wheelchair seated passengers and defines them as sitting obliquely or laterally in the vehicle.

In the absence of federal standards for procedures and equipment used in transporting students who are wheelchair-seated, many school districts have taken it upon themselves to establish guidelines and requirements. For example, many school districts are now requiring that all wheelchairs face forward in the bus and are using only equipment that has been dynamically tested at 48 km/hr (30 mph) and 20 g's. School transportation officials responsible for the transportation of students who are wheelchair-seated must, of course, be concerned not only with the tie-down and restraint equipment, but also with the types of wheelchairs being used and the manner in which the equipment is installed in the vehicle.

Efforts to get the federal government to establish standards for procedures and equipment used to transport the student with handicaps (or the motor vehicle occupant who is handicapped, in general) have met with little success to date. The general explanation for the lack of federal action is that there is little evidence of the need for such standards since there is no large "count" of injuries or fatalities.

It appears that the best hope for standards in the future rests with the Adaptive Devices Subcommittee of the Society of Automotive Engineers (SAE) that is currently working to establish an SAE Recommended Practice for "Wheelchair Tie-downs and Occupant Restraint Systems." There is also some encouragement in this direction from the International Standards Organization (ISO) that has established a special working group to facilitate an ISO Standard for wheelchair tie-downs and restraint systems. Currently, Australia has the most comprehensive standard for testing and evaluating restraint system adaptive equipment. It is expected that this document and the SAE's effort will provide significant input toward the development of an ISO standard for wheelchair restraint system adaptive equipment.

While these standard development efforts are not specifically targeted toward school transportation, they will, nevertheless, provide useful design and procedural guidelines and a basis for testing and evaluating equipment used in transportation of students with disabilities, since the full-size van is a common mode of transportation in all cases and represents the worse-case test conditions. Ultimately, it is hoped that the United States Department of Education will follow up the 1976 legislation with the establishment of a standard that specifically addresses the safe transportation of all children who are handicapped and with adequate funding for research and testing that is required to improve the state-of-the-art in transportation safety for individuals who are severely disabled.

CLOSING THOUGHTS

References concerning transportation of students who are wheelchair-seated are listed in Appendix E. Also, Appendix H contains a list of companies that market passenger tie-down/restraint systems that have demonstrated effectiveness in 48 km/hr (30 mph), 20 g impacts. Advocacy for appropriate legislation and the research programs required to develop and evaluate safer transportation equipment and methods for the child with handicaps rests with parents of children with handicaps, educators, health professionals, product designers and manufacturers, and concerned citizens.

Management through Therapeutic Positioning and Adaptive Equipment

Chapter

11

Overview of
Therapeutic Positioning

Positioning is a major part of a therapeutic program for persons with severe multiple handicaps. Proper positioning improves quality of life. It minimizes the influence of pathological forces on body posture, and, thus, helps to maintain physical status and promotes skeletal alignment. Positioning often sets the stage for performance and function. Positioning that provides a stable base of support from which to work facilitates movement patterns and active functioning. For many individuals with multiple handicaps, positioning is the key to increased independence and improved self-esteem.

Positioning may be used for several purposes. Various positions should be provided to create a variety of experiences for perceptual-motor development. Movement activities (e.g., rocking, swinging) may be combined with positioning to provide relaxation, stimulation, and leisure activities. Positioning also may be used to ease situations involving difficult transfers. For example, an individual with severe extensor thrusting patterns may be placed into sidelying or flexed prone to facilitate flexion prior to transfers from a mat or bed into a wheelchair. Also, positioning may be used in combination with active therapeutic handling (Ward, 1984). Severe cognitive impairment limits learning experiences from such active handling, but such handling should be provided for affective benefits such as nurturing and touch.

GENERAL CONSIDERATIONS

A positioning program should be designed by a team of persons who are concerned with the individual. Team members usually include an occupational therapist, physical therapist, speech-language pathologist, teacher, and caregivers. A positioning program provides a basis for therapy to become a natural part of an individual's day. Occupational and physical therapists often play key roles in adapting equipment to meet an individual's positioning needs. Details, such as the proper height of a wedge to promote stable weight shifting and activity placement to promote skilled head movement, should be determined by attending therapists.

Several factors should be considered when prescribing a positioning program. These factors include joint mobility, joint stability, respiratory status, skin condition, sensory stimulation needs, and neuromuscular and orthopaedic conditions. Social, cognitive, and affective factors also should be considered. *Positioning the Handicapped Child for Function* (Ward, 1984) is an excellent reference for detailed information about the benefits and precautions associated with positioning.

A naturalistic approach (Wise, 1989) that involves caregivers' participation in establishing a positioning program should be considered. It is important for caregivers to understand the rationale behind the program and assist in its development. A positioning program should be developed with caregivers that fits into an established schedule and routine. Furniture and objects found within the individual's environment may be used for positioning (Figure 11.1) Caregivers often supply much needed practical information that increases the likelihood of a positioning program being easy and fun to provide, as well as effective.

RECUMBENT BODY POSTURES

The three recumbent body postures described in this section include supine, prone, and sidelying.

Supine

Most persons with multiple handicaps tolerate a supine position quite well. Supine is a posture that requires low energy and little control and allows body weight to be supported over a large area. This posture often is used for a rest from prolonged sitting.

In supine, the relationship between the trunk and pelvis and lower extremities should be observed. Pelvic rotation in the coronal plane, pelvic thrust in the sagittal plane, lower extremity synergy patterns, and deformities are easily detectable. Supine provides a foundation for positioning deformities of the trunk and lower extremities. Various positioning aids can be used to maintain skeletal alignment. A headrest or pillow that positions the head in flexion, pillows under the shoulders, and bolsters under the knees are necessary to reduce extensor tone (see Figure 11.1). Supine position aids should be readily available and should be used whenever the individual is placed in supine.

Elevated supine is usually accomplished by placing a person on a wedge. This position provides an improved view of the environment. In general,

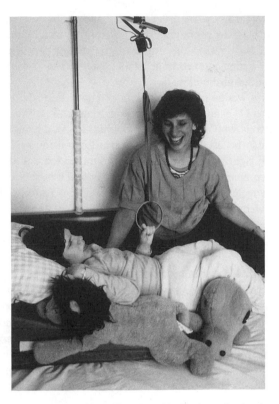

Figure 11.1. Inclined supine position. Flexed positioning in supine breaks up extensor tone. Stuffed animals are used as shoulder blocks to assist upper extremity function and to promote midline orientation.

supine positions do not promote interaction. However, visual activities may be facilitated better in supine rather than sitting for individuals with poor head control. Elevated prone may be used to strengthen trunk flexors with persons who have some vertical head righting intact (Ward, 1984). Supine should be used primarily for resting periods and for initial visual training.

Prone

There are several variations of the prone position, each having its own intent and precautions. Individual evaluation is recommended. In general, recumbent prone may be used to encourage hip extension. Careful attention should be given to monitoring respiratory function and face/head position. In the 1980s, waterbeds became popular positioning surfaces. As a safety measure, persons with severe physical impairments should never be placed on waterbeds and left unattended. Suffocation may occur in a prone position or if the head becomes lodged between the mattress and the frame.

Prone on forearms, prone over a small bolster or roll, or prone over a wedge may be used to promote upper extremity weight bearing. Careful attention should be given to the angle of the incline and the height of the bolster, roll, or wedge to encourage stable weight bearing without scapular winging or shoulder girdle elevation.

Prone over a wedge has many intents. It may be used to reduce flexed posturing (Figure 11.2) and mild hip flexion contractures. It usually is recommended for persons who demonstrate moderate to good head control (Figure 11.3). It may also be used to encourage head extension with an individual who has vertical righting responses. It is recommended that therapists select and place an accompanying activity in a manner that ensures controlled extension rather than reflexive and synergistic movement patterns (Figure 11.4). Prone over a wedge also may be used to reduce the effects of gastroesophageal reflux (see Chapter 15).

Nondirected and directed reaching at the floor level is promoted in a prone-over-a-wedge position as the arms are free to move without fighting gravity. Gravity may assist in reducing scapular retraction. Also, for persons using shoulder elevation to assist with head control, prone over a wedge with the head supported slightly frees the arms for increased movement.

Use of prone over a wedge positioning must be carefully monitored since it may inhibit respiratory capacity. This position is usually contraindicated when hydrocephalus is present, when head control is poor, or when about 70 degrees of passive shoulder flexion is lacking. Lateral supports may be needed to maintain symmetrical body alignment and support over the hips

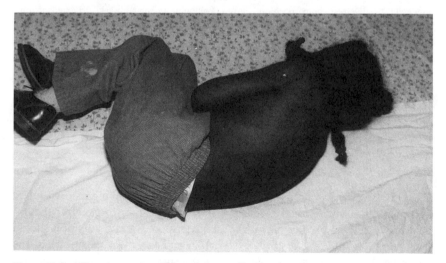

Figure 11.2.   Flexed posturing. This curled or totally flexed posture is typical of many persons with multiple handicaps. Note the flexed attitude of upper and lower extremities, head, and trunk. Sidelying, in this case, is not recommended.

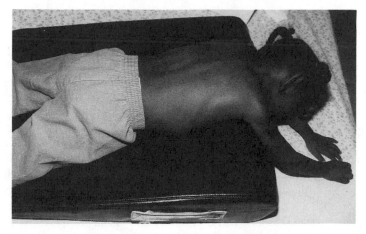

Figure 11.3. Elevated prone positioning. Elevated prone positioning usually is accomplished via a wedge. This position encourages head, trunk, and upper and lower extremity extension. This is the same child shown in Figure 11.2.

may be needed to inhibit hip flexion and/or provide a stable base of support for persons with athetosis. A support pillow under one hip will improve comfort and posture if a dislocated hip or pelvic obliquity is present. Likewise, a roll under the ankles keeps pressure off the toes and prevents legs from rotating.

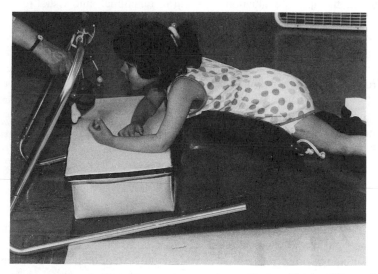

Figure 11.4. Activites facilitated by prone-on-a-wedge positioning. Weight shifting and unilateral weight bearing are facilitated as this child is encouraged to reach for the toys.

Inverted prone (i.e., position in which the head is placed lower on a wedge than hips) is used for only short time periods (usually not more than 5 minutes) to promote postural drainage. This position requires caution, since it may increase intracranial pressure in persons with hydrocephalus and promote vomiting in cases of certain digestive disorder (e.g., hiatal hernia, Sandifer syndrome). Inverted prone facilitates drooling; therefore, care should be taken to prevent saliva from collecting on the individual's ears and eyes.

Sidelying

Sidelying tends to minimize muscle imbalance; for example, it usually promotes trunk, hip, and knee flexion while reducing extensor thrusting. It often reduces the influence of abnormal reflex patterns as well. Sidelying posture should be observed along with supine and prone in order to permit a full comparison of muscle tone and asymmetry and visual responses.

Sidelying is frequently prescribed for persons with multiple handicaps because it offers a resting position in which the pull of gravity is relatively equal between the trunk flexors and extensors. Also, the lower shoulder is supported in a protracted, slightly flexed position while gravity assists in bringing the upper shoulder and arm forward so that the hands can interact in the midline.

In sidelying, gravity assists in elongating the trunk. For example, sidelying on the convexity of a scoliosis may be used provided the individual tolerates a static position and doesn't pull up against gravity. The decision to use either right of left side or alternating between the sides is based on an attending therapist's evaluation of postural, functional, and visual responses.

Positioning in sidelying usually requires two headrests or pillows—one to keep the head slightly flexed and another to support the head in line with the shoulders. Positioning body blocks help to achieve desired trunk and lower extremity alignment (see Chapter 12). Extensor tone may be minimized by rotating either the pelvis or trunk forward. Sidelying should be monitored carefully to identify pressure over small body areas and bony prominences.

Inclined sidelying may be used for feeding selected individuals (see Figure 15.3). Sidelyers may be secured to movable surfaces (e.g., swings, rocking boards) to provide a movement experience.

CLOSING THOUGHTS

Persons with multiple handicaps should be provided several positioning options throughout the day. Even those persons who spend the majority of waking hours in a seating system need an occasional change. Therapeutic positioning is a prescriptive process that should be individualized by attending therapists.

REFERENCES

Ward, D. (1984). *Positioning the handicapped child for function* (2nd ed.). St. Louis: Phoenix Press.

Wise, A. (1989, March). *Functional therapeutic positioning.* Proceeding of the Fifth Annual Conference on Developmental Disabilities, Detroit, MI.

Chapter

Trunk and
Lower Extremities

This chapter offers positioning suggestions for persons with the various postural abnormalities and deformities of the trunk and lower extremities that are described and pictured in Chapters 5 and 6. The chapter begins with a description of lower extremity synergy patterns and sensory considerations; then discusses sitting, kneeling, and standing positions; ending with suggested positioning for specific deformities.

LOWER EXTREMITY SYNERGY PATTERNS

Normally, synergy refers to muscles working together in combinations that result in an action or activity that is not within the capacity of one muscle alone. During normal development, children learn to move in and out of synergistic patterns. Persons with multiple handicaps often assume a synergistic pattern of the lower extremities and become "stuck" in that posture—an abnormal condition. Lower extremity patterns are initiated by hip positions that affect distal joints. Two basic lower extremity synergy patterns are reflected in common postural stances assumed by persons with multiple handicaps. They are flexion and extension synergies.

Flexion Synergy

Flexion synergy is characterized by an anterior pelvic tilt; hip flexion, abduction, and external rotation; knee flexion; ankle dorsiflexion; and toe extension (see Figure 6.2). Knee flexion and ankle dorsiflexion are the strongest components of hip flexion synergy.

Extension Synergy

Extension synergy is comprised of a posterior pelvic tilt; hip extension, adduction, and internal rotation; ankle plantar flexion; and toe extension (see Figure 6.1). Hip and knee extension and ankle plantar flexion are the strongest components of the extension synergy. Noting the strongest components of synergy patterns is important because control of these body parts is the key to effective positioning. Synergy positioning techniques are discussed in Chapters 8 and 11.

SENSORY CONSIDERATIONS

Sensory deficits include lack of awareness of the position of body parts, inability to relate body parts to one another, and lack of control over the force, speed, and direction of movement (Ward, 1984). Such limitations may cause a person with multiple handicaps to avoid weight bearing on a particular body part or to be unable to control or maintain a specific posture.

Reduced sensation along with an inability to shift weight makes many persons with multiple handicaps susceptible to decubiti. Decubitus formation is reduced or prevented by positioning the individual's body to avoid pressure on bony prominences and by frequent changes in positioning.

Because sensory deficits affecting positioning of the trunk and lower extremities commonly are proprioceptive in nature (i.e., responsive to pressure or stretch on muscles, tendons, ligaments, and bones), quick hard stretch pressure is contraindicated.

SITTING POSITIONS

A seated individual with various degrees of trunk support should be observed to evaluate pelvic position and trunk strength and control. The position of the lower extremities in supported and unsupported sitting should be noted. Even with a level pelvis secured in a neutral position and the trunk well supported, the lower extremities may assume an asymmetrical posture. For example, undesired hip external rotation and abduction may occur. Also, anterior and posterior pelvic tilts (discussed in Chapter 8) are easily observed in a seated position.

Unsupported persons with multiple handicaps often tend to side sit, usually on the side of maximum pathology. This posture unbalances the pelvis, thus placing the trunk in asymmetrical alignment. Unsupported floor sitting also may reveal a "reverse tailor" or "W" posture (Figure 12.1) of the limbs in which the hips are internally rotated and adducted. While this posture may produce undesirable hip rotation, it does provide a stable base of support, a level pelvic alignment, and acceptable support for the spine.

Figure 12.1. "Reverse tailor" or "W" sitting. This picture shows unsupported sitting posture in which the hips are internally rotated and adducted. While this posture may produce undesirable hip rotation, it does provide a stable base of support, a level pelvic alignment, and acceptable support for the spine.

It is common for persons with multiple handicaps to be placed alternately in recumbent and supported sitting positions. Most remain static within a posture. A few may learn to move in and out of a posture, but this is often not demonstrated in a developmental fashion. For example, instead of segmentally rolling on a mat, a supine person may sidle sideways, using back and hip extensors while remaining in a supine position. Weight shifts within a posture should be encouraged. Equipment that restricts weight shifts should not be used if an individual demonstrates this ability.

Additional therapeutic principles applicable to sitting and seating systems are discussed in detail in Chapter 8, so they will not be repeated here.

KNEELING AND STANDING POSITIONS

Supported kneeling or standing is a weight-bearing position that facilitates hip muscle cocontraction. This helps bones remain dense and maintains acetabulum depth that results in a more stable femoral-acetabular joint. Supported kneeling (Figure 12.2) is recommended for persons with good head control, fair trunk control, full hip extension, a fairly straight spine, 90 degrees of knee flexion, and no knee abnormalities (e.g., prepatellar bursitis, patella alta). Supported kneeling often is used when severe foot deformities prevent plantigrade weight bearing. In either a kneeling or standing position, an individual should be observed from an anterior, lateral, and posterior view to assess trunk control, pelvic/trunk alignment, lower extremity posture, and the adequacy of postural supports that are provided.

Persons with multiple handicaps may show either a flexed or extended standing posture. Persons with spasticity often stand with flexed hips, knees, and ankles. Their effort in maintaining standing balance tends to increase spasticity, causing hip adduction and internal rotation in combination with flexion (Bergan & Colangelo, 1985).

Figure 12.2. Supported kneeling. A Preston floor sitter, used as a kneeler, provides a comfortable kneeling surface and buttock control with the straps. Additional trunk support may be added as needed and the incline of the kneeler may be adjusted. Supervision to prevent tipping should be given since the floor sitter was not designed for the purpose of supported kneeling.

Persons who have full passive knee extension but are unable to maintain an extended leg position during standing often benefit by using temporary knee splints during this activity. Equipment commonly used for supported kneeling and standing are prone standers (Figure 12.3) and stand-in boxes. Positioning techniques and the use of such equipment have been well explored in therapeutic literature (Bergan & Colangelo, 1985; Ward, 1984) and, therefore, are not presented here. Supported kneeling or standing may be indicated in the presence of a subluxed or dislocated hip, provided limb length discrepancy is accommodated and no apparent pain or discomfort is present (Fraser & Hensinger, 1983).

As noted in Chapter 1, assisted standing transfers and assisted walking usually are the maximum lower extremity activities accomplished by most persons with multiple handicaps. Frequently, the abilities to perform these activities are lost as deformities progress. Weight bearing in a supported vertical position should be encouraged and maintained as long as possible.

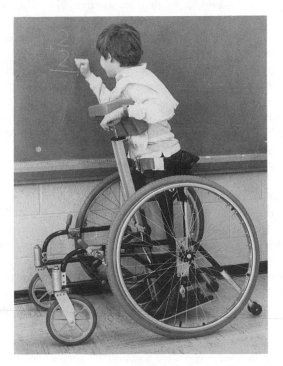

Figure 12.3.   Prone stander. This unique prone stander, The Standing Dani (TM) Wheelstand, is versatile. Persons with the ability to self-propel may do so from a standing position. The stander also may be lowered to the prone position. (Photograph courtesy of Davis Positioning Systems, Inc.)

POSITIONING FOR SPECIFIC DEFORMITIES

A number of sources have described positioning techniques for accommodating specific deformities (Bergan & Colangelo, 1985; Ward, 1984). These sources generally rely on standard positioning aids such as sandbags, rolls, bolsters, and wedges to achieve desired body support and/or control.

More elaborate body positioning aids are produced by selected manufacturers. The authors consider such aids adequate for meeting therapists' needs in positioning persons with mild to moderate handicaps and those with developmental delays. However, the aids' lack of adjustability limits their usefulness in accommodating the severe kinds of deformities that are experienced by many persons with multiple handicaps.

Therapists dealing with the severely handicapped population, then, must fall back on simpler devices that do not provide the precise control of body parts that is desirable. Or, they custom-make equipment for specific individuals. This is a time-consuming and expensive process, and the devices that result usually are not adaptable to changes in physical condition (e.g., worsening deformities, weight change, growth).

Therapists using the simpler types of positioning aids might consult the sources listed earlier for a discussion of positioning techniques. These techniques are not discussed here because the authors believe that, in the final analysis, they represent an ineffective means for meeting the special needs of persons with severe multiple handicaps. Also, mobility aids, such as scooter boards, crawlers, and tricycles, have been well described in the literature. Readers interested in mobility aids may consult Appendix F for related readings.

Instead, this section describes techniques that use equipment resulting from the authors' work, in conjunction with teachers and instructional aides, on the Trunk and Lower Extremity Positioning Project. This research was sponsored by the Wayne County Intermediate School District (WCISD) and conducted in cooperation with Danmar Products, Inc. The project's goal was to develop multipositional devices that were comprised of modular units that could be assembled easily to meet individual needs. It should be noted that the prototypes shown in this book do not represent finished products. They are presented with the idea that therapists or manufacturers may wish to use similar concepts in constructing or adapting equipment for this population.

Materials used in the project had to provide a firm yet cushioned support to counteract the force of postural abnormalities and deformities. In addition, waterproof coverings were specified since many persons with multiple handicaps are incontinent and drool. Vinyl-coated foam with an alloy core to provide strength was selected for the multipositional devices.

All devices used either the concept of a peg-type board into which the positioning aid could be fastened at regular intervals, or horizontally slotted

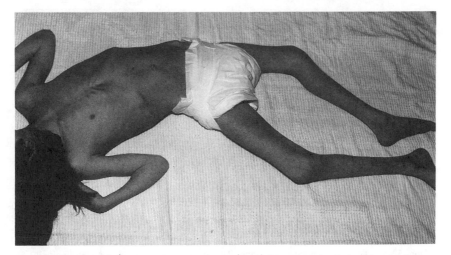

Figure 12.4. Total body C-type posture. This individual has a severe C-shaped scoliosis that involves the spine, hips, and pelvis.

panels into which positioning aids might be fastened at any point along the slot. Some devices used both concepts, with the peg-type board for upper body areas and the slotted panels for the lower extremities. The devices also could accommodate vinyl-coated foam pads and covers where bony prominences and other body parts required soft support.

Positioning for C-Shaped Scoliosis

As noted in Chapter 5, a C-shaped scoliosis often involves the trunk, hips, and pelvis. In supine, a total body may form a C shape (Figure 12.4). Supine positioning should include three-point control to help hold the spine in as symmetrical a midline posture as possible. This is achieved by placing one control point at the apex of the curve on the convex side, the second on the chest wall just under the axilla on the concave side, and the third at either the pelvis or thigh on the concave side (Figure 12.5). Other positioning aids may be added to the legs as necessary.

Sidelying, also, may be used for positioning a C-shaped scoliosis. Sidelying on the convexity of the curve may be used provided the individual relaxes into this position, allowing gravity to help straighten the spine.

Positioning for Hip Adduction Deformity

As discussed in Chapter 6, the hip adduction deformity may be accompanied by hip and knee extension, often described as scissoring legs. The goal of any positioning program is to encourage hip abduction and to maintain a separation of the lower extremities. By doing so, the head of the femur is kept well seated

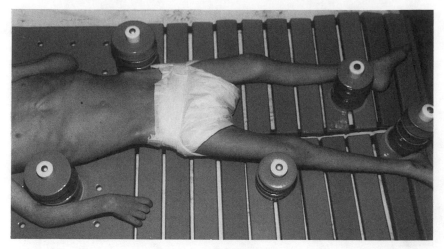

Figure 12.5. Three-point control in supine. This is the same person pictured in Figure 12.4. Three-point control is achieved by placing one positioner at the apex of the curve on the convex side, the second positioner on the chest wall just under the axilla on the concave side, and the third positioner against the thigh on the concave side. Other positioners are added to the legs as necessary to obtain an improved total body alignment.

in the acetabulum, discouraging hip subluxation and dislocation. The solution developed through the Positioning Project is described in Figure 12.6.

Positioning for Hip Abduction Deformity

The goal of positioning for hip abduction deformity is to bring the legs toward the midline and to internally rotate the hips. If left untreated, this deformity could interfere with the ability to sit in a wheelchair. Figure 12.7 shows use of a full-length body apparatus for this purpose.

Positioning for Windswept Hip Deformity

Windswept hip deformity combines flexion with abduction/external rotation of one hip and adduction/internal rotation of the opposite hip (Figure 12.8). Supine positioning is accomplished by placing the knees and hips in flexion while bringing the limbs toward a midline position. Typically, this means placing positioning aids at the lateral thigh and medial lower leg of the adducted/internally rotated hip. Figure 12.9 shows use of a slotted panel device for this purpose.

In sidelying positioning for windswept hips, the goal is proper hip alignment and a restful position. Use of this position helps to stabilize the trunk in a more neutrally aligned position. The Positioning Project achieved satisfactory results by adding certain attachments to the base positioning unit (Figure 12.10).

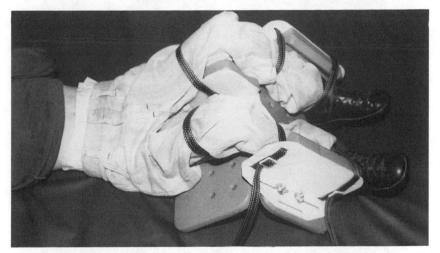

Figure 12.6. Supine positioning for hip adduction deformity. A person is placed in supine with a hinged peg-type padded board under the thighs and legs. One set of positioners is locked into the board between the person's thighs to abduct the hips. Another set is placed against the lateral aspects of the lower legs to prevent internal hip rotation. The hips and knees are placed in as much flexion as possible by elevating the hinged section of the board.

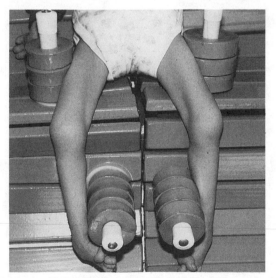

Figure 12.7. Supine positioning for hip abduction deformity. This positioning technique uses one set placed against the lateral aspects of the thighs to limit hip abduction and another set placed against the medial aspect of the lower legs to limit hip external rotation. In this case, a full body-length board is shown rather than the smaller hip/thigh board. Either would be acceptable. This is the same individual pictured in Figure 6.2.

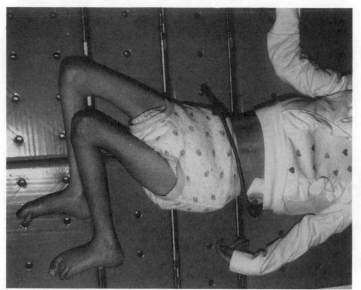

Figure 12.8. Windswept deformity. The windswept hip deformity combines flexion with abduction/external rotation of the subject's right hip and adduction/internal rotation of the left hip. Both knees are flexed.

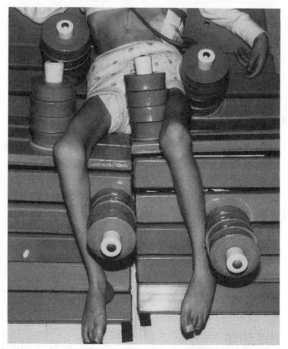

Figure 12.9. Supine positioning for windswept hip deformity. Supine positioning is accomplished using a full body-length board with separate slotted boards for the limbs. These boards are hinged under the hips and knees. Positioners are placed at the lateral thigh and medial lower leg of the abducted/externally rotated hip and at the medial thigh and lateral lower leg of the adducted/internally rotated hip to hold the legs in a straighter position. Hip and trunk supports may be added as necessary. This is the same individual pictured in Figure 12.8.

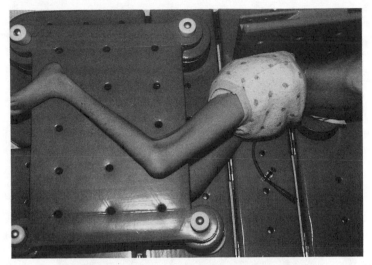

Figure 12.10. Sidelying positioning for windswept hip deformity. To accommodate sidelying positioning for the person pictured in Figure 12.8, a lower extremity shelf and back panel are attached to the base unit. A vinyl-covered foam "donut" positioner is used to protect the feeding tube.

Positioning for Hip Subluxations and Dislocations

Unilateral posterior superior or posterior hip subluxations and dislocations require individual limb positioning because one leg is shorter than the other. In either case, a goal is to equalize pressure over the buttocks, while supporting the thighs and working toward knee extension. A three-point type of control is effective, with one point above the dislocated hip and the other two points being the opposite chest wall and the opposite thigh (Figure 12.11).

In the case of anterior hip dislocations (often associated with severe extensor thrusting), the head and trunk need to be positioned in as much flexion as possible and a cover placed over the abdomen and pelvis to limit thrusting. Figure 12.12 shows how the apparatus developed in the Positioning Project accommodates this need by proving abdominal stabilization and head positioning.

CLOSING THOUGHTS

The prototypes developed during WCISD's Trunk and Lower Extremity Positioning Project are designed specifically for fixed bony deformities that are characteristic of many persons with multiple handicaps. It is anticipated that the design concepts discussed in this chapter will have applications for improving seating and recreational equipment to help persons with severe deformities enjoy a better quality of life.

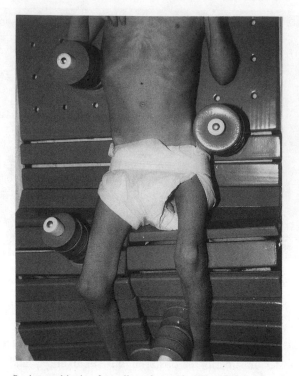

Figure 12.11.   Supine positioning for unilateral posterior superior or posterior hip subluxations and dislocations. Supine positioning must accommodate limb length differences caused by a unilateral hip dislocation. These slotted leg boards may be raised individually to place the knees and hips in flexion or lowered to achieve extension. Lower extremity boards may be hinged at any slot location. This provides the flexibility needed to cope with limb length differences and to permit the use of the device with more than one person. Positioners may be added as necessary to obtain the straightest possible body and limb alignment.

REFERENCES

Bergan, A.F., & Colangelo, C. (1985). *Positioning the client with central nervous system deficits: The wheelchair and other adapted equipment* (2nd ed.). Valhalla, NY: Valhalla Rehabilation Publications.

Fraser, B.A., & Hensinger, R.N. (1983). *Managing physical handicaps: A practical guide for parents, care providers, and educators.* Baltimore: Paul H. Brookes Publishing Co.

Ward, D. (1984). *Positioning the handicapped child for function* (2nd ed.). St. Louis: Phoenix Press.

Figure 12.12. Positioning for bilateral anterior hip subluxations and dislocations. This child's head and trunk are supported in an elevated supine position via a peg-type back support, the head is flexed using a neck/headrest, and a vinyl-covered foam pad is placed across the abdomen and pelvis to help control extensor thrusting. The lower extremities are flexed to the degree possible by elevating the knee section of the support device. Limb length differences usually are not a concern with this type of hip dislocation.

Chapter

13

___•___

Upper Extremities

Upper extremity function allows performance of self-care, work, and recreational activities. For the normal person, upper extremities may be viewed as an extension of the mind. In fact, young children stimulate motoric, cognitive, and affective development by functional use of their hands. However, upper extremity function does not develop normally in persons with multiple handicaps. Furthermore, cognitive deficits limit effective use of whatever upper extremity function does exist.

One goal of a management program for any person with multiple handicaps, then, is to achieve optimal arm and hand function within the limitations imposed by existing physical and cognitive abnormalities. Even minimal function gives persons with multiple handicaps a basis for exploring their environment, assisting in self-care, and participating in cognitive and recreational activities. The use of appropriate equipment is fundamental to achievement of this goal.

This chapter includes a discussion of general and specific postural abnormalities affecting arm and hand function. Equipment used as postural aids is described in relation to specific abnormalities. Suggestions are offered for equipment adaptation. Motivational devices also are discussed briefly. Although this chapter also deals with splinting, other orthopaedic considerations relating to the upper extremities are discussed in Chapter 7.

GENERAL OBSERVATIONS
OF POSTURAL ABNORMALITIES

Postural abnormalities in persons with multiple handicaps are caused by abnormal muscle tone, abnormal reflex activity, or a combination of these factors (Fraser & Hensinger, 1983). These abnormalities are discussed in detail in Chapters 3 and 7. Sustained postural abnormalities lead to soft tissue imbalances that, in turn, can result in contractures and skeletal pathology.

One of the most common deformities involves elbow flexion, forearm pronation, wrist flexion, and ulnar deviation. However, persons with multiple handicaps often "lock into" upper extremity synergy patterns that aggravate their postural abnormalities (Ward, 1984). Flexion synergies of the upper extremities are common among persons with multiple handicaps, although extension synergies are occasionally present. These synergy patterns inhibit isolated movements. Flexion synergy is characterized by shoulder girdle retraction, or elevation, or both; glenohumeral flexion, abduction, and external rotation; elbow flexion; forearm supination; and wrist flexion (Figure 13.1). Extension synergy is characterized by shoulder girdle protraction; glenohumeral extension, adduction, and internal rotation; elbow extension; forearm pronation, and wrist extension (Figure 13.2) (Brunnstrom, 1970).

Hand posturing is difficult to categorize due to the influence of pathological factors. Hand posture may follow expected synergy patterns (i.e., finger flexion associated with flexion synergy and finger extension associated with extension synergy). Hand posture also may be affected by primitive postural reflexes and balance between extrinsic and intrinsic hand muscles (discussed later in this chapter).

Evaluation of postural abnormalities begins with general observation of total body posture and sensory deficits. Findings suggest specific postural abnormalities to be investigated. General observation also may indicate the presence of specific joint deformities. Orthopaedic joint evaluation is appro-

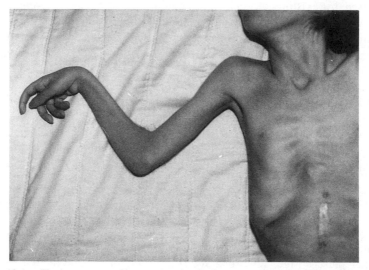

Figure 13.1.   Flexion synergy. Upper extremity flexion synergy is characterized by shoulder girdle elevation, abduction and external rotation of the humerus, elbow flexion, forearm supination, and wrist flexion.

Figure 13.2.   Extension synergy. Extension synergy is characterized by shoulder girdle pronation and depression; glenohumeral extension, adduction, and internal rotation; elbow extension;
forearm pronation; and wrist extension as shown in the photograph. This child also exhibits
extensor thrusting.

priate for each such condition. That evaluation determines whether surgical or
nonsurgical intervention, or a combination of the two, is appropriate. This
chapter deals only with detection and management of postural abnormalities.

Teaching caregivers passive handling techniques (Finnie, 1975), providing proper positioning through equipment, and offering motivational devices
are important aspects of therapy for persons with multiple handicaps. Other
forms of therapy used with this population include range-of-motion exercises
and neurodevelopmental techniques. Passive range-of-motion exercises help
maintain tendon length. Neurodevelopmental techniques encourage total
movement patterns (Bobath, 1978; Erhardt, 1982b; Howison, 1983; Trombly
& Scott, 1977), but these techniques may not be appropriate with individuals
who have severe cognitive impairments. Patterning techniques (i.e., repeti-
tion of the desired action over and over with trainer assist gradually decreasing) are effectively used in cases where cognitive impairment is involved.
Positioning, especially sitting positioning, through adaptive seating devices
(discussed in Chapter 8) may improve functional motoric progress of grasping
skills (Hulme, Gallacher, Walsh, Niesen, & Waldron, 1987).

Evaluation Considerations

Standard developmental evaluations are of limited value with persons with
multiple handicaps, most of whom do not follow normal developmental sequences. Their severe pathologies involve orthopaedic, reflex, and postural

abnormalities that lead to fixed deformities. However, the Erhardt Developmental Prehension Assessment, intended as a developmental assessment, may be a useful guide to analyzing quality of movement and specific components of reach and grasp.

Upper extremity evaluation should include passive and active range-of-motion testing. Goniometric measurements (American Academy of Orthopaedic Surgeons, 1965; Norkin & White, 1985; Trombly & Scott, 1977) should be taken to establish baseline joint mobility and to permit subsequent comparisons. Range of unresisted motion also should be noted in order to monitor the development of deformities. Measurements should be taken in a variety of positions (e.g., sitting, sidelying, supine) to note the influence of primitive postural reflexes on range of motion. Videotaping is suggested to document arm and hand posture and to provide a basis for "before and after" treatment analysis (Shaffer, 1983). Periodic videotaping is a useful tool to record subtle changes in positioning that occur over time.

Total Body Posture

Abnormal postural patterns can be detected most accurately by observing a person with multiple handicaps in both recumbent and sitting positions. Abnormal posture often changes with positioning. This is due to the effects of gravity and of primitive postural reflexes in relation to the position of the body and head in space (see Chapter 3).

Recumbent Body Posture

Many persons with multiple handicaps function most efficiently on a horizontal plane (Ward, 1984). Observation of an individual in all three recumbent positions—supine, prone, and sidelying—yields useful information about abnormal muscle tone, body asymmetry, the presence of obligatory postural reflexes, pathological synergies, and the presence of skeletal deformities such as pelvic obliquity, spinal deformities, and hip subluxation or dislocation. These abnormalities may limit an individual's ability to tolerate or maintain a position conducive to upper extremity movement and function. (Positioning suggestions for the trunk and lower extremities are presented in Chapter 12.)

Sitting Body Posture

Most persons with multiple handicaps spend at least a portion of each day in a sitting position, thanks, in part, to advancements in seating systems. An individual should be observed with varying degrees of trunk support to evaluate the relationship between trunk/head posture and upper extremity posture and movement. A positive correlation exists between trunk abnormalities and restricted use of upper extremities. For example, an individual with a hypotonic trunk and a functionally collapsing spine may use the upper extremities to support the torso and to maintain a sitting posture. Also, a weak trunk may lead to abnormal pelvic posturing in an attempt to support the torso in an upright position. This has a cascading effect on the upper extremities. For example, a seated person with a posteriorly tilted pelvis often forms a functional trunk hyperkyphosis to maintain an upright posture that promotes shoulder girdle protraction and elevation to support the head. This, in turn, limits side reaching. A seated person with an anteriorly tilted pelvis may form a functional trunk hyperlordosis to maintain an upright sitting posture that causes scapulae retraction and limits midline hand use. In both examples, therapeutic management begins with stabilizing the pelvis in a neutral position and providing enough trunk and head support to facilitate upper extremity use (see Chapter 8).

Sensory Deficits

Persons with multiple handicaps typically experience multiple sensory impairments. These impairments combine to limit purposeful upper extremity activities. Severe cognitive impairment also is common among this population. Such impairment may rule out use of formal sensory testing that requires active participation by subjects. Even so, observation of response to sensory stimulation is possible. Persons should be observed for visual, tactile, and auditory abilities and deficits.

Hyposensitivity is a sensory deficit that is experienced by many persons with multiple handicaps. It is typified by diminished peripheral response to touch, temperature, and pain; an inability to process sensory stimuli; or both. Persons with an inability to sense pain should have safety devices built into their positioning systems to protect the upper extremities from accidental injury. Also, hyposensitivity often limits splinting options, and continual monitoring is necessary whenever splinting in employed.

Tactile defensiveness is an aversive response to touch resulting from an integrative defect in tactile perception (Ayers, 1964, 1972; Montgomery & Richter, 1977). If tactile defensiveness is present, the individual may not be able to tolerate restricted positioning. In such cases, activities should be chosen that allow the person some control over the offered sensory input. For example, a variety of toys may be placed near the person for independent exploration rather than physically assisting the individual to touch a specific toy. Another technique effective with tactile defensive persons is deep pressure touching with gradual fading toward a lighter touch. Materials that the person comes in contact with on wheelchairs, toys, or daily living aids should be carefully evaluated based on the individual's responses. For example, some persons accept contact with smooth material, such as vinyl, more readily than coarser materials like terrycloth or wool.

EVALUATION AND MANAGEMENT
OF PROXIMAL POSTURAL ABNORMALITIES

General observation of total body posture and sensory deficits must be combined with evaluation of specific postural abnormalities to tailor an appropriate management plan. The following paragraphs discuss common proximal postural abnormalities affecting upper extremity function in persons with multiple handicaps. Although discussed separately, such abnormalities often appear in combination. Equipment used to support and prepare the upper extremities for optimal movement and function is discussed in relation to the specific postural abnormalities to which the equipment applies. This information should be used in conjunction with Chapter 11, Overview of Positioning.

Shoulder Girdle Retraction

Shoulder girdle retraction is common among persons with multiple handicaps. Specific postural components usually include shoulder girdle elevation, posterior positioning of the clavicles, scapular adduction, glenohumeral extension and external rotation, elbow flexion, and an inability to disassociate scapulae movement from shoulder movement (Figure 13.3).

Two of the most common causes of shoulder girdle retraction are associated reactions upon initiation of upper extremity movements and general body hypertonus (Bergen & Colangelo, 1983). Another cause is increased extensor tone, often associated with the presence of a supine tonic labyrinthine reflex

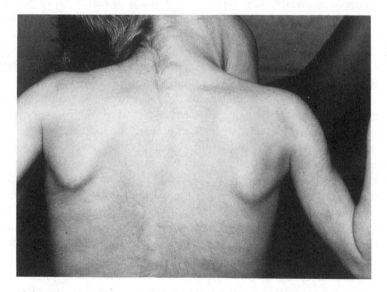

Figure 13.3.   Shoulder girdle retraction. Shoulder girdle retraction restricts glenohumeral flexion and horizontal abduction, thus limiting midline use of the hands.

(TLR) (see Chapter 3) that triggers retraction in response to the position of the person's head in space (Trefler, 1984). Persons with poor trunk control also may use shoulder girdle retraction to assist in maintaining an upright trunk posture and to support the head (Bergen & Colangelo, 1983).

Specific components of shoulder girdle retraction should be individually analyzed. Equipment and positioning techniques vary depending on the specific postural component or components involved.

Managing Shoulder Girdle Retraction

Recumbent Positions The prone-over-a-wedge position may be used to counteract shoulder retraction. This position allows gravity to assist the scapulae in maintaining a neutral posture. Other prone positioning devices such as prone scooter toys or wedges with shoulder guides also may be used to reduce shoulder girdle retraction.

Supine positioning is not recommended for activity if a retracted shoulder girdle is present. This position is especially contraindicated if the supine TLR is positive. In such a case, trunk extensor tone is increased and shoulder girdle retraction is encouraged as the person struggles against the effects of the TLR.

Sidelying can be used to counteract shoulder girdle retraction with appropriate positioning aids. The horizontal and vertical surfaces of a sidelying device hold the lower (i.e., weight-bearing) shoulder in a flexed position and gravity assists in bringing the top arm toward midline. A pillow or neckrest should be used to position the head in slight flexion. Objects of interest should be presented to the person to encourage use of hands at midline within his or her visual field (Figure 13.4).

Sitting Positions Proper sitting positioning is fundamental to upper extremity management. It begins with ensuring that the trunk is supported adequately and obtaining the straightest possible alignment of the pelvis and trunk. Supporting the neck in slight forward flexion helps prevent neck hyperextension that could trigger extensor patterns.

Angular inserts or wing supports may be added to a wheelchair back or to the wraparound part of a wheelchair tray to place slight forward pressure against the scapulae, shoulders, and upper arms (Bergen & Colangelo, 1983; Ward, 1984). The shape of the device, its location, and the amount of pressure exerted by the wings should be determined by attending therapists on an individual basis. In some cases, gentle forward pressure behind the scapulae is adequate to enhance upper extremity function. In other cases, the heads of the humeri and the upper arms need to be supported also. Care must be taken to avoid too much forward pressure on the humeri. This can produce glenohumeral internal rotation and limit upper extremity movement. Pressure exerted on the scapulae and humeri may be varied through materials used in the supports (e.g., plastic versus wood, low- versus high-density foam) and

Figure 13.4. Sidelying position. Sidelying positioning promotes shoulder girdle protraction, which allows midline positioning of the hands.

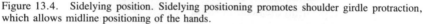

placement of the devices. Chair inserts and wing positioners may be used in conjunction with an H harness system (see Chapter 8). The H harness provides counterpressure and prevents the entire trunk from being pushed forward (Bergen & Colangelo, 1983). An H harness may be positioned to provide slight downward pressure if shoulder girdle elevation accompanies retraction.

An alternative to using chair inserts or wing-type supports is a shoulder protractor belt (Erhardt, 1982a). This consists of a belt placed around a person's trunk and elastic arm cuffs designed for midhumerous placement. The cuffs are tied to the belt at midline by connecting straps (Figure 13.5). The arm position in relation to midline may be altered by loosening or tightening the straps. Resistance to retraction may be varied by the type of material (i.e., different elastics versus webbing) used for the straps. A "figure 8"-style belt also may be used to bring the arms into midline (Reymann, 1985a). Use of a shoulder protractor belt should be individually assessed—it is not effective on all persons with shoulder girdle retraction. Such belts appear to be especially useful with persons having mild to moderate involvement. Com-

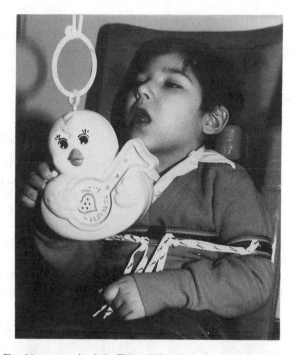

Figure 13.5. Shoulder protraction belt. This training device is used to encourage midline use of the hands. During initial training, nonelastic straps, such as the shoelaces pictured, may be used attached to cuffs placed at midhumerus level to hold the arms at midline. Later, elastic straps may be introduced to encourage greater arm movement.

mercial corner sitters also are available that, by the nature of their shape, promote scapular protraction in mildly to moderately involved individuals.

Caregivers also may position the shoulders manually. To do so, caregivers hold the shoulders in a depressed position by gentle pressure on the top of the person's shoulders. Inward rotation of the humerus may be achieved by slight forward pressure against the outside of the person's upper arm.

Shoulder Girdle Protraction

Shoulder girdle protraction is characterized by a forward position of the humeral heads causing the shoulders to appear rounded. Glenohumeral internal rotation, elbow extension, and forearm pronation often accompany this condition.

One cause of shoulder girdle protraction is generalized hypotonia with the trunk falling forward in response to gravity (Bergen & Colangelo, 1983). Another common cause is specific hypertonicity of the scapular adductors. The hypertonicity creates an imbalance between shoulder girdle protractors and retractors that commonly results in the forward (i.e., protracted) position of the humeral heads being combined with scapular adduction (i.e., retraction) (Figure 13.6). The shoulders may be depressed or elevated depending upon the position of the head. Often the shoulders are depressed when the head is flexed and elevated to support the head in a hyperextended position. The protracted position keeps the arms close to the trunk, limiting glenohumeral abduction. Prolonged protracted posture may lead to limitation of shoulder motion.

Managing Shoulder Girdle Protraction

Recumbent Positions Persons with shoulder girdle protraction usually demonstrate greater movement of their upper extremities in a supine position than persons with shoulder girdle retraction. At rest, in a supine position, gravity helps the shoulder girdle fall into a neutral position. However, in a supine position, pillows should be placed under the head to free shoulders for mobility. Prone-on-forearms positioning may be considered if the shoulder girdle is strong enough to support upper extremity weight bearing.

Sidelying usually is not indicated per se for persons who exhibit shoulder protraction. However, sidelying may be desirable for other postural abnor-

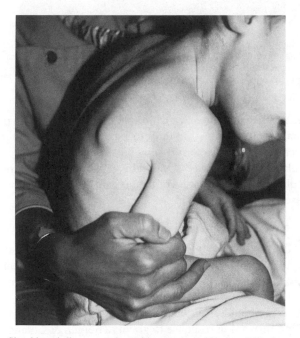

Figure 13.6. Shoulder girdle protraction with scapulae adduction. This is a typical rounded shoulder posture of many persons with multiple handicaps. Note that the shoulder girdle is protracted and the scapula is retracted (producing a winged appearance). This child's shoulders depress when the neck flexes and elevate slightly when the neck hyperextends.

malities (e.g., positioning for scoliosis) that take precedence over shoulder protraction consideration.

Sitting Position An erect trunk is the most important consideration in providing seating support for a person with shoulder girdle protraction. This may be accomplished in several ways. A chest plate may provide sufficient trunk support. Or, reclining a wheelchair seat 10–15 degrees may prevent a weak trunk from falling forward. An H harness may be sufficient to pull the heads of the humeri and clavicles back into a neutral position when the involvement is mild. The H harness shoulder strap should be secured so as to provide downward pressure if shoulder girdle elevation is present.

Padded shoulder straps may be effective in positioning the shoulders of persons with moderate involvement. They exert support over a wider area than does an H harness, and the padding protects against skin breakdown over bony prominences. Commercially available shoulder pommels may be effective in maintaining a slightly hyperkyphotic trunk upright, especially if the shoulder protraction is accompanied by weak trunk extensors.

Shoulder Girdle Elevation

Shoulder girdle elevation is characterized by an upward (e.g., hunched) posturing of the shoulders, causing the shoulders and head to appear to be united (Figure 13.7). Trunk, shoulder, and neck muscle hypertonicity and compensation for poor head control are common causes of shoulder girdle elevation. When shoulder elevation is used to stabilize the head, normal head/neck elongation is inhibited and functional use of the upper extremities is compromised (Bly, 1983). Shoulder girdle elevation may appear with or without retraction. It occurs occasionally with protraction. (Refer to the pertinent section if protraction or retraction accompanies elevation.) The following discussion pertains to elevation with scapulae in a neutral position.

Management of Shoulder Girdle Elevation

Recumbent Position A supine position that maintains symmetrical trunk alignment reduces the need to use the shoulders to support the head. Appropriate positioning may be accomplished by placing bolsters or sandbags along each side of the torso to stabilize the trunk, placing a bolster under the knees to support the knees and hips in flexion, and placing a pillow under the head to support the neck in slight flexion.

Sitting Position Symmetrical pelvic and trunk alignment is necessary to enhance trunk and head control (see Chapter 8). Once this has been achieved, addition of an appropriately anchored (below shoulder level) H harness provides a downward force that helps to overcome shoulder elevation. A head support system may help to stabilize the head, thus encouraging the shoulders and arms to assume a more normal position. Head control and separate shoulder and arm motion may be facilitated by reclining a wheelchair

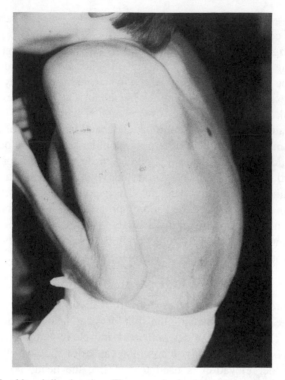

Figure 13.7. Shoulder girdle elevation. The person's shoulders hike up to support the head, giving the appearance of the head and shoulders as a unit. Note that the shoulder girdle also is protracted and the spine is hyperkyphotic.

10–15 degrees. This is particularly helpful in cases where shoulder girdle elevation is used to support the head.

Hypotonicity

Generalized hypotonicity of the trunk and upper extremities interferes with antigravity activities such as sitting and reaching. In addition, persons with hypotonic shoulder musculature are susceptible to shoulder dislocation and subluxation. Care should be taken to lift such individuals by the trunk instead of pulling on the arms (Fraser & Hensinger, 1983). A lifting belt placed around the trunk may be indicated for large individuals.

Management of Hypotonicity

Recumbent Positions   Sidelying and prone-over-a-wedge positioning allow gravity to assist in maintaining symmetrical trunk alignment and arm/hand function. In sidelying, it may be necessary to place a pillow or foam pad under the head and neck to avoid pushing the weight-bearing shoulder into protraction. Supporting the head and neck in line with the spine reduces pressure on the shoulder and prevents an anterior subluxation of the gleno-humeral joint (Ward, 1984). The use of a four-point over-a-bolster position may help stabilize and strengthen the shoulders.

Sitting Position   Persons with hypotonic trunks need support when sitting to prevent hypotonic posture and shoulder protraction. Chest supports or shoulder pommels used in conjunction with a lap belt are often used for this purpose. Selecting trays and tables that support the arms at a correct height can help in avoiding postural problems. If the trays are too low, they will be ineffective; if they are too high, shoulders may become elevated. Tray and table height specifications should be determined by the attending therapist.

Athetosis

Athetosis is characterized by fluctuating muscle tone with involuntary random movements that are especially severe in the arms and hands. Athetosis is a manifestation of brain damage commonly associated with cerebral palsy. In persons with multiple handicaps, athetosis often combines with ataxia or spasticity. Securing other body parts may enhance controlled upper extremity movement by providing a stable base for purposeful arm movements. Efforts should be directed toward helping the individual to perform a limited number of functional movement patterns, rather than emphasizing a variety of movements.

Management of Athetosis

Recumbent Positions   Supine and sidelying positions may be used to facilitate controlled movement of athetoid upper extremities. In supine, the trunk should be stabilized by use of a wide strap attached to weights that are placed on each side of the trunk. Commercially available sidelyers have positioners to stabilize the trunk. Use of a headrest in supine and a neckrest in sidelying is recommended to stabilize the head in a midline position.

Sitting Position   In sitting position, the trunk and head may be stabilized using an appropriate chest and head support (see Chapter 8). Feet may be secured to the footplates of a wheelchair to inhibit leg motion. Even if bilateral athetoid movement of the arms is present, unilateral hand activities can be achieved. This can be accomplished by restricting movement of one hand while the other hand is used for function. A dowel may be attached to a tray, table, or other work area to provide a grasping surface that can be used to stabilize one hand while the other hand is used for activities. Also, a wheel-chair tray or table may be used to block movement of one arm (Trefler, 1982). If severe athetosis persists in the arms and hands despite these positioning techniques, the head or feet may prove more successful for functional activities.

In some persons, athetosis may be associated with joint hypermobility. Such persons have more success in attempting activities that require movement of one joint while other joints are stabilized. For example, a task requiring hand movement can be accomplished more proficiently if the elbow is stabilized on a work surface.

Asymmetry

In persons with multiple handicaps, the asymmetrical tonic neck reflex (ATNR) is the major postural abnormality that leads to asymmetry of the upper extremities. The ATNR usually results in shoulder girdle retraction, glenohumeral external rotation, and elbow extension on the face side. This posturing allows only unilateral hand function and interferes with midline use of hands and visual attending skills. Since head rotation triggers the reflex, the head should be stabilized in midline. Then, activities should be presented at the midline to encourage bilateral use of the hands and visually directed reaching. In cases of severe involvement, midline positioning may not be effective in changing upper extremity posturing caused by an ATNR. In such cases, an ATNR may be used for unilateral reaching. Before encouraging ATNR unilateral reaching, an attending therapist should determine whether the ATNR is obligatory, it is most likely permanent, and that bilateral reaching is unrealistic.

Management of Asymmetry

Recumbent Positions   Stabilization of the head can be achieved in supine, prone, and sidelying positions. Neck- and headrests may be used in conjunction with supine mat positions. For example, commercially available lateral head support systems offered for travel wheelchairs may be removed and placed under the head to prevent rotation. In prone, the head may be supported in midline by a facerest device with cutout portions for the eyes, nose, and mouth. Neckrests are ideal for supporting the head in midline during sidelying positioning. Pillows may be placed behind the head to hold the neck in flexion. A vacuum-molded or custom headrest may be necessary in severe cases.

Sitting Position   Head and neck support systems (see Chapter 8) may be used with wheelchairs and classroom chairs to stabilize the head in midline. Headrests that allow for rotation of the head should be avoided when possible. Trays with shoulder protraction blocks may promote midline orientation. If severe deformities are present, arm positioning systems may be needed to maintain adequate arm circulation and to protect an extended arm during transport (Figure 13.8).

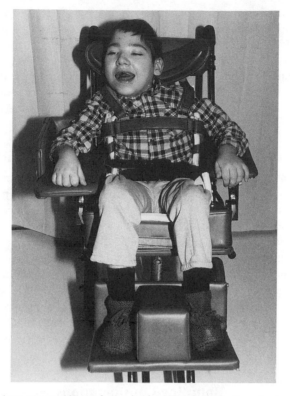

Figure 13.8. Armrests provide comfort and safety. This individual's armrests are enlarged to provide adequate resting areas. The side guard on the right armrest prevents extension of the elbow caused by a persistant asymmetrical tonic neck reflex.

EVALUATION AND MANAGEMENT
OF DISTAL POSTURAL ABNORMALITIES

Proximal upper extremity (e.g., shoulder girdle, upper arm) synergy patterns often lead to abnormal distal (e.g., forearm, hand) postures. For example, the common flexor synergy pattern includes elbow flexion/forearm pronation components. This limits forearm rotation and also makes wrist extension difficult. Maintaining supination, either through passive range-of-motion exercises or active reaching, is necessary if rotational movement is desired. It is important to differentiate between movement components, such as isolating forearm pronation from glenohumeral internal rotation or isolating forearm supination from glenohumeral external rotation, to determine appropriate management activities.

The use of equipment for proximal positioning, although it affects the shoulder girdle area, often has a minimal effect on distal parts (Seeger, Caudrey, & O'Mara, 1984). This section begins with a discussion of the relationship between spastic extrinsic/intrinsic hand muscles, then offers splinting considerations, followed by a description of specific distal postural abnormalities (e.g., elbow flexion, wrist extension, wrist flexion, extrinsic/intrinsic hand spasticity relationship, extended hand, weak hand, flexed spastic hand, and thumb-in-palm).

Extrinsic/Intrinsic Hand Spasticity Relationship

Examination of the wrist and hand includes testing for dominant spasticity between extrinsic and intrinsic hand muscles. Extrinsic hand muscles (e.g., flexor pollicis longus, brevis) originate in the forearm and insert in the hand. Intrinsic hand muscles (e.g., lumbricals, interossei, thenar, hypothenar muscles) originate and insert within the hand. Usually, persons with multiple handicaps experience extrinsic muscle tightness that results in wrist deformities. Intrinsic muscle tightness may be present as well, compounding the extent of hand deformity. The absence of intrinsic muscle spasticity has implications for treatment and splinting. If relaxation of intrinsic musculature occurs with wrist extension and thumb abduction, then functional gains in grasping may be made through placing-and-holding treatment techniques and splinting.

Splinting Considerations

Recent studies indicate that hypertonus and soft tissue deformities of the elbow, wrist, and hand are reduced by the use of splints (Mathiowetz, Bolding, & Trombly, 1983; McPherson, Kreimeyer, Aalderks, & Gallagher, 1982; Mills, 1984; Snook, 1979). However, splinting should be used with persons with multiple handicaps only if the splint improves function, hygiene, and ease of care. Splinting should not be used just because a muscle imbalance exists.

General splinting guidelines concerning the principles of mechanics, fit, and construction (Brand, 1984; Cannon et al., 1985; Malick, 1976; Mayerson, 1971) should be followed during the fabrication process. For example, edges should be smoothed and corners rounded for wearing comfort. Also, areas that are intended to exert pressure on a bodily part should be as wide as practicable to maintain even pressure distribution. Special adaptations may be necessary for splints used by persons with multiple handicaps. For instance, straps should be permanently attached to the splint with rivets to prevent loss. Padding should be placed over the rivets and straps to ensure comfort. Vinyl-covered foam padding may be used for hygiene management. Also, buckles may replace Velcro if the individual inappropriately attempts to remove the splint. A professional checklist for assessing comfort and function is recommended (Hill, 1988). Most persons with multiple handicaps cannot express discomfort and should be closely monitored for edema and circulation difficulties. Caregivers should be trained in the use and application of a splint. Splinting is contraindicated if monitoring is erratic. Prolonged unsupervised splint usage could result in pressure ulcers and joint ankylosis.

Nighttime may be preferred by some doctors and therapists for splint usage since stretching occurs while the person is relaxed during sleep. Nighttime usage also allows the elbow or hand to be free of the splint during the day. However, night splinting may be inappropriate in an institutional setting because the number of personnel on duty often is insufficient to monitor splint usage. Persons with multiple handicaps may demonstrate a "gadget intolerance" or extreme tactile sensitivity. In such cases, splinting should be avoided.

Splinting is most effective in conjunction with a therapy program. Relaxation and range of motion should be performed before application of a splint. An active reaching or exercise program also should be developed to compensate for the lack of movement in antagonist muscles commonly found in spastic limb posturing. Severe cognitive deficits make it difficult to achieve functional gains through splinting. Therefore, use of splints with this population should be carefully evaluated and monitored.

Serial casting has been discussed in the treatment of spasticity (Cherry & Weigard, 1981; King, 1982; Yasukawa & Hill 1988). It generally is contraindicated in this population due to the difficulties of monitoring and the lack of functional outcome caused by cognitive impairment. Serial casting, also, is contraindicated in cases of extreme tone (i.e., rigidity).

Elbow Flexion

Elbow flexion posturing with forearm pronation is common to persons with multiple handicaps. Individuals with slight elbow flexion contractures experience little inconvenience. However, this deformity often is progressive and tends to worsen during periods of growth (Bleck, 1979). Elbow contractures of more than 45 degrees usually interfere with positioning the hand for function (Shaffer, 1983). A severely contracted elbow is subject to maceration in the elbow crease and interferes with dressing.

Therapy specifically for the elbow joint consists of passive range-of-motion exercises. Use of slow, steady pressure helps to improve or at least maintain present mobility. A positioning program should include a total body relaxation effect (see Chapter 11). Functional movement of the extremity should be attempted from positions of total body relaxation. Ideally, such exercises should be included in an early intervention therapy program before a contracture develops. After a contracture develops, hygiene management is an important consideration.

The typical elbow flexion/forearm pronation deformity eliminates rotary action at the elbow. The individual tends to substitute through lateral trunk flexion during reaching. Trunk stabilization is used to discourage this substitution. Active reaching should be encouraged through the use of motivational devices (discussed in Chapter 14).

A splint may be employed to maintain the elbow in extension during early stages of an elbow flexion contracture. The splint should hold the elbow in midrange (with neither the flexor nor the extensor on maximum stretch). This midrange positioning avoids constant facilitation of elbow flexors (Barnes & Crutchfield, 1972). Splints should be carefully fitted and well padded in the forearm area and use should be monitored closely. Splints are contraindicated if spasticity is severe or if a contracture is too rigid. Under such conditions, splinting would put too much pressure on the forearm (King, 1982). Occasionally, such a positioning device is used with a psychologist's or behavioral specialist's programming to inhibit hand-to-mouth behavior. This is advantageous with persons who damage their hands through constant sucking or biting. Elbow splints offer an alternative to mitts and allow for functional use of the hands.

When the spasticity is so severe that splinting is contraindicated and hygiene management becomes difficult, surgical release of the biceps tendon may be indicated. Use of open-cell foam spacers in the elbow crease may be indicated to decrease maceration if surgery cannot be performed or is delayed. Absorbent powder or cornstarch may be applied to the foam to keep the area dry. Short-sleeve shirts or loose-fitting long-sleeve shirts should be worn to allow air to circulate around the macerated area.

Wrist Extension

Wrist extension posturing is relatively rare, but will occasionally be encountered. Splinting is seldom indicated as functional gains rarely result, and the wrist extension posturing does not present a hygiene problem. Also, splinting of the dorsum of the hand that has many bony prominences and little adipose tissue is not well tolerated by individuals with multiple handicaps. Treatment for a fisted hand, which may accompany wrist extension posturing, is discussed later in the chapter.

Wrist Flexion

Wrist flexion is often accompanied by ulnar deviation due to the relative strength of the flexor carpi ulnaris and the weakness of the antagonists. Position of the fingers varies. Wrist posturing has a critical effect on grasp and release. In mild cases, with primary involvement in extrinsic flexors, placing-and-holding training techniques may yield a more controlled grasp and release. This is accomplished by placing the wrist in a neutral or slightly extended posture to break up overflow from the forearm musculature.

Many persons with moderate involvement use the mechanical action (i.e., tenodesis) of wrist extension to assist with grasping, and wrist flexion to assist with releasing. Splinting usually is not indicated in such cases since it would interfere with function. Tenodesis splints may be used occasionally. However, these require a fair amount of cognition and perceptual motor skills for use.

When wrist flexor tightness is due to extrinsic musculature involvement, a wrist cock-up splint with thumb abductor is effective in decreasing tone at the wrist and allowing increased hand function (Figure 13.9). Thumb abduction is an important component for reducing flexor spasticity in the arm (Bobath, 1978). If intrinsic tightness is present as well as extrinsic hypertonicity, less functional gains will be achieved from splinting. In such cases, treatment should focus on adapting toys, appliances, and so forth (through use of adapted switches) to facilitate functional use of the hand. Occasionally, a splint may serve as a pencil/crayon holder or pointer (Figure 13.10). For example, a hand splinted in extension is more functional with a utensil holder than attempting to use a utensil holder with a flexed wrist.

Finger flexion may accompany wrist flexion posturing. Hygienic management to prevent maceration of the palm is a primary consideration. Hand cones (Farber, 1982) may be added to wrist cock-up splints to facilitate finger extension and allow air to circulate around the palm (Figure 13.11).

Splinting may be used as an evaluation technique prior to wrist arthrodesis surgery. A splint can simulate the wrist fusion to determine what effect the surgery would have on the person's functional abilities.

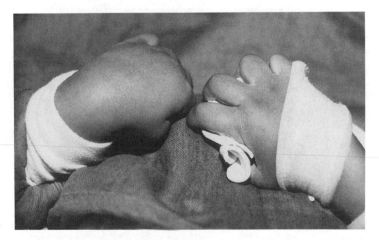

Figure 13.9.   Wrist cock-up splint with thumb abductor. This splint is used to position the wrist in extension and the thumb in abduction.

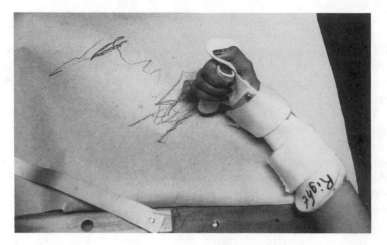

Figure 13.10. Splint serves as holder. A resting pan splint is used to place this person's hand in a functional position for simple activities. A pointer, crayon, or marker may be placed in the end of the hand cone.

Extended Hand

Extension at the metacarpophalangeal (MCP) joint is common among persons with multiple handicaps. It does not present hygiene problems, as does the flexed hand. In the extended hand, the palmar grasp reflex often is absent and no active grasping is elicited. If such is the case, objects can be secured into the person's hand with elastic straps. Objects such as bells, rattles, and

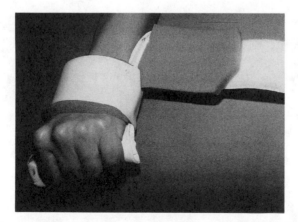

Figure 13.11. Hand cone on wrist cock-up splint. A hand cone may be added to a wrist cock-up splint to facilitate wrist and finger extension and allow air to circulate around the palm. Note that extra padding has been added since most persons with multiple handicaps cannot self-monitor or self-adjust straps for comfort.

maraca-type toys are good choices since they give auditory feedback for movement of the upper extremity.

Weak Hand

Quite commonly, a person with multiple impairments demonstrates a weak or nonfunctional grasp. This may be due to the effects of the ATNR, generalized hypotonicity, or athetosis. The ATNR results in a weak grasp with arm and hand posturing affected by the position of the head. For example, when head rotation causes the arm to extend, the hand tends to open. Grasping objects may be adapted to accommodate this condition by enlarging the object and decreasing its weight. For example, built-up handles may be added to an object to increase its size (Figure 13.12). Weight of an object may be reduced by using foam, Styrofoam, sponge, or similar lightweight materials. A strap may be used to secure a toy in the palm of the hand (Figure 13.13). Stabilizing the wrist and using placing-and-holding therapy techniques may also facilitate grasping. This is especially effective if athetosis or joint hypermobility is present.

Squeeze toys are often a good choice for use with persons having weak grasp. The person can be patterned by a trainer to exhibit a grasping action and will receive auditory feedback from the toy.

Figure 13.12.   Built-up handle on a commercially available toy. Simple adaptations, such as enlarging handles with foam or splinting materials, make a functional difference for many persons with multiple handicaps.

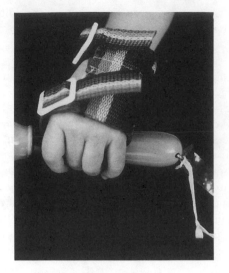

Figure 13.13. Toy holder. This toy holder is used to secure a toy into the palm of a hand. Adjustable Velcro loops hold the toy to the palmar strap. A stabilizing strap is placed around the wrist (available from Danmar Products, Inc.).

Flexed Spastic Hand

The flexed hand is characterized by flexion at the metacarpophalangeal, proximal interphalangeal, and distal interphalangeal joints. It is caused by spasticity of the long and short finger flexor muscles. Also, a positive tonic grasp reflex may contribute to this condition. The flexed position of the fingers and thumb can lead to hygiene problems and maceration in the palmar area.

Persons with a flexed spastic hand demonstrate a sustained grasp and have difficulty opening the hand. Toys with small diameters, such as a rattle, may fit into a tightly fisted hand. The use of hand cones may be indicated. Theoretically, hand cones inhibit finger flexion and facilitate extension (Farber, 1982). However, this effect should not be anticipated in cases of severe involvement. Realistically, an individually fitted hand cone may reduce maceration and allow air to circulate around the palmar surface. Cornstarch may be sprinkled on the cone prior to use. The cornstarch helps dry a moist palm. In the event cones cannot be tolerated, open-cell foam rolls may be used instead. The diameter of the roll and density of the foam may be increased as tolerance develops. The effect of the soft foam versus a hand cone should be evaluated on an individual basis. Palm-Guard, made of aliplast and fleece (available from AliMed, Inc.), helps protect the palm from contracted fingers. Some therapists have found that a spasticity reduction splint (Snook, 1979) is effective with a flexed hand. This splint holds the wrist extended, thumb extended and abducted, and fingers abducted and extended (Bobath, 1978). This position helps reduce hand spasticity.

The prognosis for function of a severely flexed hand is poor. In such cases, alternate body areas (e.g., elbow, arm, head, knee) or the fisted hand may be used to operate communication devices or adapted toys and switches (see Appendix G).

Thumb Adduction

Thumb adduction is the posturing of the thumb against the side of the hand. Thumb adduction posture limits effective grasping due to the lack of thumb opposition. The thumb loop (Hill, 1988) and Sof-Splint (Reymann, 1985b) may be used with individuals who reach out and interact with objects. Both splints are semidynamic orthoses in that they have no moving parts, but position the hand and wrist in such a way that optimal movement may be elicited (Hill, 1988).

Thumb-In-Palm

Thumb-in-palm (i.e., cortical thumb) posturing consists of an opposed thumb that rests in a flexed position in the palm (Figure 13.14). It is caused by intrinsic muscle spasticity. It may occur with or without joint deformity and finger flexion. It should be differentiated from an adducted thumb deformity in which the thumb is held in an extended position against the side of the palm. Although both deformities prevent opposition and pincer grasp, the thumb-in-palm deformity is the more troublesome of the two to persons with

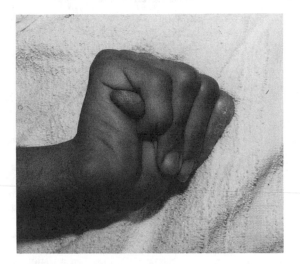

Figure 13.14. Thumb-in-palm deformity. The thumb-in-palm deformity (i.e., cortical thumb) describes the position assumed by the thumb. In this case, the fingers have flexed over the thumb making it difficult to keep the hand clean.

multiple handicaps. The tightly flexed position often results in maceration of the thenar web and presents difficulty to caregivers in providing hand hygiene.

In the early stages of the deformity, toys that are held in place by elastic straps may be placed between the thumb and first finger to abduct the thumb. In deformities that involve moderate spasticity with little shortening of the thenar tendons, C-bar splints (Mayerson, 1971) are effective in preventing maceration and preserving the thumb web space. Once intrinsic thumb muscles have begun to shorten, splinting is no longer as effective and may place too much pressure on the tendons. Open-cell foam spacers may be used to help prevent maceration in severe deformities. In such cases, surgical procedures often are considered (Shaffer, 1983).

CLOSING THOUGHTS

General and specific postural evaluations are fundamental to preparing individuals with multiple handicaps for upper extremity movement and function. Evaluation results lead to a program of physical management that centers around positioning and adaptive equipment. Proper positioning controls proximal postural abnormalities, stabilizes the body for arm/hand activities, and may facilitate functional use of the upper extremities. In some cases, splinting may be used to help control distal postural abnormalities.

REFERENCES

American Academy of Orthopaedic Surgeons. (1965). *Joint motion method of measuring and recording*. Chicago: Author.

Ayers, A.J. (1964). Tactile function: Their relation to hyperactive and perceptual motor behavior. *American Journal of Occupational Therapy, 18*, 6–11.

Ayers, A.J. (1972). *Sensory integration and learning disorders*. New York: Psychological Corporation.

Barnes, M.R., & Crutchfield, G.A. (1972). *The neurophysiological basis of patient treatment: Vol. I, The muscle spindle*. Atlanta, GA: Stokesville Publishing Co.

Bergen, A.R., & Colangelo, D. (1983). *Positioning the client with central nervous system deficits: The wheelchair and other adapted equipment*. Valhalla, NY: Valhalla Rehabilitation Publications.

Bleck, E. (1979). *Orthopaedic management of cerebral palsy*. (Saunders Monographs in Clinical Orthopaedics, Vol. 2). Philadelphia: W. B. Saunders.

Bly, L. (1983). *The components of normal movement during the first year of life and abnormal motor development*. Chicago: Neuro-Developmental Treatment Association. (P.O. Box 14613, Chicago, IL 60614)

Bobath, B. (1978). *Adult hemiplegia: Evaluation and treatment*. London: William Heinemann Medical Books.

Brand, P. (1984). The forces of dynamic splinting: Ten questions before applying dynamic splints. In J.M. Hunter, L.H. Schneider, E.J. Macklin, & A. Callahan (Eds.), *Rehabilitation of the hand*. St. Louis: C. V. Mosby.

Brunnstrom, S. (1970). *Movement therapy in hemiplegia.* New York: Harper & Row.

Cannon, N.M., Foltz, R.W., Koepfer, J.M., Lauck, M.F., Simpson, D.M., & Bromley, R.S. (1985). *Manual of hand splinting.* New York: Churchill Livingstone.

Cherry, D., & Weigard, G. (1981). Plaster drop-out casts as a dynamic means to reduce muscle contracture. *Physical Therapy, 61,* 1601–1603.

Erhardt, R.P. (1982a, June). *A NDT approach to hand dysfunction.* Proceedings of Continuing Education Opportunities, Ann Arbor, MI

Erhardt, R.P. (1982b). *Developmental hand dysfunction.* Laurel, MD: Ramsco Publishing Co.

Farber, S.D. (1982). *Neurorehabilitation: A multisensory approach.* Philadelphia: W.B. Saunders.

Finnie, N.R. (1975). Handling the young cerebral palsied child at home. New York: E.P. Dutton.

Fraser, B.A., & Hensinger, R.N. (1983). *Managing physical handicaps: A practical guide for parents, care providers, and educators.* Baltimore: Paul H. Brookes Publishing Co.

Hill, S.G. (1988). Current trends in upper-extremity splinting. In R. Boehme (Ed.), *Improving upper body control* (pp. 131–164). Tuscon, AZ: Therapy Skill Builders.

Howison, M.V. (1983). *Occupational therapy with children—cerebral palsy.* In J.L. Hopkins & H.D. Smith (Eds.), *Willard and Spackman's occupational therapy* (6th ed.) (pp.643–681). Philadelphia: J.B. Lippincott.

Hulme, J.B., Gallacher, K., Walsh, J., Niesen, S., & Waldron, D. (1987, July). Behavioral and postural changes observed with use of adaptive seating by clients with multiple handicaps. *Physical Therapy, 67*(7), 1060–1067.

King, T. (1982, October). Plaster splinting as a means of reducing elbow flexor spasticity: A case study. *American Journal of Occupational Therapy, 36*(10), 671–673.

Malick, M.H. (1976). *Manual on static hand splinting.* Pittsburgh: Harmarville Rehabilitation Center, Inc.

Mathiowetz, V., Bolding, D.J., & Trombly, C.A. (1983, April). Immediate effects of positioning devices on the normal and spastic hand measured by electromyography. *American Journal of Occupational Therapy, 37*(4), 247–254.

Mayerson, E.R. (Ed.). (1971). *Splinting theory and fabrication.* Clarence Center, NY: Goodrich Printing and Lithographers.

McPherson, J.J., Kreimeyer, D., Aalderks, M., & Gallagher, R. (1982, October). A comparison of dorsal and volar resting hand splints in the reduction of hypertonus. *American Journal of Occupational Therapy, 36*(10), 664–670.

Mills, V.M. (1984, February). Electromyographic results of inhibitory splinting. *Physical Therapy, 64*(2), 190–193.

Montgomery, P., & Richter, E. (1977). *Sensorimotor integration for disabled children: A handbook.* Los Angeles: Western Psychological Services.

Norkin, C.C., & White, D.J. (1985). *Measurement of joint motion: A guide to goniometry.* Philadelphia: F.A. Davis.

Reymann, J. (1985a, June). Arm band control for upper extremity posture. *Developmental Disabilities Special Interest Section Newsletter, 8*(2), 4. Rockville, MD: American Occupational Therapy Association.

Reymann, J. (1985b, June). The Sof-Splint. *Developmental Disabilities Newsletter, 8*(2), 4.

Seeger, B.R., Caudrey, D.J., & O'Mara, N.A. (1984). Hand function in cerebral palsy: The effect of hip flexion angle. *Developmental Medicine and Child Neurology, 26*(5), 601–606.

Shaffer, J.W. (1983). Hand and upper extremities. In G.H. Thompson, I.L. Rubin, & R.M. Bilenker (Eds.), *Comprehensive management of cerebral palsy* (pp.221–229). New York: Grune & Stratton.

Snook, J.H. (1979, October). Spasticity reduction splint. *American Journal of Occupational Therapy, 33*(10), 648–651.

Trefler, E. (1982), Arm restraints during functional activities. *American Journal of Occupational Therapy, 36*(9), 599–600.

Trefler, E. (Ed.). (1984). *Seating for children with cerebral palsy.* Memphis: The University of Tennessee Center for the Health Sciences, Rehabilitation Engineering Program.

Trombly, C.A., & Scott, A.D. (1977). *Occupational therapy for physical dysfunction.* Baltimore: Williams & Wilkins.

Ward, D.E. (1984). *Positioning the handicapped child for function: A guide to evaluate and prescribe equipment for the child with central nervous system dysfunction* (2nd ed.). St. Louis: Author.

Yasukawa, A., & Hill, J. (1988). Casting to improve upper extremity function. In R. Boehme (Ed.), *Improving upper body control* (pp.165–188). Tucson, AZ: Therapy Skill Builders.

Chapter

Adaptive Devices
for Function

with Judy C. Arkwright

Technology for persons with handicaps is expanding rapidly. Adaptations of existing technology are being designed for use with persons with severe multiple impairments. Such adaptations include motivational activity devices; adapted switches, toys, and appliances; communication systems and computers; and work skill tools.

MOTIVATIONAL ACTIVITY DEVICES

One of the greatest challenges to professionals working with persons with multiple handicaps is to select (and often to create) motivational activities. Visual or hearing impairments, or both, along with severe cognitive deficits, can severely limit activity selection. Devices that stimulate multiple senses may be selected, designed, and incorporated into daily activities by attending team members (including parents). There are many commercially available toys and other objects that provide auditory, tactile, and visual stimulation in response to actions such as light touch, batting, pulling, or squeezing (see Appendix G).

Until the mid 1980s, therapists with limited electronic knowledge were confined to adapting battery-operated devices or using tape recorders equipped with remote jacks. Control units now are available (see Appendix G) that allow an adapted switch to connect safely to an electrical appliance

Judy C. Arkwright, M.A., C.C.C.-S.L.P., is a Speech and Language Therapist and Technology Consultant to Wayne County Intermediate School District in Wayne, Michigan.

(Figure 14.1), such as a fan, blender, lamp, microwave oven, food processor, vibration devices, light displays, mixers, and vacuums. This is a major safety advance since direct contact with the electrical current is prevented. This mechanism is an alternative to costly environmental control units previously used to activate appliances. Simple technology affects play, enhances sensory skills, assists cognitive and communication development, and encourages participation in kitchen activities and work skills.

ADAPTED SWITCHES, TOYS, AND APPLIANCES

Radios, tape recorders, small appliances, and battery-operated toys connected to adapted switches represent a major advancement in motivational activities for persons with multiple handicaps. Adapted switches are used to bypass normal on-off switches found on battery operated devices. (On-off switches require precise hand function and motor control that is too advanced for persons with multiple handicaps.) Adapted switches can be made or purchased to accommodate any body or body part movement that an individual is capable of controlling. Activating motions may include head (Figure 14.2) and chin movement (Figure 14.3), batting arm movement, pulling, pushing, rolling, or such hand movements as pincer grasp. The use of switches provides opportunities for motivational activities and allows for play with nonhandicapped peers. For example, a child may use a switch to turn on a "Lights Alive" or "Lite Brite" toy that is being used by a nonhandicapped sibling or friend. Companies are now offering adapted toys appropriate for adolescents

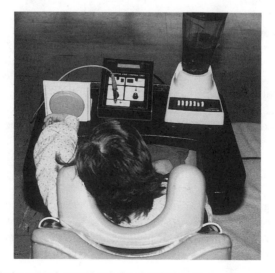

Figure 14.1. Environmental control unit for electrical appliance. Use of a control unit and adapted switch allows this student to safely operate an electrical appliance with only a light touch.

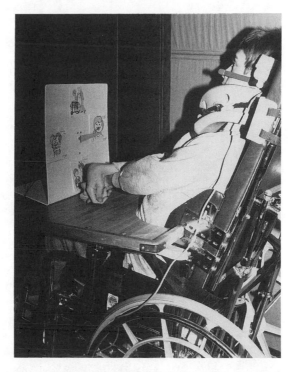

Figure 14.2.   Adapted communication device. This person with nonfunctional upper extremities operates his communication device by using his head.

and adults. A number of commercially available switches and motivational devices are listed in Appendix G.

One should be aware of the type of connector on the switch before ordering. Connectors are not standardized among commercial companies and may include various size jacks or sandwich-type interfaces. Adapters often need to be ordered with a switch or toys.

Homemade devices are much less expensive than those commercially available, encourage therapist/team creativity, and permit adaptation to an individual's needs. However, homemade devices tend to work less consistently and fail more often than commercial products.

Selection considerations for switches include volitional control and speed and reliability of an action that is needed to activate the switch. The motor action (e.g., arm or head motion) should enhance an individual's ability to maintain visual contact with the device to which the switch is connected (Figure 14.4). Motor actions that increase associated reactions, motor overflow, and abnormal reflex reactions should be avoided. Other considerations for switch selection include mounting capabilities, sensitivity,

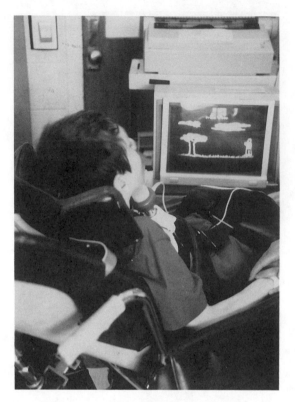

Figure 14.3. Chin switch activates computer. A chin switch is used to activate this cause-effect computer program.

shape, size, and color of the switch. Timers may be used to allow a device to stay on for a predetermined period once a switch is activated. Feedback, in the form of a "click," often is helpful to let the user know the switch has been activated (Levin & Scherfenberg, 1987).

COMMUNICATION SYSTEMS

Communication among human beings is a process most people take for granted. Communicating basic needs, wants, thoughts, and dreams for a person with a severe physical handicap often is an ongoing challenge. The major challenge for professionals and family members assisting the person with handicaps is the identification of a strategy that enables the person's communication intent to develop. Intent and skills to communicate develop and expand through opportunities to act on the environment and to control the people and events in life.

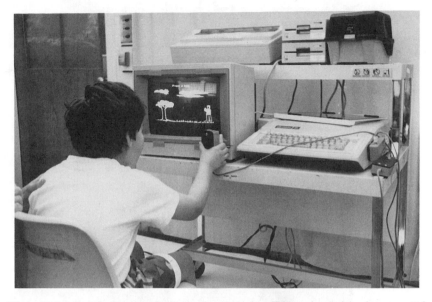

Figure 14.4. Switch placement facilitates visual attention. This touch switch has been mounted in front of the computer monitor to direct this child's visual attention to the screen.

A person with severe impairments with limited or no intelligible speech requires an alternative means to communicate, and, in turn, act on his or her environment. The field of alternative communication systems is presenting new opportunities for these individuals to communicate. An individual may communicate through hand sign language paired with vocal approximations, or through a communication board. The communication board may be comprised of common objects, photographs, simple drawings, bliss symbolics, rebus symbols, letters, words, and/or phrases. Often, a total communication approach works best, as a person is offered all strategies that are successful for him or her.

Technology now is capable of adding artificial voice to a nonverbal person's communication system. These systems are called Voice Output Communication Aides (VOCA) (Figure 14.5). VOCAs are available in single and multiple switch devices, direct select touch panels, and in a variety of scanning arrays (see Appendix G). VOCAs vary in complexity, size, and price. Synthesized speech is used as well as recorded speech.

The communication system is accessed through the person's most effective body part movement. Appropriate device and switch selection is crucial. A multidisciplinary or transdisciplinary evaluation must assess an individual's present skill level of language and communicative intent, as well as projected potential. It is important to determine the individual's most controllable ac-

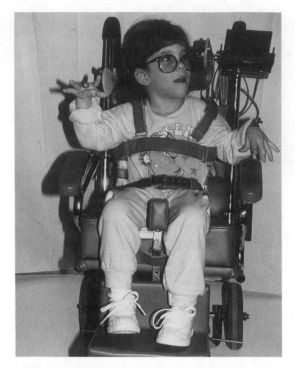

Figure 14.5. Student uses an Audio Scan, a Voice Output Communication Aide (VOCA). This child operates this type of VOCA by turning her head. A visual display is not required with the Audio Scan. VOCAs provide increased communication potential for students who are nonverbal and/or have volitional movement dysfunction.

tion, range of motion, accuracy of action, and the speed and force needed to access a given device and switch. Identifying a system that is accepted and accessible in all environments for the individual and family is the most important factor in selecting a communication system.

COMPUTER-ASSISTED INSTRUCTION

Computer-assisted Instruction (CAI) is the use of computers as a teaching tool. Computers may be used to teach individuals across all cognitive and content areas. Individuals with severe physical impairments require a variety of instructional strategies to learn. CAI has been demonstrated to promote an individual's learning potential and to improve skill attainment.

The computer may be accessed through a keyboard, single or multiple switches, touch panel, touch window, or voice input. There are a large variety of commercially adapted software programs accessed through adaptive input modes. Adapted firmware programs are available to adapt a keyboard program to a switch or to alter the cognitive level of a software program to meet the needs of an individual. Appropriate adaptive devices, switches, and software program selection is critical. (See Appendix G for resource information.)

Computers may be used to present a simple attending or cause-effect program. Turn taking, initiating interaction, identification, response to commands, matching, and classifications are a few skills successfully taught with CAI. Math, reading, science, and other subjects also are taught through CAI. A creative teacher, therapist, or parent can use the computer as one of their teaching tools in almost any area.

Why is CAI so effective with individuals with severe impairments? It motivates people. The software programs combine visual and auditory stimulation. The graphics and voice feedback capture and maintain a person's attention. Learning becomes fun. The person is motivated and physically capable of accessing and, in turn, controlling his or her learning process. Teacher dependency is reduced as the computer prompts the individual to respond. Computer interaction is consistent with positive reinforcement of correct responses.

The computer facilitates access to the educational process for persons with severe impairments. The computer also opens avenues of social-leisure activities. A well designed computer system for an individual who is severely impaired includes a communication system, environmental control, as well as a means to access his or her learning process and social-leisure activities.

WORK SKILLS

The ability to perform functional work related activities is important in building self-esteem and self-worth. There are many creative ways in which most persons with severe physical handicaps can contribute in a working environment. The keys to success is choosing work activities based on the person's interests, motivation, cognitive skills, and motor abilities and segregating those tasks into small components.

During the early years of life, therapists, parents, and caregivers strive to help a person with multiple handicaps develop fine motor and manipulative skills. As a child matures, the focus of "therapy" shifts from performing specific isolated motor skills to learning work-related tasks that often require therapeutic adaptation of devices and the environment.

Most persons with severe multiple handicaps do not function independently in a work situation. Yet, such persons can contribute by doing one part of a job (i.e., partial participation). For example, an individual may complete a final part of a packaging job by placing items in a shipping box. Many persons with severe impairments are successful composite workers (Levin & Scherfenberg, 1986). A composite worker shares work with another person. For example, a pencil sharpening job may require one person to place and hold the pencil in an electric sharpener while the person with physical handicaps turns on a switch to activate the sharpener.

ADAPTED DEVICES FOR WORK SKILLS

The use of adapted devices by a person with multiple handicaps facilitates participation and increases success. Examples of such devices are jigs, tubs, and grids. Jigs are special guides that keep paper aligned. Jigs may be used with staplers, three-hole punches, self-inking stampers, and similar devices to increase accuracy and lessen motor skill levels that are required for a task (Figure 14.6). Recessed tubs may be used for sliding objects during sorting. Grids outline designated items and are used for counting.

CLOSING THOUGHTS

This chapter offered a brief introduction to adapted devices for function. An extensive list of references is provided in Appendix E for those who wish to explore this subject in detail. Appendix G lists companies that market commercially available switches, toys, and related products. In addition, Appendix G provides computer hardware and software resources along with infor-

Figure 14.6.   Jig facilitates use of electric stapler. A jig attached to a stapler keeps paper aligned and eliminates error. Increased self-esteem and independent work skills are developed through functional work activities such as stapling.

mation regarding communication devices especially useful for persons with severe multiple handicaps.

REFERENCES

Levin, J., & Scherfenberg, L. (1987). *Selection and use of simple technology in home, school, work and community settings.* Minneapolis: ABLENET.

Levin, J., & Scherfenberg, L. (1986). *Breaking barriers.* Minneapolis: ABLENET.

SECTION

V

Management of Activities of Daily Living

Chapter

15

Feeding and Eating

Much of the day of a person with multiple handicaps is taken up with feeding, dressing, toileting, bathing, grooming, and oral hygiene. All persons with multiple handicaps require some level of assistance with these activities. Some remain totally dependent upon care providers for even their most basic personal needs. Others gain varying degrees of independence. For totally dependent persons, basic daily tasks such as diapering or bathing provide an opportunity for social stimulation and showing affection. For higher functioning individuals, development of self-help skills is of primary importance in facilitating cognitive development and building self-esteem.

This chapter focuses on devices that are used by or with persons with multiple handicaps during activities of daily living. Recommendations are presented relating to therapeutic management, and suggestions are offered for equipment adaptation and fabrication. Emphasis is placed on feeding since the majority of this population experiences complex and frustrating difficulties with eating, drinking, and the digestive process. Adequate nutritional intake is a life-sustaining necessity for these persons.

FEEDING

Mealtime is a social occasion for nonhandicapped persons. It is a time to relax, to enjoy food, to converse, and to be with family or friends. The same should generally hold true for persons with handicaps. Most therapists believe that it is beneficial for persons with mild and moderate handicaps to socialize during mealtime. Contact with others presents an opportunity to watch and model eating skills after less handicapped or nonhandicapped persons. Similar concepts hold true for persons with multiple handicaps; however, special planning may be needed to permit a successful mealtime experience.

227

Extensive physical abnormalities—including spasticity, athetosis, skeletal deformities, hydrocephalus, and retained primitive postural reflexes—often combine to make independent feeding impossible for individuals with multiple handicaps. In addition, many such persons may require chopped, mashed, ground, or pureed foods due to chewing and swallowing difficulties. The vast majority of these persons are dependent upon caregivers for varying degrees of assistance during the eating process (occasionally tube feeding may be necessary). For the purposes of this book, dependent feeders are defined as those who demonstrate oral-motor difficulties and lack the ability to place food in the mouth. The goals of a management plan for dependent feeders are to supply adequate nutritional intake and to improve oral-motor function while eating. Assisting feeders are those who accept food well and whose oral-motor skills are sufficiently developed to allow chewing and swallowing without therapeutic intervention. Assisting feeders also have upper extremity motor control that allows hand-to-mouth activity. Goals of therapy management for assisting feeders are to learn hand-to-mouth feeding patterns and to develop use of utensils to self-feed.

Feeding Evaluation

Evaluation for feeding programs includes obtaining background information; conducting a preliminary examination of the mouth; assessing oral function; noting responses to various food thicknesses, textures, utensils, and presentation; and assessing the effects of positioning. Several evaluation sessions should be conducted. Sufficient time should be allowed to evaluate several feeding variables (e.g., positioning, food, texture, food presentation, utensils).

Background Information

Background information includes postural, reflex, and gross motor components that affect an individual's functioning. Caregivers should be interviewed to learn about the setting in which the person is fed (e.g., social, sensory, affective considerations); the time allowed for feeding; feeding methods used; management difficulties that are experienced; and positions used for feeding. Medications that an individual is taking should be reviewed for side effects that may affect feeding. Such side effects may cause vomiting, interference with normal gastrointestinal flow, relaxation of the lower esophageal sphincter, and interference of calcium metabolism (Bray, Barks, & Beckman, 1987). Cognitive and communication functioning should also be ascertained.

Preliminary Examination of the Mouth

A preliminary examination should include inspection of the teeth, gums, and palate. Malocclusion and a high arched palate are common among this population. Facial asymmetries and mandible subluxation may be present. Gum hypertrophy may appear as a side effect of Dilantin and other seizure control medications. Jaw and/or tongue asymmetry may also be present due to the effects of an asymmetrical tonic neck reflex. Oral sensitivity should also be noted.

Oral Assessment

An oral assessment includes several components. Breathing patterns are noted. The presence of primitive oral-motor reflexes (discussed later in this chapter) is identified. Developmental aspects of jaw, tongue, and lips are considered. (*The Pre-Speech Assessment Scale* [Morris, 1982b] is especially suitable for in-depth information in this area.) However, it should be noted that oral-motor pathology, present in most persons with multiple handicaps, limits the value of developmental information.

An oral functional examination is especially important for persons with severe multiple handicaps. This examination should include answers to the following questions: Do lips actively remove food from the spoon? Is tongue movement controlled enough to shape a bolus and move the bolus to the back of the mouth for swallowing? Is jaw action present for mastication? What is the response of the jaw, tongue, and lips when liquid is presented? How much spillage of food and liquid is present? Stratton's (1981) *Behavioral Assessment Scale of Oral Function in Feeding* is useful in this regard. It may be helpful to evaluate the time for oral transit of food from placement in the mouth to swallow initiation. A comparison of the effects of various positions, foods, and texture changes should be included in the assessment.

Food Textures

A feeding evaluation should include the individual's response to various food thicknesses and textures. Thickness may be increased by adding potato flakes to food or Thick-It ® or other similar commercial products to liquid. Binasol^{T.M.} 81 Starch may be used to thicken liquids and is available from several distributors (Stratton, 1989). A Jello product also may be added to liquid. Textures may be changed by placing a small amount of finely mashed food with a binder food, such as combining mashed noodles with blended noodles to create a noodle dish. Textures may be first introduced by using foods that stay together in a bolus, such as mashed bananas or mashed squash. The most difficult textures to handle are foods that separate in the mouth such as rice or mashed vegetables.

Utensils, Cups, and Tumblers

An evaluation should include trials of various utensils, cups, and tumblers to assess their effect on oral-motor function. Size, configuration, and material of a cup or tumbler will effect the presentation of liquids. The type of utensil, the amount of food given, and the placement of food should be analyzed in relation to utensils. Typically, food is placed between the molars or on various areas of the tongue (e.g., anterior, medial, lateral). Depending upon the area of food placement, various oral-motor responses will be elicited. Analysis should include observation of lip, cheek, jaw, and tongue movements to determine which presentation style promotes the desired result.

Positioning

Position changes may affect oral-motor function (Hulme, Shaver, Acher, Mullette, & Eggert, 1987); therefore, a feeding evaluation should include effects of changing the individual's position. In general, positioning should be evaluated to determine which supported posture reduces the effects of pathological primitive reflexes and excess muscle tone. Specific suggestions are presented later in this chapter. Positioning within the environment should be evaluated with the goal of creating situations that are comfortable and easy for caregivers to implement. Once a total body position is determined, a head position that facilitates desired oral-motor responses should be established. Wheelchair evaluations should include consideration of anticipated feeding positions if feeding is to take place with an individual seated in a wheelchair. Caution should be taken against placing tight belts across the abdomen during feeding sessions.

Videofluoroscopy

Videofluoroscopy is a radiological technique used to evaluate the movement of food through the pharynx and esophagus and thereby permit evaluation of aspiration risks. Evaluation of the pharyngeal and esophageal stages of swallowing requires radiographic studies. Videofluoroscopy is a modified barium swallow radiographic procedure. It differs from a traditional barium swallow in that the radiograph remains focused on the oral and pharyngeal areas to assess activity before, during, and after a swallow. Barium is given in small controlled amounts with the test recorded on videotape to allow repeated review without further radiation exposure to the individual. Videofluoroscopy should be conducted if there is question or concern about the safety of food or liquid intake. Aspiration is the penetration of food or liquid into the airway below the level of the true vocal folds. Common clinical signs of aspiration include congestion, recurrent pneumonias, excessive mucus secretions, and unexplained fevers (Logemann, 1983). It should be noted that aspiration may be asymptomatic (e.g., silent aspiration). Aspiration may occur before, during, or after swallowing (Logemann, 1985). It most commonly occurs before or after swallowing in the severely handicapped population. Aspiration before a swallow is due to poor tongue control that allows food portions to collect in the airway prior to swallowing, or due to a delayed or absent swallow reflex. Aspiration occurring after a swallow may result from asymmetrical pharyngeal deformities, a strong asymmetrical tonic neck reflex, a severe reflux, or an incomplete swallow of the bolus with food remaining in the pharynx after a swallow.

Videofluoroscopic examination reveals the speed, efficiency, and safety of food movement. This procedure, ordered by a physician, requires a team approach including a radiologist, a swallowing therapist who usually is a specially trained speech pathologist, the therapist most familiar with the individual being tested, and caregivers. Changes in food thickness and texture, along with positioning, should be incorporated into the radiological examination to assure complete assessment and to permit planning of appropriate management approaches. The examination should be conducted with the individual in the same position (ideally in the same wheelchair or positioning device) in which feeding normally occurs. This allows for replication of normal feeding conditions and gives a true picture of the problem. Forethought may be required regarding a chair (or modifications for a chair) that will fit in the radiographic equipment.

It should be noted that videofluoroscopic examinations usually are performed in general hospitals where radiologists and swallowing therapists tend to be most familiar with acute care patients. By contrast, individuals with multiple impairments are chronic care clients. Special criteria should be used with this population to decide on oral versus tube feeding. Slow oral transit times should be expected. It is not unusual to require 45 minutes per meal. Oral feeding should be encouraged for social reasons if caregivers are willing to spend sufficient time feeding and if food can be taken safely. In some cases, tube feedings may be deemed necessary to provide adequate nutrition and to hydration or prevent aspiration. However, it may be possible to continue providing specified foods or liquids by orally supplementing the tube feeding. Decisions regarding oral versus tube feedings reflect a consensus of the attending team.

Evaluation of Assisting Feeders

Typically, developmental scales are used for self-feeding evaluation. Criterion-referenced assessments (*Callier-Azusa Scale* [Stillman, 1978]; *Carolina Curriculum for Handicapped Infants and Infants at Risk* [Johnson-Martin, Jens, & Attermeier, 1986]) may be more adaptable to the needs of persons with multiple handicaps than norm-referenced tests (*Bayley Scales of Infant Development* [Bayley, 1969], *Denver Developmental Screening Test* [Frankenburg & Dodds, 1969]) (Copeland & Kimmel, 1989). Developmental tests should be adapted since severe deformities do not allow for the progression of normal developmental sequences. For example, a child may never grasp a spoon independently, but may become an assisting feeder by using a palmar cuff or adapted sandwich holder. An evaluation should include analysis of positioning. Such an analysis provides information about support needed to provide a stable base, facilitate control, and allow functional movement. An evaluation should also determine the types of utensils, tumblers, plates, and table or tray to be used as well as the position of the feeding equipment within the environment.

General Program Development

Once an evaluation is complete, a general management program is developed that emphasizes a team approach. It is important for the attending therapist to model training and feeding techniques and to be available to answer questions and give additional advice on a frequent basis. In addition, written instructions supplemented by photographs or illustrations should be provided to caregivers (Lewis, 1984). Although many oral-motor treatment programs exist, those most applicable to individuals with multiple handicaps center on external factors. These factors include type, consistency, and placement of food; rate of feeding and food amount; environmental adaptations; consideration of manual jaw control; and providing appropriate therapeutic positioning.

Team Approach

A management plan may be designed by a team consisting of an occupational therapist, speech-language pathologist, a physical therapist, and caregivers. In many situations, an occupational therapist is responsible for the development of feeding programs because management programs focus on positioning, selecting utensils, adapting food, and choosing methods of food presentation. However, in some settings, a speech-language pathologist may conduct feeding programs and often an occupational therapist and speech-language pathologist may work together. Also, a speech-language pathologist may enhance an individual's mealtime socialization by using communication systems designed to indicate personal food choices or by encouraging sound play following the oral stimulation of eating. Caregivers are an integral part of plan development. Their understanding of why a plan is being developed facilitates implementation.

The assistance of a dietician, nurse, and physical therapist can help an occupational therapist meet an individual's feeding needs. Nutritional planning by a dietician who is trained in the needs of persons with multiple handicaps is conducive to an effective feeding program. A nurse may use food as a means of giving medications and may also supervise tube feedings. A nurse also may assist in coordinating a physician's recommendations if a gastroesophageal reflux is present. An attending physical therapist may provide postural drainage prior to eating and may help position an individual for his or her meal. Other professionals, such as physicians, dentists, and psychologists may provide consultation.

Food Type and Texture

Food type and texture should be decided on an individual basis. Many caregivers seem to have a false impression that persons with multiple handicaps, much like babies, require liquids or runny foods. Most persons may handle thickened food with less coughing and spilling than runny food. Poor oral control and sensory impairments may create a situation in which liquids place the person at risk of aspiration. Yet, often, such persons may be able to handle thickened foods adequately. It should be noted that a blockage of the airway could occur if foods are overly thickened or given in large quantities. Generally, food and liquid should be presented in small amounts. The temperature and tastes of food must be considered. Adding salt or spices to foods may help stimulate oral movement in hypotonic individuals. Cold temperatures may increase spasticity and, therefore, may need to be avoided with some persons. Sensory properties of food should be considered. Are foods grainy, lumpy, or smooth? Do they stay together as a bolus? Does the food melt in the mouth? Does it break up into pieces? Adding a food thickener or a binder food may enhance the success of assisting feeders (Morris & Klein, 1987). Methods for changing food types and textures were discussed earlier in this chapter.

Rate of Feeding and Food Amount

The rate of food presentation (i.e., time between spoonfuls of food) should be specified in a feeding plan. Some persons need extra time for swallowing due to poor oral transit of food to the back of the mouth. Others need extra time between spoonfuls, allowing for two or more swallows to clear the food from the pharyngeal area and to prevent aspiration. The frequency of liquid presentation during the meal may be important.

The amount of food presented affects oral control. In general, a small bolus will facilitate more controlled oral-motor action. There may be instances, however, where a large mouthful of food will facilitate mouth closure and lip activity in children who are able to produce these movements (Morris & Klein, 1987).

Environmental Adaptation

Environmental adaptation during feeding is an important aspect of a physical management program for persons with multiple handicaps. Experience shows that persons with handicaps eat more successfully in a relaxed atmosphere. This may be encouraged by playing soft music and creating a group setting. Mealtime also may require concentration. When an individual with multiple handicaps is learning a new eating skill, isolation in an area of a room where distractions are minimal may be necessary. Once the desired skill is learned, he or she may rejoin a group for mealtime socialization. In order to help an individual develop and maintain a positive attitude toward feeding, many therapists prefer to avoid performing specific oral-motor treatment techniques (such as those designed to decrease a hyperactive gag, improved tongue control, and improve lip closure) at mealtime. Such treatment techniques may be performed by providing a food experience at another time during the day.

Manual Jaw Control

Manual jaw control often is needed to facilitate oral control and to minimize spillage, thereby aiding adequate nutritional intake. It also may be an effective treatment technique for developing chewing or improving lip closure with persons who do not follow directions or who are unable to perform motor imitations. Jaw control may be provided with or without manual head sup-

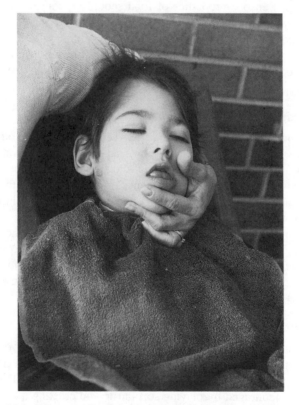

Figure 15.1. Manual jaw control with head stabilization. This person's head is cradled by the caregiver's arm. The caregiver's index finger rests lengthwise on the chin just under the lower lip with the middle finger placed under the chin and the thumb placed on the side of the face. The caregiver's other hand is free for feeding.

port. The person's head is cradled by a caregiver's arm (Figure 15.1) when using manual head support. The caregiver's index finger rests lengthwise on the chin just under the lower lip, with the middle finger placed under the chin just behind the anterior tip of the mandible, and the thumb placed on the side of the face (Wilson, 1978). The caregiver's other hand is free for feeding. Usually, manual head and jaw control is applied with the caregiver seated beside the individual. A frontal approach may be used if slightly flexed symmetrical head support is provided by a headrest or if no manual head stabilization is needed. In these cases, the caregiver's thumb is placed in the center of the person's chin and the index finger is placed under the person's chin to control jaw movement (Howison, 1983). If lip control is desired in addition to jaw control, then the thumb should be placed on the chin under the bottom lip, the index finger on the cheek, and the middle finger lengthwise under the chin just behind the mandible (Conner, Williamson, & Siepp, 1878) (Figure 15.2). Therapists and caregivers trained in using manual jaw control techniques facilitate the feeding process with dependent feeders (Mueller, 1975). The amount of manual control may be reduced as jaw and lip actions improve.

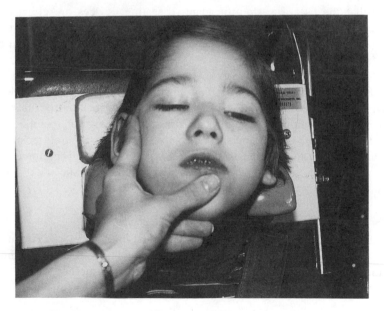

Figure 15.2. Manual jaw control without head stabilization. A modular head support system inhibits the ATNR and prevents neck hyperextension. Feeding, via a frontal manual jaw control approach, is used by this caregiver. Note that the placement of the caregiver's thumb is used to facilitate lip closure.

Therapeutic Positioning

Mealtime is *not* the time for a person with multiple handicaps to put effort into developing gross motor skills, such as trunk or head control. Appropriately, placed positioning aids allow an individual to concentrate energy on eating skills without trying to support and control body parts. For example, a person with athetoid movements of the extremities may need his or her feet secured to footplates in order to permit some degree of arm control. To obtain necessary head control, persons may need more trunk support than would be required at other times during the day. In some instances, complete head stabilization may be necessary to facilitate mouth and tongue movements. Self-feeders may need trunk or chest supports in order to maintain a stable sitting posture and to free the hands for use. Such supports should not restrict breathing or press tightly against the individual's abdomen.

Proper positioning can make the feeding process productive for both the person with handicaps and the care provider. Proper positioning provides support and control to the trunk, head, legs, and arms, allowing attention and energy to be focused on oral-motor skills. Positioning also breaks up or limits total synergy or reflexive patterns and, thus, encourages isolated movements of the arms, head, and oral musculature (Mueller, 1972). Hulme et al. (1987) found that the use of custom-fit adaptive seating devices are effective in improving some components of eating and drinking. Specifically, food and liquid spillage decreased, acceptance of textures increased, and skill in cup drinking improved.

Usually, positioning is achieved by use of equipment, aided, at times, by manual support given by a caregiver. Positioning requirements should be determined through the joint efforts of attending physical and occupational therapists. The following paragraphs address positioning for specific problems that are likely to be encountered. Most of the positioning techniques presented pertain to both dependent and assisting feeders. Therefore, techniques applicable only to dependent or assisting feeders are specifically identified in the following discussion.

Specific Program Management

Specific program management requires a detailed look at specific conditions that cause feeding difficulties. These conditions include gross motor abnormalities, primitive postural reflexes, presence of oral-motor reflexes, and abnormal oral-motor pathology.

Gross Motor Components

Spasticity   Persons with multiple handicaps with spasticity often assume a position in which the neck and head are extended. This position makes swallowing difficult. In addition, neck extension may contribute to aspiration by allowing food to move more readily into the airway (Howison, 1983). Swallowing is a complex process that requires careful evaluation (Log-emann, 1983). In most cases, positioning in which the head is slightly flexed (i.e., about 5–15 degrees) facilitates swallowing and reduces extensor hyper-tonus. Upright positioning and a forward head position, in general, helps to protect food from going into the airway. However, causing the head to flex more than 15 degrees may inhibit swallowing. It is important to note how the recommended head position for swallowing affects breathing. A few individ-uals require slight neck extension to maintain a clear pharyngeal airway for breathing (Morris, 1982a), but, in general, head extension is avoided during feeding because it opens the airway, thereby placing an individual at risk of aspiration. Correct head positioning should be determined by the attending therapist. In many cases, a videofluoroscopy is needed to determine the exact effects of positioning. In order to gain accurate, functional information, the therapist should use various positioning devices to mimic the positions used during the radiographic study.

For a feeding program, the amount of support necessary to hold the head in slight flexion varies according to the degree of head control. For example, an individual with fair head control using a standard wheelchair may need only a commercially available headrest extension. An individual with poor head control or severe spasticity who is capable of sitting in a standard or travel wheelchair may require a neck support or head support (see Chapter 8). In the presence of a severe total extensor pattern, it may be necessary to protract the shoulders in addition to neck flexion positioning. (A severe exten-sor pattern, including neck extension, tends to increase lip retraction and tongue thrusting.) Shoulder protractors (see Chapter 13) or rolled towels may be placed behind the shoulders (Howison, 1983). A modular chest support (see Chapter 8) may be needed to secure the shoulders in a flexed, nonele-vated position and to prevent forward leaning. Shoulder elevation often pro-duces chest tightness. This may be controlled by the yoke section of the chest support. Manual jaw support also may be considered for dependent feeders. Manual therapeutic techniques yield maximal functional gain only when posi-tioning equipment is used to maintain the desired effect (Ward, 1984).

For persons restricted to a recumbent posture, slight neck flexion may be achieved by supine positioning in a bean bag or in a semireclined or fully reclined wheelchair with the head supported by a pillow or special head support. (Bean bags should not be used with persons exhibiting total body flexion since the bags position the trunk and legs in flexion.) Torticollis may be present in some individuals. Positioning in such cases should focus on maintaining a stable body position.

Sidelying may be functional since it reduces the effects of many primi-tive postural reflexes of hypertonicity. Positioning an individual on a sidelyer or a wedge will aide digestion (Figure 15.3). Proper body alignment and

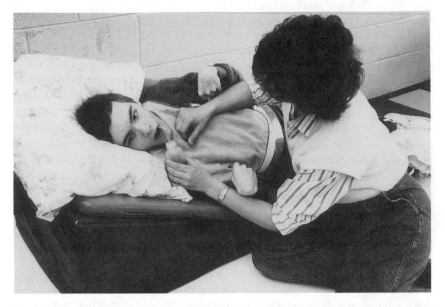

Figure 15.3. Elevated sidelying position for feeding. Positioning an individual on an elevated sidelyer or a wedge, as pictured, with symmetrical body alignment and slight head flexion, facilitates digestion. Weight bearing on the right side is preferred for gastric emptying.

slight head flexion is recommended. Weight bearing on the right side is preferred for gastric emptying unless orthopaedic restrictions prohibit right sidelying. Food presentation is typically at the top cheek at the first molar or further back between cheek and teeth. Liquids are presented by syringe or gravity squeeze bottle (Bray, Beckman, & Barks, 1987). A drawback to sidelying feeding is an increase in food spillage if oral control is poor.

Severe Extensor Thrusting   In cases of severe extensor thrusting, the body should be stabilized in a flexed supine or sitting position with the hips ideally in more than 90 degrees of flexion. This may be accomplished by use of a wedged wheelchair seat. A wedge placed under the legs of a person in a supine position also helps reduce thrusting. While flexion tends to reduce extensor tone, it may not affect shoulder retraction and associated mouth and lip position. Since shoulder girdle retraction, open jaw or jaw thrust, and lip and tongue retraction are part of the total body extensor pattern, shoulder protractors and a neckrest that holds the head in flexion may be needed. Shoulder protractors (see Chapter 13) provide external support to the posterior shoulder girdle and humerus, thereby positioning the shoulders in protraction. (Generally, shoulder protractors are used to block shoulder girdle retraction with higher functioning assistance or self-feeding.)

Athetosis   Persons with multiple handicaps frequently experience athetoid movements of their legs, arms, and head. For persons with athetosis of the arms and legs, restricted limb movement may facilitate head control. This may be accomplished by temporary supports that are removed after mealtime. For example, padded straps may be used to secure the feet to the footplate of a wheelchair, and a wheelchair tray may be used to block movement of the arms (Trefler, 1982). By adding a neckrest or a head positioner, the head is held in a static midline position, allowing the person more control of the oral-motor areas. Dependent feeders may require manual jaw control. Some athetoid dependent feeders who require additional head control respond well to a collar-type head support. Assisting feeders may benefit from an elevated table height for initial training. Also, shoulder protraction blocks or a shoulder protraction belt (see Figure 13.5) may be used to increase midline orientation. Assisting feeders also may benefit from the stability of a prone stander (see Chapter 12) to support the trunk and lower extremities during feeding.

Hydrocephalus   Persons with hydrocephalus must bear the weight of an enlarged head. The constant energy and work needed to support this head in an upright position detracts from eating concentration. The most common devices recommended are those that stabilize the head in a midline position. The use of a head support with an occiput shelf for safe head weight bearing and to prevent neck hyperextension (see Chapter 8) may be appropriate during feeding. Supporting the weight of a large head frees energy for movement or oral musculature.

Hypotonic Muscle Tone   Persons with weak muscle tone usually have poor trunk and head control. In a supported sitting position, pelvic and trunk alignment must be addressed first (as discussed in Chapter 8). A floppy head may require the support provided by a head positioner during feeding. The positioner provides a stable base for the head and facilitates controlled oral muscular movement. Caregivers should be aware that low facial and oral tone may allow food to pool between the cheeks and gums. Assisting feeders, especially, need adequate trunk support. Chest supports may be used during feeding and removed once mealtime is over. Also, raising a table or tray to midchest height level encourages trunk extension and may also enhance controlled arm movement (Howison, 1983). Adding spices, sourness, or tartness to foods may increase sensory input with hypotonic individuals (Morris & Klein, 1987).

Medical Conditions   The following are medical conditions that affect a feeding program.

Respiratory Difficulties   Chronic coughing and gagging are commonly experienced by persons with multiple handicaps. These conditions exist because of general inability to clear mucus secretions from the lungs and tracheobronchial tree and because of frequent respiratory infections (Galka, Fraser, & Hensinger, 1980). Coughing and choking may indicate aspiration. A videofluoroscopic study should be conducted to rule out aspiration. Excessive coughing due to mucus may be controlled by using postural drainage positions prior to feeding, by placing the person's head in a slightly flexed position while eating, and by alternating warm liquids and food during the meal. Floor feeder seats (e.g., the "Tumble Forms" seat available from J. A. Preston Corp.) provide an excellent base for feeding because they can be used to position a person at various angles, from supine to 90 degrees. However, floor feeder seats generally have no neckrest and often allow the head to fall into hyperextension. Adding a neckrest to the floor feeder seat supports the head in a slightly flexed position. After feeding, an individual should remain seated to aid digestion.

If excessive coughing and gagging continue, in spite of positioning corrections, and aspiration has been ruled out, other factors should be considered. Is blended food too thin and runny? Does chopped food contain lumps that separate too easily? Is the food being placed directly on the tongue? If so, is this stimulating a hyperactive gag reflex? Is there oral hypersensitivity? Persistent coughing and gagging that remain unaffected by therapeutic intervention warrant medical examination.

Gastroesophageal Reflux   Gastroesophageal reflux is the backwash of the stomach contents into the esophagus. Typical symptoms include frequent vomiting and burping, pain, the inability to burp, or aspiration. Food refluxing into the pharynx presents a risk of aspiration. Failure to thrive, respiratory complications, esophagitis, and anemia are complications of a persistent reflux (Aguilina, 1987). Management of a gastroesophageal reflux may include incorporating dietary changes, giving smaller meals more often, and positioning programs or medications to facilitate emptying of the stomach into the intestines. Typical positioning following meals involves upright sitting, inclined supine (angle usually determined by a physician), or inclined sidelying on the right side. Morris and Klein (1987) suggest use of a pronestander or a prone-over-a-wedge position at a 30–45 degree angle. Morris and Klein also suggest pressure on the stomach while the person is in the recommended positions as an aid in digestion. This technique has proved effective in the authors' experience. Surgical intervention often is necessary in more severe cases.

Primitive Postural Reflexes

Certain primitive postural reflexes—specifically the asymmetrical tonic neck reflex, the symmetrical tonic neck reflex, and the tonic labyrinthine reflex—may interfere with feeding. Reflex-inhibiting postures help control abnormal posturing.

Asymmetrical Tonic Neck Reflex   The asymmetrical tonic neck reflex (ATNR) is particularly troublesome for assisting feeders because the reflex interferes with hand-to-mouth movements. Asymmetry may be controlled by securing or placing the person's nondominant hand on a dowel or a plate at midline. Also, manual shoulder control provided by a caregiver may be required to maintain stability (Mueller, 1975). Encouraging hand-to-mouth activity with dependent feeders may prevent oral tactile hypersensitivity (Howison, 1983). The ATNR "fencing" posture may also cause asymmetry of the jaw and tongue. Since the ATNR is triggered by head rotation, head support devices are recommended to maintain the head in a midline position while allowing slight neck flexion (see Chapter 8). However, in cases of severe ATNR, the head may be pulled to one side. Bringing the head to midline during feeding may allow food to pool in the vallecular spaces on the affected side, placing the individual at risk of aspiration. A videofluoroscopic examination is necessary to establish the feeding position in such a severe case.

Symmetrical Tonic Neck Reflex   The symmetrical tonic neck reflex (STNR) affects a person's ability to maintain a stable seated position. In sitting, neck extension causes the arms to extend and legs to flex, while neck flexion causes the arms to flex and legs to extend. The STNR is particularly troublesome to assisting or self-feeders because neck flexion or extension interferes with hand-to-mouth activity. A neck collar or head support that holds the head in an upright position decreases the effects of the STNR. Also, the addition of a tray or another surface to support the elbows in a flexed position assists in maintaining sitting stability. A wheelchair tray placed at midchest level counterbalances the kyphotic trunk posture often associated with the STNR.

Tonic Labyrinthine Reflex   The tonic labyrinthine reflex (TLR) causes the head to be either too far extended or too far flexed for controlled swallowing. The TLR appears to be triggered by the head's position in relation to gravity. In sitting, the TLR supine is activated when the head falls backward at a 90-degree angle to the horizontal (Conner et al.,1978). Neck extension increases synergy patterns and tends to inhibit swallowing, limit respiration, and decrease the ability of assisting feeders to accomplish hand-to-mouth movement (Howison, 1983). A supported sitting position with manual head control or a headrest system supporting the head in slight forward flexion is needed to counteract the effects of the TLR.

Oral-Motor Reflexes

Oral-motor reflexes are normal primitive reflexes that become pathological when not integrated. They include biting, rooting, gagging, and sucking-swallowing. Stable positioning of the trunk and head in a position as symmetrically neutral as possible facilitates the development of controlled tongue, jaw, and lip movement. In the presence of extremely severe pathology, body positioning may not inhibit the effects of pathological reflexes. However, a stable body position with careful positioning of the head and neck facilitates the feeding process.

Bite Reflex The bite reflex is a phasic bite release pattern that occurs upon stimulation of the gums and teeth (Morris, 1982a). It should be differentiated from the abnormal tonic bite pattern (discussed later in this chapter). A rubber-coated spoon with a shallow bowl or a spatula spoon may be used to help place food in the mouth without touching teeth or gums. Also, a treatment program should be designed to promote more mature oral patterns.

Rooting Reflex The rooting reflex is an orientation of the head and mouth to a tactile stimulus applied to the side of the mouth (Barnes, Crutchfield, & Heriza, 1979). It tends to be strongest when the individual is hungry. The rooting reflex may be triggered by a caregiver using manual jaw control. Manual jaw control should be discontinued if placement of the trainer's hand on the face elicits lateral head movement. A neck collar may be used to support the head in midline. Such a collar does not come in contact with the sides of the face, therefore, does not trigger this reflex.

Gag Reflex The gag reflex is a gag response to tactile stimulation applied to the posterior aspect of the tongue or soft palate (Howison, 1983). Normally, it is present at birth and gradually diminishes somewhat as chewing develops. It serves a protective mechanism against the injection of foreign objects, but doesn't affect normal feeding. A hyperactive gag (stimulated by tactile input to oral areas other than the posterior tongue or soft palate), however, does affect feeding. Specific treatment programs (Conner et al., 1978; Farber, 1974; Howison, 1983; Morris, 1982a) are geared to correct the cause of the hyperactive gag. Positioning to facilitate swallowing by supporting the head slightly forward is recommended for persons with multiple handicaps.

Suck-Swallow Reflex A suck-swallow reflex is characterized by lip closure, followed by rhythmical movements of the tongue and jaw upon tactile stimulation to the lips. This reflex allows liquid to be transferred to the back of the throat for swallowing (Howison, 1983). It is present at birth and gradually diminishes as sucking becomes voluntary. However, in persons with multiple handicaps, sucking is usually impaired prenatally or from birth.

Abnormal Oral-Motor Components

Besides pathological oral-motor reflexes, other abnormal components that may be encountered include lack of lip closure, jaw thrust, tongue thrust, lack of tongue lateralization, tonic bite, weak sucking, passive or inactive swallowing, nasal regurgitation, oral hypersensitivity, and decreased sensation. One text in particular, *Pre-Feeding Skills: A Comprehensive Resource for Feeding Development* (Morris & Klein, 1987), is most applicable for this population. Some practical suggestions for management are provided in the following paragraphs since many commonly used treatment techniques are not appropriate for individuals with cognitive impairment. These suggestions are especially suitable for individuals living in situations where management is directed at maintaining adequate nutritional intake and making the feeding process as simple as possible for caregivers.

Lack of Lip Closure   A lack of lip closure may be due to low muscle tone, generalized oral spasticity, or lip retraction (i.e., a pulling back of the lips and cheeks toward the ears, often associated with increased extensor tone). Poor lip closure makes it difficult for the lips to assist in taking food from a spoon or liquid from a cup. Positioning for feeding should be evaluated with extensor tone reduced as much as possible. A spoon with a shallow bowl should be chosen for feeding. Feeding should not be hurried. The caregiver should wait for the person's lips to assist. If there is no response, manual jaw control and lip closure may be necessary for training and to secure food or liquid in the mouth. Thickened liquids and foods will help reduce food spillage.

Jaw Thrust   Jaw thrust is characterized by an abnormally strong downward extension of the lower jaw (often associated with head extension or total body extensor patterns). Use of manual jaw control may be needed to maintain jaw closure, train for an increase in the graded jaw action, and decrease food spillage. Slight forward flexion of the head and shoulder, and a hip angle greater than 90 degrees, may help inhibit jaw thrusting. Check for the presence of oral hypersensitivity.

Tongue Thrust   Tongue thrust is an abnormally strong protrusion of the tongue. Often, the tongue initiates a swallow with an anterior rather than posterior movement (Logemann, 1983). The tongue may appear thick and bunched. This appearance makes it difficult to insert a nipple or spoon in the mouth. Also, the tongue may thrust beneath a cup (Morris, 1982a). In milder cases, a slight downward pressure on the tongue with a spoon (when tongue is inside the mouth) inhibits tongue thrust and encourages lip activity. Thickened food and use of smaller amounts may be advisable. Techniques to promote tongue lateralization may be helpful in milder cases. This is discussed later in this chapter. Jaw and lip control may be used to keep the tongue from pushing food out of the mouth and to reinforce mouth closure. In more severe cases or with older clients whose tongue mobility is unlikely to be improved, spillage can be reduced by thickening food and placing it to alternate sides of the mouth between the molars and the cheek. Proper positioning with the head in flexion should be maintained.

Lack of Tongue Lateralization   Lack of tongue lateralization is identified by predominant "in and out" movements of the tongue. In such cases, food should be thickened and placed in alternate sides of the mouth to encourage side-to-side tongue movement and to decrease food spillage. Texture or spicy, sour, or tart tastes added to the food may enhance sensory awareness and facilitate tongue movement. In addition, manual jaw control may be employed to inhibit the in and out tongue movement.

Reduced Tongue Movement   Tongue movement that is reduced due to hypertonicity or hypotonicity may prevent formation of a cohesive bolus of food or prevent holding a bolus of food in the mouth. As a result, food separates and may fall into the pharynx prior to initiation of a swallow, placing the person at risk of aspiration. Management techniques include thickening food, assuring that textured food has a binder food added in order to slow the rate of feeding to allow adequate time between spoonfuls, and positioning the head in slight flexion. Liquids may cause more of a problem than food since reduced sensation or sensory processing may contribute to an individual being unaware that liquid is falling into the pharynx. If this is the case, liquids should be presented from a syringe or thickened.

Reduced Tongue Elevation   Reduced tongue elevation may result in food collecting on the hard palate. Caregivers should be aware of this for hygiene purposes.

Tongue Retraction   Tongue retractions may be present as part of a neck hyperextension, shoulder girdle retraction pattern. Positioning the hips, shoulders, and head in slight flexion may reduce tongue retraction.

Tonic Bite   A tonic bite is an abnormally strong closure of the jaw, often obligatory, that occurs upon tactile stimulation of the teeth and gums. This is often seen in individuals with primitive reflex pathology and extensor thrusting. Use of a spatula spoon allows for accurate food placement in the mouth with minimal tactile contact to the teeth and gums. Supporting the trunk and head in a stable midline, flexed position is recommended. If a bite should occur while spoon feeding, caregivers should simply wait for relaxation to occur before removing the spoon. A program to reduce hypersensitivity (carried out at other than mealtimes) may be indicated.

Weak Sucking   Weak sucking occurs when a nipple consistently can be pulled out of the mouth or when a sucking pattern is inefficient (Morris, 1982a). Extra-long nipples may help stimulate sucking. Nipples with an enlarged hole may be needed. If the hole needs to be substantively enlarged, a cup may be preferred in order to control the flow of liquid into the mouth. Therapists should experiment with different kinds of nipples (discussed later in this chapter) to determine the most appropriate type for an individual. It should be noted that many individuals with multiple handicaps do not demonstrate a true suck. Often, alternate methods of presenting liquid (e.g., cup, syringe) may be explored with the person's therapist.

Delayed Swallowing   Delayed swallowing occurs when the bolus of food hits the posterior tongue and a swallow is not elicited immediately. There often is leakage of food off the base of the tongue into the vallecular region. Occasionally, the swallow is not triggered until food enters the pharynx. Delayed swallowing places an individual at risk of aspiration, and videofluoroscopic evaluation is recommended to help determine appropriate management (e.g., posture, presentation of food, consistency of food). Some helpful techniques may include placing food or fluid between the person's cheek and gum, positioning the food between the molars and the cheek, or providing a small amount of fluid after a bit of food (Bray, Beckman, & Barks, 1987).

Inactive Swallowing Inactive swallowing exists when liquid or food flows down the pharynx without active muscle action (Morris, 1982a). Use of thick liquids and varying food consistency along with lip closure techniques may result in less food spillage. Techniques to facilitate swallowing may be evaluated for possible use (Conner et al., 1978; Farber, 1974; Howison, 1983; Morris, 1982a; Mueller, 1972). The head should be maintained in slight flexion.

Nasal Regurgitation Nasal regurgitation is movement of liquid or food through the nose during feeding. It may occur if a cleft palate or abnormalities in structure or movement of the soft palate exist. Nasal regurgitation also may occur due to timing problems or food overflow. In such cases, management strategies include reducing the size of the bolus, thinning the food, and placing the individual more upright. If the etiology is either an oral timing difficulty or structural problem, the risk of aspiration should be explored.

Oral Hypersensitivity Oral hypersensitivity is an excessive or adverse response to oral stimulation. Oral hypersensitivity is common among persons with multiple handicaps. If hypersensitivity is present, desensitization procedures should be used prior to feeding. Desensitization procedures are well defined in current literature (Conner et al., 1978; Farber, 1974; Howison, 1983; Morris, 1982a; Morris & Klein, 1987; Mueller, 1972). Such treatment may be administered at times other than during meals.

Decreased Sensation Impaired processing of sensory input is common among persons with multiple handicaps. This, in combination with poor tongue mobility, causes difficulties when drinking liquids. Individuals may be unaware of liquid falling into the pharynx. In some cases, it may help to thicken liquids since they provide greater tactile and proprioceptive cues (Morris & Klein, 1987). Liquids also may be placed toward the back of the mouth by syringe or squirt bottle to elicit a swallow before spillage of liquids into the pharynx occurs. A videofluoroscopic evaluation may be needed to assess the extent of the problem and to assure that there is adequate airway protection when liquid is presented via a syringe or squirt bottle.

Tube Feeding

Occasionally tube feedings may be necessary. Tube feedings may be used in cases where individuals have a normally functioning gastrointestinal tract, but are unable to orally ingest adequate nutrients to meet metabolic demands (Cataldo & Smith, 1982). A nasogastric tube (i.e., nose to stomach) may be used for temporary problems. It may cause adverse oral responses and should be paired with positive oral sensory experiences. Long-term tube feeding techniques most commonly used with persons with multiple handicaps involve the gastrostomy (i.e., permanent opening between the stomach and outside surface of the abdominal wall) and jejunostomy (i.e., permanent opening between the small intestine and outside surface of the abdominal wall) feeding routes (S. Schuster, personal communication, September 27, 1988). Tube feedings may either supplement oral feeding to help maintain adequate nutrition and hydration or be the sole source of feeding. The authors have noticed that children who have changed from oral feedings to tube feedings, exclusively, demonstrate a significant regression in oral-motor patterns. Prolonged exclusive tube feedings often lead to difficulties in controlling saliva. Studies are needed to determine the relationship between tube feedings and the regression in oral-motor patterns and to document the functional effects of oral stimulation programs conducted after tube feeding is initiated. The authors also have observed that supplemental tube feedings reassure caregivers that adequate nutrition is being received. This reassurance leads to a more relaxed and pleasant oral feeding experience for all concerned.

Positioning is an important consideration during tube feedings. An individual's head and upper torso should be inclined at least 30 degrees during tube feeding to reduce risk of gastroesophageal reflux and aspiration. This positioning should be maintained for approximately one hour after feeding. Many options are available for positioning including the person's seating system, the Preston floor sitters, the Rifton youth chairs, bath chairs, corner chairs, or inclined wedges. After tube feeding positioning, right sidelying with the head and torso on an incline of at least 30 degrees is also an option. Also, social factors should be introduced with tube feeding to create a pleasant social experience. Many caregivers pair olfactory experiences with tube feedings. An example of this is the use of scented lip balms (Figure 15.4).

Feeding Equipment

Most individuals with multiple impairments use specially adapted equipment during feeding. Those who are totally dependent require specially designed bottles, cups (Figure 15.5), and spoons (Figure 15.6). A wider variety of feeding aids is used with those capable of active participation in the feeding process. Commonly used items include plates with food guards and suction cups, spoons with adapted handles, sandwich holders, and specially designed cups. Complex feeder systems have become available that permit self-feeding by some persons with multiple handicaps. The following paragraphs discuss adapted feeding equipment in more detail. Feeding equipment is available from several supply sources. All the equipment mentioned below is available from Fred Sammons, Inc. or Maddax, Inc., unless otherwise indicated.

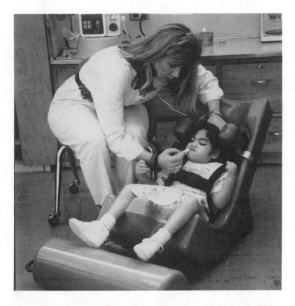

Figure 15.4.   Tube feeding with oral stimulation. Mealtime for tube feeders can be a social and sensory experience. A scented lip balm is being placed on the lips of this individual who is unable to take any food by mouth.

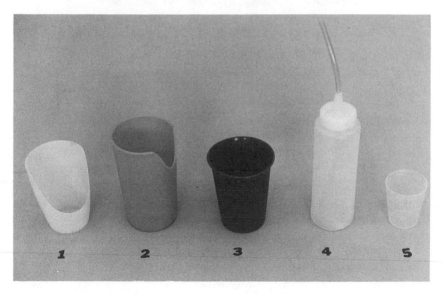

Figure 15.5.   Cups, tumblers, and bottle. A variety of cups and tumblers are available from companies that carry feeding aids. Those pictured are: 1) small, flexible cut-out cup, 2) large cutout cup, 3) Tupperware Bell Jar Tumbler, 4) squeeze bottle made by placing plastic (i.e., aquarium-type) tubing through the top of a new (unused) plastic cosmetic bottle, and 5) 2-ounce flexible tumbler.

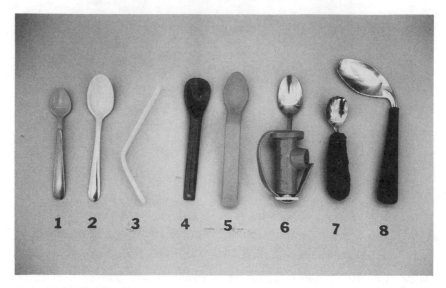

Figure 15.6. Utensils. Pictured are a sampling of eating utensils appropriate for many persons with multiple handicaps. They are as follows: 1) coated infant spoon, 2) coated adult spoon, 3) spatula spoon, 4) maroon spoon, 5) rubber spoon, 6) spoon with foam built-up handle, 7) built-up child's spoon, and 8) built-up handle offset spoon for right hand.

Bottles and Nipples

Parents of persons with multiple handicaps often find it convenient to use commercially available bottles such as Nuk, Gerber, and Evenflo for bottle feeding. However, the use of regular baby nipples may present difficulties. For example, a regular nipple may not be long enough to make contact with the posterior tongue surface. An extra-long nipple allows a caregiver to place liquid at the back of the mouth, thereby stimulating sucking action. Regular baby nipples may not provide adequate lip contact to stimulate lip closure. Nuk Orthodontic Nipples have a large bulbous portion that provides extra contact stimulation to the lips. Such nipples may be indicated for persons who have difficulty closing the lips because of tongue protrusion (Wilson, 1978). Crosscut nipples are available to accommodate thick liquids. The hole on these nipples may be enlarged if needed, as per the attending therapist's specifications. Bottle straws are available that allow individuals with an active suck and swallow ability to take liquids with the head in an upright position (thereby discouraging neck hyperextension).

Gravity feed bottles (e.g., plastic squeeze bottles) are semiflexible, allowing finger pressure to force liquid upward through the bottle and attached tube while the bottle is held in an upright position. A gravity feed bottle allows care providers to regulate liquid flow and release small amounts into a desired area of the mouth. This is often considered for use when severe oral deformities prohibit adequate lip and jaw closure. Gravity feed bottles also are useful in cases of extremely poor tongue control and sensory deficits. Liquid presented from a squeeze bottle to the back of the mouth may facilitate a more active swallow. Squeeze bottles (see Figure 15.5) may be made inexpensively by placing polyethylene plastic (i.e., aquarium-type) tubing through the top of a new (unused) plastic cosmetic bottle—available at most drug or variety stores. Nurses may find squeeze bottles or syringes useful when placing liquid medicine in the back of a person's mouth.

Cups and Tumblers

A variety of covered glasses and cups are available from companies that carry feeding aids. They are useful with assisting feeders who are experiencing mild to moderate lack of hand-to-mouth coordination. Cup covers with spouts (available for young children in many local stores or in transparent plastic in many rehabilitation catalogs) may be helpful in advancing a person with handicaps from bottle to cup drinking. Cup size appropriate for an assisting feeder is indicated by the ease with which the individual grasps the cup in the hand. Small cups without handles are easy for some individuals to control. Some assisting feeders may need a two-handled cup because of a weak or poorly controlled grasp.

Addition of a straw may facilitate independent drinking for persons with poor head control or limitations in active arm movements. The length, flexibility, and softness of the straw should be determined by the attending occupational therapist. A soft straw helps prevent injury to the face or mouth. A short straw is easier to use during early training. (Gravity feed bottles [see above] and commercially available juice boxes facilitate training of straw usage since a trainer can assist in partially moving the liquid into the straw.) A flexible straw may be needed to bend into a desired direction, but lacks the stability of a rigid straw. In such a case, a straw holder may be used in conjunction with a flexible straw for added stability. A thick-walled polyethylene straw (i.e., aquarium tubing) limits air intake (Mueller, 1975). However, straw drinking tends to increase neck hyperextension and should be used only as recommended by the attending occupational therapist. Tilting glass holders may encourage an upright head position and increase independence for some individuals.

Cups with a weighted bottom return to an upright position after being tipped or moved. This type of cup is recommended for initial training in cup drinking, for persons with visual impairment who have difficulty with the "up" concept, and for persons with athetoid arm movements.

Generally, a cup diameter should be about the same or slightly larger than the length of the mouth to encourage jaw and lip closure. The cutout plastic tumbler (see Figure 15.5) is one of the most commonly used with dependent feeders. The tumbler has a cutout on one side for the nose so an impaired person can drink without extending the neck. This feature also allows a caregiver to monitor and control the quantity of fluid going into the mouth (Mueller, 1975). Large and small cutout tumblers are commercially available. Regular translucent plastic tumblers may be cut out and the raw edge sanded (carefully). Clear cutout cups are preferred. They allow the caregiver more control over the direction in which liquids are introduced in the mouth and observation of liquid flow. The Sassy Infa-Trainer Training cup is a clear cup with a large lip that allows a trainer to adjust the flow of liquid. Tupperware and others offer flexible polyethylene tumblers. Two-ounce tumblers appear to be especially appropriate with young children. Their flexibility also helps direct fluid into the mouth of older persons.

Tupperware manufactures a rolled edge tumbler (i.e., Bell Jar Tumbler) that facilitates lip closure by making broad contact with the lips. Tupperware also offers lids with spouts for rimmed tumblers that may be useful for decreasing spillage. This tumbler is especially helpful for assisting feeders who use a "normal" oral pattern for drinking liquids.

Spoons

The utensil used most commonly by persons with multiple handicaps is a spoon. The attending therapist should try a number of spoon styles with an individual to determine the best choice. A wide variety of utensils is commercially available from manufacturers carrying adapted feeding supplies, including angled (offset) spoons, sporks (combination spoon and fork), and lightweight or weighted utensils with built-up, vertical or horizontal handles (see Figure 14.6). An ideal spoon is small enough to allow for accurate placement of food in the mouth and has a shallow bowl. In some instances, commercially available products will not meet an individual's needs. In such cases, the attending occupational therapist may consider adapting a spoon. The most common adaptations include building up handles or adding palmar cuffs for self-feeding training with persons who have a weak grasp.

Spatula-Type Spoons   Spatula-type spoons (see Figure 15.6) are often used for sensorimotor management of persons with tactile sensitivity, tongue thrust, sucking reflex, and gag reflex. They are made of plastic and designed with a shallow bowl that directs only a small amount of food into the mouth. A spatula spoon may be used to inhibit tongue thrust by pressing the bottom of the spoon against the anterior portion of the tongue. The flat undersurface of the spoon also encourages lip closure. This kind of spoon has also proven to be beneficial for use with persons showing a tonic bite reflex. Its flat profile allows a caregiver to get food into the mouth and withdraw the spoon without touching the teeth and eliciting the bite reflex. Using the spoon to stimulate one side of the tongue followed by placing food between the molars on the same side of the mouth encourages development of tongue lateralization.

Plastic- or Nylon-Coated Spoons   Plastic- or nylon-coated spoons are indicated when a person exhibits oral hypersensitivity due to tactile defensiveness or to gum hypertrophy associated with Dilantin usage. Such spoons prevent accidental contact of the metal to the teeth or gums, are less conductive of hot and cold, and reduce the transmission of these sensations to mouth surfaces. There are a variety of coated spoons on the market, available in child as well as adult sizes from companies carrying activity-of-daily-living equipment. Plastic-coated baby-size spoons are sold at many drug and grocery stores. Use of plastic-coated spoons should be well monitored, as the plastic will eventually crack or peel off. Maroon spoons from Therapy Skill Builders are plastic spoons in a narrow shape with a shallow bowl. Rubber spoons can withstand the force of a moderate tonic bite and are also gentle to the teeth and gums. However, the added depth of the rubber spoon requires use in situations where the oral opening is large enough to accommodate the larger bowl. The bent shape of the handle on commercially available rubber spoons (see Figure 15.6) (available from Fred Sammons, Inc.) are useful for some self-feeders. These spoons also have a long handle that allows easy trainer prompting during pattern feeding. In addition, the soft bowl of the rubber spoon is recommended for athetoid self-feeders who may injure the mouth with a regular spoon.

Sandwich Holders

Sandwich holders are useful when a person is capable of hand-to-mouth movement but lacks the hand control needed to grasp food. For example, when such a person uses his or her hand to pick up a cookie, uncontrolled grasp is likely to cause the cookie to crumble. Sandwich holders enable such persons to enjoy limited self-feeding with finger foods. Sandwich holders, generally available, are designed for adult persons with quadriplegic involvement. While these may be appropriate for adolescent or adult persons with multiple handicaps, young persons may need a smaller size. A small sandwich holder may be fabricated using splinting material (Figure 15.7).

Plates

A variety of plates are available, including scoop dishes, plates with add-on guards, and plates with integral food guards (e.g., inner lip plates) to help a person with handicaps keep food on a plate. The shape of scoop dishes vary; round dishes accommodate random scooping action and narrow ones are used for a controlled horizontal scooping pattern. Plates with suction cups on the underside successfully stabilize the plate on a table and protect against sliding or overturning by persons with uncoordinated hand movement. Other techniques for stabilizing plates includes the use of Dycem, which is a nonslip plastic mat for use under a plate, or a wet towel under the plate.

Figure 15.7.   Small sandwich holder. This child uses a small sandwich holder that was fabricated using splinting material. She is capable of hand-to-mouth movements, but lacks the hand control needed to grasp foods.

Wheelchair Trays

Wheelchair trays are used commonly by assisting and independent feeders and less commonly by dependent feeders. A tray may double as a meal table and a work surface. In some cases, a wheelchair tray may be used to support a communication system. Also, a wheelchair tray may help to position the upper extremities and shoulder girdle, thereby increasing arm and hand function (see Chapter 13). A wheelchair tray should not be used to support a weak trunk (Bergen & Colangelo, 1985).

Most wheelchair manufacturers offer trays as an optional item. Therapists often find it convenient to order a matching tray when placing the wheelchair order. This ensures easy attachment to the wheelchair armrests and a coordinated appearance of the wheelchair and tray unit. Commercially available trays are made of wood or plastic. Wood trays are sturdy, but tend to be heavy and may lack cosmetic appeal. A wood tray may be best for self-abusive persons because it is easily padded (see Chapter 8) and will withstand jarring and scratching. Clear plastic trays offer visibility, but tend to scratch and cloud. They fracture relatively easily if dropped and are difficult to repair when damaged. Both wood and plastic trays may be adapted with positioning aids to facilitate upper extremity function. For example, appropriately placed grasping pegs (position determined by the attending occupational therapist) may be added to accommodate associated movements of the nondominant arm. For assisting and independent feeders, grasping a peg with the nondominant hand steadies the trunk, in turn, yielding improved dominant hand and arm control. Humeral wings (see Chapter 13) may be used in conjunction with a wheelchair tray to prevent shoulder retraction and support the arms in a more functional midline position (Bergen & Colangelo, 1985).

Feeding Systems

Sophisticated feeding systems have grown out of collaboration between occupational therapists and rehabilitation engineers. Because good cognitive skills and limited oral-motor pathology are needed to use an automatic feeder, most persons with multiple handicaps are not candidates for using such devices. Trial use of this type of equipment is recommended before purchase.

CLOSING THOUGHTS

Feeding programs emphasize maintenance of the person's nutrition and hydration needs through a positive experience for the individual and the caregiver. Therapeutic intervention often takes the form of changing external factors, such as positioning; type, consistency, and placement of food; rate of feeding; and types of utensils used. Therapists should have access to a large selection of feeding equipment to try with each individual. Catalogs from such companies as Fred Sammons, Inc.; Cleo, Inc.; Maddax, Inc.; Medical Equipment Distributors, Inc.; AliMed, Inc.; and Achievement Products, Inc. offer a variety of feeding aids. Catalogs are an excellent starting resource for professionals who are working for the first time with persons with multiple handicaps. They also are a valuable resource for experienced professionals, enabling them to keep current on commercially available feeding products. Most catalogs are updated annually.

REFERENCES

Aguilina, S.S. (1987). Gastroesophageal reflex: Problem or nuisance? *Journal of Pediatric Health Care, 1*, 233–239.

Barnes, M.R., Crutchfield, C.A., & Hcriza, C.B. (1979). *The neurophysiological basis of patient treatment: Vol. II, Reflexes in motor development.* Atlanta, GA: Stokesville Publishing Co.

Bayley, N. (1969). *Bayley Scales of Infant Development.* New York: Psychological Corporation.

Bergen, A.R., & Colangelo, D. (1985). *Positioning the client with central nervous system deficits: The wheelchair and other adapted equipment* (2nd ed.). Valhalla, NY: Valhalla Rehabilitation Publications.

Bray M., Barks, L.S., & Beckman, D. (1987). Crisis intervention for persons with severe eating difficulty [Monograph]. *Problems with Eating—Interventions for Children and Adults with Developmental Disabilities*, 65–83.

Bray, M., Beckman, D., & Barks, L.S. (1987). Mealtime interventions for persons with compromised oral-motor function [Monograph]. *Problems with Eating—Interventions for Children and Adults with Developmental Disabilities*, 85–113.

Copeland, M.E., & Kimmel, J.R. (1989). *Evaluation and management of infants and young children with developmental disabilities*. Baltimore: Paul H. Brookes Publishing Co.

Cataldo, C.B., & Smith, L. (1982). *Tube feedings: Clinical application*. Columbus, OH: Ross Laboratories.

Conner, F.P., Williamson, G.G., & Siepp, J.M. (Eds.). (1978). *Program guide for infants and toddlers with neuromotor and other developmental disabilities*. New York: Teacher's College Press.

Farber, S. (1974). *Sensorimotor evaluation and treatment procedures for allied health personnel* (2nd ed.). Indianapolis: Purdue University at Indianapolis Medical Center.

Frankenburg, W. K., & Dodds, J. B. (1969). *Denver Developmental Screening Test*. Denver, CO: LADOCA Project and Publishing Foundation.

Galka, G., Fraser, B.A., & Hensinger, R.N. (1980). *Gross motor management of severely multiply impaired students: Vol. II, Curriculum model*. Baltimore: University Park Press.

Howison, M.V. (1983). Occupational therapy with children—cerebral palsy. In G. Hopkins & H.D. Smith (Eds.), *Willard & Spakman's occupational therapy*, (pp. 643–681). Philadelphia: J.B. Lippincott.

Hulme, J.B., Shaver, J., Acher, S., Mullette, L., & Eggert, C. (1987). Effects of adaptive seating services on the eating and drinking of children with multiple handicaps. *American Journal of Occupational Therapy, 41*(2), 81–89.

Johnson-Martin, N., Jens, K. G., & Attermeier, S. M. (1986). *Carolina curriculum for handicapped infants and infants at risk*. Baltimore: Paul H. Brookes Publishing Co.

Lewis, J. A. (1984). Effectiveness of parent training for feeding intervention: The parents' perspective [Monograph]. *Developmental Disabilities Special Interest Section Newsletter, 7*(4), 1–2.

Logemann, J. (1983). *Evaluation and treatment of swallowing disorders*. San Diego, CA: College-Hill Press.

Logemann, J. (1985). *The diagnosis and treatment of dysphagia: An inservice training manual*. Gaylord, MI: Northern Speech Services.

Morris, S.E. (1982a). *The normal acquisition of oral feeding skills: Implications for assessment and treatment*. Central Islip, NY: Therapeutic Media.

Morris, S.E. (1982b). *Pre-speech assessment scale: A rating scale for the measurement of pre-speech behaviors from 0–2 years*. Clifton, NJ: J.A. Preston Corp.

Morris, S.E., & Klein, M.D. (1987). *Pre-feeding skills: A comprehensive resource for feeding development*. Tucson, AZ: Therapy Skill Builders.

Mueller, H. (1972). Facilitating feeding and prespeech. In P. H. Pearson & C. E. Williams (Eds.), *Physical therapy services in the developmental disabilities* (pp. 283–310). Springfield, IL: Charles C Thomas.

Mueller, H. (1975). Feeding. In N.R. Finnie (Ed.), *Handling the young cerebral palsied child at home* (pp. 113–132), New York: E.P. Dutton.

Stillman, R. (1978). *Callier-Azusa Scale.* Dallas, TX: Callier Center for Communication Disorders.

Stratton, M. (1981). Behavioral assessment scale of oral function in feeding. *American Journal of Occupational Therapy, 35*(11), 719–721.

Stratton, M. (1989). *Swallowing.* Advanced Lecture Presentation at the Fifth Annual Conference on Developmental Disabilities, Southfield, MI.

Trefler, E. (1982). Arm restraints during functional activities. *American Journal of Occupational Therapy, 36*(9), 559–600.

Ward, D.C. (1984). *Positioning the handicapped child for function: A guide to evaluate and prescribe equipment for the child with central nervous system dysfunction* (2nd ed.). St. Louis,: Phoenix Press, Inc.

Wilson, J.M. (Ed.). (1978). *Oral-motor function and dysfunction in children.* Chapel Hill: University of North Carolina at Chapel Hill.

Chapter
16

Hygiene

Hygiene consists of dressing, toileting, grooming, and oral hygiene. The majority of persons 'with multiple handicaps are not capable of independence in self-care skills. However, if a person is able to participate in any portion of dressing, grooming, or hygiene tasks, caregivers should encourage the greatest possible degree of independence. The neurodevelopmental principle of providing proximal stability to enhance distal movement may be applied to assisting dressers (Boehme, 1983). For example, a care provider may support the pelvis of a person who is reaching to place an arm in a sleeve of a coat. Pelvic stability facilitates upper extremity reaching movements. The focus of this discussion, however, centers on adaptive clothing appropriate for totally dependent persons with multiple handicaps.

DRESSING

Selection of clothing for persons with multiple handicaps should accommodate deformities and make the dressing process as easy as possible for caregivers. During dressing, caregivers should be instructed to place the person's most affected limb into a garment first. This sequence should be reversed during undressing (i.e., least affected limb out first). Positioning of the individual being dressed should be considered to ease caregiving. For example, the person being dressed should be placed at a height that is comfortable for the caregiver to reach. Dressing an individual on a waterbed may be easier than on a solid surface due to the maneuverability of the person on a dynamic surface. Sidelying position may be used to lessen pathological forces of primitive reflexes.

Outerware

Capes are preferred rather than coats for individuals with spasticity or contractures that interfere with limb movement needed for dressing. (Cape availability is listed in Appendix F.) If using a coat, an oversized one is recommended for ease in placing a contracted or tight limb into a sleeve. Usually it is inadvisable for a person to wear a coat while seated in a custom seating system. For therapeutic reasons, many customized wheelchairs are designed to fit a person with handicaps closely (Fraser & Hensinger, 1983). Therefore, if a cape is not available, a coat or jacket may be placed on the child backwards. Coats should not be worn inside an orthosis because such seats are designed to fit close to the body. An oversized coat may be placed around the outside of a seating orthosis. Many caregivers report they leave the coat in the chair between the orthosis back and the wheelchair (Figure 16.1). Once the individual is placed in the orthosis, the arms are carefully placed in the coat. In extremely cold weather, blankets or lap covers made for wheelchair users (see Appendix F) may be used along with slipper socks or foot warmers.

Daily Clothing

Clothes may need to be a bit oversized or be made of stretchable material for ease in placing a contracted limb into a sleeve or pant leg. Neck openings may have to accommodate an enlarged head. Shirts made of cotton blends are best because they absorb perspiration caused by sitting in a wheelchair or against a vinyl surface. Women may be more comfortable in camisole-type underwear rather than in bras. This is especially helpful for persons with scoliosis, whose shape usually causes the bra to fit poorly. Trousers with metal protrusions,

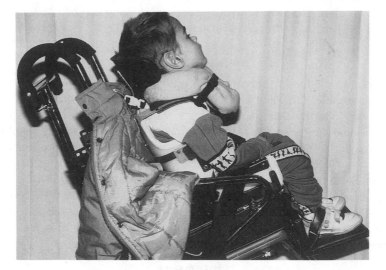

Figure 16.1.   Use of a coat with orthotic seating. A seating orthosis is designed to fit close to the body; therefore, an oversized coat may be placed behind the orthosis and in front of the wheelchair frame for ease of dressing.

such as jean pocket decoration, may cause skin breakdown. Elastic waist pull-on sweat type pants are advisable and available in many stylish varieties. Loose trouser legs are recommended for persons who use long leg braces. Reinforcements, such as iron-on patches, may be needed over stress areas (Lamb, 1984).

Shoe Adaptation

High-top orthopedic shoes, mentioned in Chapter 6, can be modified for a person with multiple handicaps. Laces may be replaced by Velcro closures (Figure 16.2) for easy application. A Velcro strap may be added across the anterior portion of the ankle (i.e., under the shoe's tongue) to hold the foot into the shoe. Clear plastic inserts in the heel area allow care providers to check for the proper placement of the foot in the shoe. Individuals who crawl and creep often cause premature wearing on the tops of the shoes. In such cases, steel toes can be added to prolong the life of expensive orthopaedic shoes. Foot warmers (see Appendix F) or warm slipper socks may be used in colder climates with non–weight-bearing individuals.

TOILET AIDS

The majority of persons with multiple handicaps are incontinent and remain so their entire lives (Fraser & Hensinger, 1983). Some may learn to indicate the need to use a bathroom, but still require assistance from caregivers in toileting.

Incontinent persons who cannot be placed in a sitting posture, usually wear large cloth or disposable diapers. Persons who can tolerate a sitting

Figure 16.2.   Velcro closures on shoes. The laces on these high-top orthopedic shoes have been replaced with Velcro for easy application and removal.

posture, who remain dry for several hours, and who have cognitive awareness should be placed on an adapted toilet on a scheduled basis throughout the day or immediately if need is indicated. Behavior modification methods have been successful in toilet training persons with mental retardation (Foxx & Azrin, 1973). Toilet training methods are not discussed in this book. Instead, this text deals with aids that facilitate optimum use of whatever controlled bowel and bladder function is possible for an individual with multiple handicaps.

Bedpans

Persons with multiple impairments who are restricted to a recumbent position may learn to use a bedpan. A padded coating provides a nonslip contact surface, thus reducing the likelihood of pressure marks and discomfort caused by cold metal.

Toilet Chairs

Equipment that is designed to provide proper trunk and head support reduces fear of falling and allows an individual to concentrate on bowel and bladder functions. Proper fit of a toilet chair is important. Persons with spasticity, especially, require positioning to reduce overall hypertonus so that abdominal muscles may relax enough to eliminate. Persons with low muscle tone require a stable sitting position to facilitate elimination. The best seating arrangement for toilet training supports an individual in a stable, but relaxed posture (Finnie, 1975). A wide variety of toilet seats are available, such as those offered by Gunnell, Inc.; Lumex; Childsafe; Everest and Jennings; Fred Sammons; Kaye Products; and Rifton.

While such commercially available toilet chairs generally are useful for persons with multiple handicaps, they are expensive, and budgets may not permit their purchase for trial or training purposes. Instead, existing equipment may be modified by the attending therapist at considerable cost savings. Toilet chairs may be made by modifying an unused or old travel wheelchair (Figure 16.3) or a Kindergarten Chair. The seat on the chair pictured was removed and replaced with a toilet seat made of foam that has been coated with a urine-proof vinyl coating. In some cases, an individual's wheelchair may be adapted to accommodate a removable potty seat. Also, the "Sleek Seat," a commercially available seat commonly used by children with neuromotor dysfunction, has been modified successfully to accommodate a toilet seat (Ottenbacher, Malter, & Weckwerth, 1979).

Toilet Seats

A few persons with multiple handicaps may have sufficient trunk control to use a regular potty seat or toilet. Small toilet seats are readily available at general merchandise stores. They may be placed over a standard-size toilet seat to make the hole smaller for children or small adults. Toilet seats may be

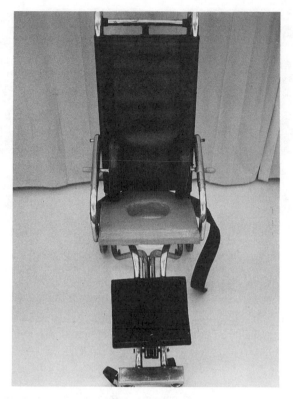

Figure 16.3. Modified toilet chair. This toilet chair was made by removing the seat of an old travel-type wheelchair and replacing it by a hand-made foam seat that was covered with a vinyl dip. Materials for seat construction are included in the Therapy Materials Kit from Danmar Products, Inc. (221 Jackson Industrial Drive, Ann Arbor, MI 48103)

adapted by padding the seat with foam and covering it with vinyl dip. The vinyl-coated padding reduces the possibility of slipping and provides seating comfort. For added support, a person may face the toilet tank (Jaeger, 1989). Behavior problems, such as rectal digging or smearing, may be controlled by adding a tray to prevent the person's hands from reaching the perineal area.

Deflectors

Deflectors may be attached permanently to a potty seat or may be removable. Permanent deflectors may make it difficult for caregivers to place a person on the toilet. However, permanently attached deflectors may be the only option for a person who has hand function and is intent on manipulating the deflector. Deflectors may be made from moldable plastics such as Orthoplast (Figure 16.4) or cut-off bottoms of plastic detergent bottles. Regular cleansing of deflectors with bleach is recommended for sanitation purposes. Caregivers

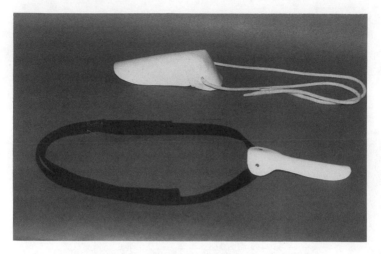

Figure 16.4. Deflectors. These deflectors are made from a moldable plastic (e.g., orthoplast). Straps are attached for tying around the user's waist to prevent displacement during toileting.

sometimes tie such removable deflectors around the user's waist to prevent them from being displaced during toileting. Deflectors also can be made that slide under a toilet seat.

Bathing Aids

Bathing aids designed to support persons with handicaps range from portable bath aids for the person's bed to bathtub seats. Inflatable shampoo sinks and inflatable bathtubs (used in a bed) are available for persons who cannot be transferred to a tub or shower. Persons with multiple handicaps often require the total support provided by large reclined bath chairs or bath tables. These are readily available commercially in various sizes and varieties. Local equipment vendors often lend these chairs to therapists for trial use with individuals. Trial use of bathing aids in the home is recommended before purchase. Hydraulic tub lifts may be beneficial with some persons. Nursing homes commonly use shower carts for persons who are restricted to a recumbent position. Hand-held shower extensions offer a practical addition to a shower. A pamphlet entitled *Bathing Techniques for Children who have Cerebral Palsy* (Dunaway & Klein, 1988) offers many practical suggestions for home bathing.

In classroom settings, many persons using standard wheelchairs often are unable to reach a sink. In such cases, a dishpan may be placed on a cutout table in front of the person to allow for training in hand- and face-washing skills. If the individual's wheelchair can be positioned near a standard sink, handle adaptation—commercially available or made from moldable plastic such as splinting material—may enable the person to turn the water on and off. Inability to hold onto a bar of soap, a common problem experienced by persons with multiple handicaps, may be solved by placing the soap in a nylon knee-high stocking or onion bag and tying the open end of the stocking around the faucet or using soap on a rope. Pump-type soaps may be used by some individuals.

GROOMING AND ORAL HYGIENE

Hair combs, brushes, and toothbrushes are available with built-up handles or palmar cuffs for persons capable of assisted self- care. Grooming aids may be individually modified similar to eating utensils.

Dental Considerations

Consistent, frequent oral hygiene and a low-sugar diet reduce tooth decay, diseased gums, and halitosis. Also, regular dental visits are important. Unhealthy teeth and gums also increase drooling, a problem common to persons with multiple handicaps (Green, 1970). While some individuals may assist in brushing their teeth, thorough cleaning includes both brushing and flossing. This should be carried out by caregivers after meals.

Tooth Brushing

A soft bristle toothbrush with rounded tips is recommended. Use of toothpaste is not necessary, but can be used. Fluoride in the paste may benefit the individuals. A small amount of toothpaste may be placed on the toothbrush. Small amounts of fluoride in the toothpaste may be swallowed without harm, but large quantities should be avoided. Placing the person in a prone or semiprone position with the head slightly extended allows a care provider direct visibility into the mouth. A mouth prop may be used to stabilize an open mouth during cleaning and prevent bitten fingers. (Mouth props may be made by taping tongue blades together or may be obtained from dentists.) Rinsing may be accomplished by squirting water from a plastic squeeze bottle fitted with a spout into the mouth. The water may be allowed to dribble out or be swallowed. If gum or oral sensitivity precludes use of a soft toothbrush, "Toothettes" are a practical alternative. Toothettes are disposable plastic sticks with a foam end that can be used to clean teeth. They are available from medical suppliers. A gauze square or washcloth initially may be used with an individual who cannot tolerate a toothbrush.

Mouthguards

Dentists may assist in preventing damage from self-abusive behaviors such as biting. A common intervention involves fabrication and use of a mouthguard to prevent self-injury or injury to others resulting from biting.

Drool Control

Persons with multiple handicaps often experience drooling. Research has indicated a variety of possible causes for drooling (Copeland & Kimmel, 1989), and largely responsible for this behavior is impaired oral-motor function (Camp-Bruno, Winsberg, Green-Parsons, & Abrams, 1989). Contributing factors include inefficient swallowing (Ekedahl, Mansson, & Sandberg, 1974; Sochaniwskyj, 1982), poor lip closure (Palmer, 1947; Sittig, 1947), infantile tongue thrusting (McCracken, 1978), poor body posture (Diamant & Kumlien, 1974; Makhani, 1974), poor jaw stability (Ray, Bundy, & Nelson, 1983), and tactile deficits and/or mouth breathing (Burgmayer & Jung, 1983; Schmidt, 1976). Copeland and Kimmel (1989) cite several studies that allude to hypersalivation (Ekedahl, 1974; Rapp, 1980; Wilkie, 1967) and hypersalivation due to medications (Crysdale, 1980; Ekedahl, 1974).

Drooling is difficult to eliminate in persons with multiple handicaps. Some success in decreasing drooling has been demonstrated in cases caused by poor jaw control and lack of mouth closure, especially in individuals who are hypotonic. Training involves patterning through manual jaw control procedures for jaw and lip closure that, in turn, facilitates swallowing of excess saliva (Ray et al., 1983). Training should be performed consistently by caregivers and often requires extended time periods before results are obtained. Persons with weak oral musculature or malocclusion may benefit from use of a lip halter that supports the lower lip and facilitates jaw closure (Nelson, Pendleton, & Edel, 1981). This encourages swallowing. A cap with a chin strap may be used with hypotonic children to promote jaw-lip closure during snack times (Morris & Klein, 1987). Drool control training may be effective through activities that increase specific oral-motor function of jaws and lips. Training to increase sensory awareness of the oral area is not usually successful with persons with multiple handicaps. Behavior management techniques have been reported to be used to decrease drooling (Drabman, Cordua, Cruz, Ross, & Lund, 1979; Rapp, 1980; Trott & Maechtlen, 1986). However, many such behavior management programs are quite time consuming for caregivers.

Medication in the form of synthetic anticholinergics may be an alternate method of decreasing drooling (Camp-Bruno et al., 1989). Surgical procedures may also be considered (Brody, 1977; Crysdale, 1980; Goode & Smith, 1970; Wilkie, 1967, 1970). However, the severity of oral pathology found in many persons with multiple handicaps makes prognosis for improvement poor following surgery. In general, these types of procedures have been found to be only partially successful (Copeland & Kimmel, 1989).

Presently, functional treatment consists of modifying the person's environment to maintain good hygiene. Drool-proof materials should be used around the neck and chest area (e.g., vinyl-covered chest positioners and head supports, mentioned in Chapter 8, and vinyl-backed bibs). Plastic webbing and buckles should be used on equipment rather than Velcro. Good oral hygiene coupled with regular dental care helps reduce bacteria present in drool.

CLOSING THOUGHTS

Ordering, adapting, and fabricating equipment for activities of daily living have been and will continue to be important responsibilities of attending therapists. Meeting the adaptive equipment needs of persons with multiple handicaps requires attending therapists to apply practical working experience and to be creative in individual problem-solving situations, concentrating on ideas that work well under actual situations, rather than theoretically ideal solutions. A trial-and-error approach is best. "Cookbook" answers do not exist. Therapists are encouraged to maintain working relationships with equipment manufacturers and vendors who can give invaluable assistance in finding answers to complex equipment problems that require technologically oriented solutions.

REFERENCES

Boehme, R. (1983). Self-care assessment and treatment from an NDT perspective. *Developmental Disabilities Special Interest Section Newsletter, 16*(4), 1–3. (American Occupational Therapy Association, Rockville, MD)

Brody, G.S. (1977). Control of drooling by translocation of parotid duct and extirpation of mandibular gland. *Developmental Medicine and Child Neurology, 19,* 514–517.

Burgmayer, S., & Jung, H. (1983). Hypersalivation in severe mental retardation. *International Journal of Rehabilitation Research, 6,* 193–197.

Camp-Bruno, J.A., Winsberg, B.G., Green-Parsons, A.R., & Abrams, J.P. (1989). Efficacy of benztropine therapy for drooling. *Developmental Medicine & Child Neurology, 31,* 309–319.

Copeland, M.E., & Kimmel, J.R. (1989). *Evaluation and management of infants and young children with developmental disabilities.* Baltimore: Paul H. Brookes Publishing Co.

Crysdale, W.S. (1980). The drooling patient: Evaluations and current surgical options. *Laryngology, 90,* 775–783.

Dunaway, A., & Klein, M.D. (1988). *Bathing techniques for children who have cerebral palsy.* Tucson, AZ: Therapy Skill Builders.

Diamant, H., & Kumlien, A. (1974). A treatment for drooling in children with cerebral palsy. *Journal of Laryngology and Otology, 88,* 61–64.

Drabman, R.S., Cordua, Y., Cruz, G., Ross, J., & Lund, S. (1979). Suppression of chronic drooling in mentally retarded children and adolescents: Effectiveness of a behavioral treatment package. *Behavior Therapy, 10,* 46–56.

Ekedahl, C. (1974). Surgical treatment of drooling. *Acta Otolaryngologica, 77,* 215–220.

Ekedahl, C., Mansson, I., & Sandberg, N. (1974). Swallowing dysfunction in the brain damaged with drooling. *Acta Otolaryngologica, 78*(1–2), 141–149.

Finnie, N.R. (1975). *Handling the young cerebral palsied child at home.* New York: E.P. Dutton.

Foxx, R.M., & Azrin, N.H. (1973). *Toilet training the retarded: A rapid program for day and nighttime independent toileting.* Champaign, IL: Research Press.

Fraser, B.A., & Hensinger, R.N. (1983). *Managing physical handicaps: A practical guide for parents, care providers, and educators.* Baltimore: Paul H. Brookes Publishing Co.

Goode, R.L., & Smith, R.A. (1970). The surgical management of sialorrhea. *Laryngology, 80,* 1078–1089.

Green, A. (1970). Preventive care guide for multihandicapped children: Dental care begins at home. *Rehabilitation Literature, 31,* 10–12.

Jaeger, D.L. (1989). *Transferring and lifting children and adolescents.* Tucson, AZ: Therapy Skill Builders.

Lamb, J.M. (1984). Family use of functional clothing for children with physical disabilities. *Rehabilitation Literature, 45*(56), 146–148.

Makhani, J.S. (1974). Dribbling of saliva in children with cerebral palsy and its management. *Indian Journal of Pediatrics, 41,* 272–277.

McCracken, A. (1978). Drool control and tongue thrust therapy for the mentally retarded. *American Journal of Occupational Therapy, 32*(2), 79–85.

Morris, S.E., & Klein, M.D. (1987). *Pre-feeding skills: A comprehensive resource for feeding development.* Tucson, AZ: Therapy Skill Builders.

Nelson, E.C., Pendleton, T.B., & Edel J. (1981). Lip halter: An aid in drool control. *Physical Therapy, 61*(3), 361–362.

Ottenbacher, K., Malter, R., & Weckwerth, L. (1979). Toilet seat arrangement for children with neuromotor dysfunction. *American Journal of Occupational Therapy, 33,* 193.

Palmer, M.F. (1947). Studies in clinical techniques II—Normalization of chewing, sucking and swallowing reflexes in cerebral palsy. *Journal of Speech Disorders, 12,* 415–418.

Rapp, D. (1980). Drool control: Long-term follow-up. *Developmental Medicine and Child Neurology, 22*(4), 448–453.

Ray, S.A., Bundy, A.C., & Nelson, D.L. (1983). Decreasing drooling through techniques to facilitate mouth closure. *American Journal of Occupational Therapy, 37*(11), 749–753.

Schmidt, P. (1976). Feeding assessment and therapy for the neurologically impaired. *AAESPH Review, 1*(8), 19–27.

Sittig, E. (1947). Chewing method applied for excessive salivation and drooling in cerebral palsy. *Journal of Speech Disorders, 12,* 191–194.

Sochaniwskyj, A.E. (1982). Drool quantification: Noninvasive technique. *Archives of Physical Medicine and Rehabilitation, 63,* 605–607.

Trott, M.C., & Maechtlen, A.D. (1986). The use of overcorrection as a means to control drooling. *American Journal of Occupational Therapy, 40*(10), 702–704.

Wilkie, T.F. (1967). The problem of drooling in cerebral palsy: A surgical approach. *Canadian Journal of Surgery, 10,* 60–67.

Wilkie, T.F. (1970). The surgical treatment of drooling: A follow-up report on five years experience. *Plastic and Reconstructive Surgery, 45,* 549–554.

Appendix

A

Physical and Occupational Therapy Service Delivery Model Resources

The following is a list of physical and occupational therapy service delivery model resources that are applicable for educational settings.

A Resource Handbook for Physical and Occupational Therapists in Educational Settings. Available from The Kansas Chapter, American Physical Therapy Association, 1237 Belle Terrace, Topeka, KS 66604.

Guidelines for Occupational Therapy Services in School Systems. Available from the American Occupational Therapy Assication, Inc., Rockville, MD 20852.

Waukesha Delivery Model: Providing Occupational/Physical Therapy Services to Special Education Services. Available from Publication Sales, Department of Public Instruction, P. O. Box 7841, Madison, WI 53707-7841.

Wayne County Intermediate School District's Physical Therapy Service Delivery Model. Available from Wayne County Intermediate School District, 33500 Van Born Road, Wayne, MI 48180.

Appendix

B

— . —

Manufacturers/Distributors of Seating Equipment

Glenda Atkinson

Readers interested in detailed current information regarding commercially available seating for persons with disabilities may contact ABLEDATA, 4407 Eighth Street, NE, The Catholic University of America, Washington, DC 20017, (202) 635-5826/635-5887 TDD. ABLEDATA has a computerized listing of products and manufacturers on-line. At present, it offers the most comprehensive database of this kind in the United States.

This appendix lists addresses and telephone numbers of manufacturers/distributers of commercially available seating equipment found helpful in the author's clinical experience. This information is provided for the reader's convenience. This is not as an exhaustive list of companies providing seating products.

Adaptive Engineering Lab., Inc.
Bldg. 2A, Unit 3
4403 Russell Road
Linwood, WA 98037
AliMed, Inc.
68 Harrison Avenue
Boston, MA 02111
(800) 225-2610

Canadian Posture and Seating Centre (1988), Inc.
15 Howard Place
P.O. Box 1473
Station C
Kitchener, Ontario,
Canada N2G 4P2
(519) 743-5352

Glenda Atkinson, P.T., is a faculty member at the University of Central Arkansas, Department of Physical Therapy, and serves as a seating consultant to several facilities in the central Arkansas area.

Columbia Medical Mfg. Co.
P.O. Box 633
Pacific Palisades, CA 90272

Consumer Care Products
6405 Paradise Lane
Sheboygan, WI 53085
(414) 467-2393

Creative Rehabilitation Equipment
513 N.E. Schuyler Street
Portland, OR 97212
(800) 547-4611

Cyclo Manufacturing Co.
1438 S. Cherokee Street
Denver, CO 80223
(303)744-3600

Danmar Products, Inc.
221 Jackson Industrial Drive
Ann Arbor, MI 48103
(313) 761-1990

Davis Positioning Systems, Inc.
1376 Merle Street
Burton, MI 48509
(313) 742-0581

Dynamic Systems, Inc.
Rt. 2, Box 18213
Leicester, NC 28748
(704) 683-3523

Everest and Jennings
3233 E. Mission Oaks Blvd.
Camarillo, CA 93010
(805) 987-6911

Freedom Designs
18165 Napa, #8
Northridge, CA 91325
(818) 886-2932

Gunnell, Inc.
221 N. Water Street
P.O. Box 1694
Vassar, MI 48768-9986
(800) 551-0055

Invacare Corp.
2302 113th Street Suite 100
Grand Prairie, TX 75050
(800) 527-3804

J.A. Preston Corp.
60 Page Road
Clifton, NJ 07012
(919) 688-1601

Jay Medical, Ltd.
P.O. Box 18656
Boulder, CO 80308-8656
(800) 648-8282

Kaye Products
1010 E. Pettigrew Street
Durham, NC 27701-4299
(919) 688-1601

Luxury Liners
14747 Artesia Blvd.
Bldg. 18
La Mirada, CA 90638
(800) 247-4203

Metalcraft Industries, Inc.
399 N. Burr Oak
Oregon, WI 53575
(608) 835-3232

Miller's
283 E. Market Street
Akron, OH 44308
(216) 376-2500

Mobility Plus, Inc.
215 N. 12th Street
P.O. Box 391
Santa Paula, CA 93060
(800) 325-7397

Modular Medical Corp.
1558 Hutchinson River Pkwy. East
Bronx, NY 07012
(800) 631-7277

Motion Designs, Inc.
1075 Cole
Clovis, CA 93616
(800) 523-8166

Ortho-Kinetics, Inc.
P.O. Box 2000
Waukesha, WI 53187
800-558-2151

Orthotic and Prosthetic Specialties, Inc.
9811 Mallard Drive, #112
Laurel, MD 20708
(301) 470-3344

Otto Bock Orthopedic Industry
4130 Hwy. 55
Minneapolis, MN 55422
(800) 328-4058

Pin Dot Products
8100 N. Austin Avenue
Morton Grove, IL 60053
(800) 451-3553

Quadra Wheelchairs, Inc.
31117 Via Colians
Westlake Village, CA 91362
(800) 824-1068

Rehab Equipment Systems
Manufacturing Division
1828 Yale Avenue
Seattle, WA 98101
(206) 624-3123

Rehabilitation Designs, Inc.
1492 Martin Street
Madison, WI 53713
(800) 792-3504, ext. 1234

Safety Rehab.
147 Eady Court
Elyria, OH 44036
(800) 421-3349

Scandinavian Mobility Products
P.O. Box 1221
Southampton, NY 11968
(516) 287-1108

Scottie Seating Systems
430 Roberson Land
San Jose, CA 95112
(408) 947-0431

Snug Seat, Inc.
P.O. Box 1141
648-B Matthews-Mint Hill Road
Matthews, NC 28106
(704) 847-0772

Stainless Medical Products
9389 Dowdy Drive
San Diego, CA 92126
(800) 238-6678

Summit Seating Systems
9231 Laramie Avenue
Skokie, IL 60077
(312) 966-2696

Tumble Forms, Inc.
60 Page Road
Clifton, NJ 07012
(201) 777-8004

Appendix

C

Glossary

Abduction Sideways movement of the limbs away from the midline of the body.

Acetabular dysplasia Abnormal development of the large cup-shaped cavity on the lateral surface of the os coxae in which the head of the femur articulates.

Acetabulum A large cup-shaped cavity on the lateral surface of the os coxae in which the head of the femur articulates.

Acquired Refers to condition produced by influences originating outside the person—not genetic in origin.

Active range of motion Independent movement of arms, legs, head, and trunk.

Activities of daily living The process of exerting energy to accomplish tasks necessary for self-care (e.g., eating, dressing, personal hygiene).

Acute Sharp or poignant; of relatively short duration.

Adaptive behavior The effectiveness or degree with which the individual meets the standards of personal independence and social responsibility expected of his or her age and cultural group.

Adduction Sideways movement of the limbs toward the midline of the body.

Aerophagia Spasmodic swallowing of air followed by eructations; often occurs in conjunction with functional gastrointestinal disturbances.

Agonist A prime mover; a muscle opposed in action by another muscle.

Alignment Arranged in a straight line.

Ambulation The act of walking.

Antagonist A muscle that acts in opposition to another muscle.

Anterior Toward the front of the body.

Anterior pelvic tilt Movement in the frontal plane that causes the part of the trunk around the hips (pelvis) to be positioned forward of its neutral position.

Anteversion The forward tipping or tilting of an organ.

Antigravity Reducing, canceling, or protecting against the effect of gravity or having weight.

Arm Includes shoulder through elbow.

Arthritis A general term used to describe a variety of conditions in which pain and inflammation occur in and around joints.

273

Arthrodesis The surgical fixation of a joint by a procedure that promotes the proliferation of bone cells.

Asphyxia A condition caused by lack of air in the lungs; suffocation.

Aspiration Material penetrating the larynx and entering the airway below the true vocal folds.

Associated reaction Stimulation to one part of the body causes uncontrolled responses in another part (e.g., fisting of the right hand causes involuntary fisting of the left hand).

Asymmetrical Characterized by dissimilarity in corresponding parts or organs on opposite side of the body that are normally alike in appearance.

Asymmetrical Tonic Neck Reflex An automatic act in which turning the head sideways causes extension of the arm and leg on the side of the body to which the face is turned and flexion of the arm and leg on the opposite side of the body.

Ataxia Irregularity of muscle action; inability to coordinate voluntary muscular movement (e.g., wide base, staggering gait).

Athetosis Repeated involuntary movements that are purposeless, but often associated with deliberate movements; especially severe in the hands.

Atrophy A wasting away; a reduction in the size of a cell, tissue, muscle, organ, or body part.

Auditory Relating to or experienced through hearing.

Augmentative communication systems Aids, such as communication boards or gestures, that enhance or add to a nonspeaking person's ability to communicate.

Baseline An experimental condition or phase; initial period of observation in which the natural frequency of the occurrence of a specific behavior is obtained.

Behavior Any act, or collection of acts, by a person.

Behavior modification Techniques designed to alter existing behavior in some predetermined manner.

Biceps A muscle having two heads (e.g., biceps brachii [biceps muscle of the arm] and biceps femoris [biceps muscle of the thigh]).

Bilateral Pertaining to both sides of the body.

Bolus A rounded mass of food.

Bony prominences Points of the body where the bone has little tissue covering.

Bony surgery The surgical cutting of bone to realign or fuse a joint.

Calcaneus The irregular quadrangular bone at the back of the tarsus, also called os calcis or heel bone.

Calcaneus deformity A condition in which the forefoot is pulled upward and the heel downward.

Callous Hard.

Capitate Head shaped.

Cardiopulmonary Pertaining to the heart and lungs.

Cast A positive copy or likeness of an object.

Central nervous system The part of the nervous system primarily responsible for controlling voluntary motion and thought processes. It is comprised of the brain and spinal cord.

Cerebral palsy A condition involving disabilities in movement and posture that results from damage to the brain before or during birth, or in infancy.

Cerebrovascular accident Pathology involving the blood vessels in the cerebrum causing brain damage.

Cervical A term pertaining to the neck, or to the neck of any organ or structure.

Circumduction A smooth, coordinated circular movement that revolves around a given point; a movement that contains elements of flexion, abduction, extension, and adduction.

Clavicle The bone articulating with the sternum and scapula; commonly called the collar bone.

Clonus Alternate muscle contraction and relaxation in rapid succession.

Cocontraction The mutual coordination of antagonist muscles (e.g., flexors and extensors) in maintaining a straight limb.

Cognitive Refers to the act or process of perceiving or knowing.

Concavity A hollowed-out area on the surface of an organ or other structure.

Congenital Refers to conditions that are present at birth, regardless of their causation. These conditions may originate before or at birth.

Contracture A permanent shortening of a muscle-tendon unit (e.g., muscle, tendon, and/or joint capsule) due to spasticity or paralysis, resulting in less than normal range of motion of a joint.

Convexity A rounded somewhat elevated area on the surface of an organ or other structure.

Coronal plane Situated in the direction of the sutures; a longitudinal plane or section passing through the body at right angles to the median plane.

Comesis The art of increasing or preserving beauty.

Coxa valga Increased angle of the femoral head, neck, and shaft.

Curriculum The courses offered by an educational institution; a set of courses constituting an area of specialization.

Curvature Deviation from a rectilinear direction; deviation of the spine from its normal direction or position.

Decubitus ulcer An ulcer of the skin; commonly called a bedsore.

Deformity A distortion or malformation of any part of the body.

Degenerative disease A condition or illness characterized by progression from a higher to a lower level of body function.

Deinstitutionalization The name given to a movement to eliminate large impersonal facilities where persons with mental retardation and handicaps reside. Alternatives to institutionalization involve having these persons remain within the family unit or reside in a small group home.

Developmental age The age, in months, at which an individual can perform a specific action. For example, a child normally learns to stand independently at about 12 months of age. If a 15-year-old person just learned this skill, he or she would be considered to be functioning at a 12-month developmental age level in relation to this skill.

Developmental assessment A test that identifies the state of an individual's maturation (i.e., adaptive, motor, or social functioning in relation to normative patterns).

Developmental curriculum A series of related studies that focus on gross motor, fine motor, perceptual, cognitive, social, and self-help skills.

Developmental disabilities   Functional deficits measured in performance rather than based on diagnostic category. A popular generic term used to describe a wide range of disabilities and may refer to physiological body functions as well as cognitive or psychological impairments and mental retardation.

Developmental skills   Actions (e.g., rolling, crawling, creeping, walking, reaching) that an individual is expected to perform within a given range of time according to the standards of his or her culture.

Diagnosis   The art of distinguishing one disease from another or determining the nature or cause of disease.

Diplegia   Muscle involvement of similar parts of the body; often refers more to legs than arms.

Dislocation   A term applied to a joint to indicate that the surfaces of the bones that form it are no longer in contact or are displaced.

Distal   Away from the center of the body or a point of reference.

Dominant side   Part of the body (e.g., right or left) used most often and with greater skill and coordination than the opposite one.

Dorsiflexion   A backward bending of the hand at the wrist or lifting the forefoot.

Down syndrome   A condition characterized by a flat face; small, low-bridged nose; upward slanted folds of skin at the inner corners of the eyes; and moderate mental deficiency associated with chromosomal abnormality. Down syndrome is diagnosed by chromosomal studies and identified as trisomy 21.

Dynamic   Active.

Dysplasia   Abnormal development of a body part.

Dystonic   Pertaining to disordered tonicity of muscles.

Electromyography   The recording and study of the intrinsic electrical properties of skeletal muscle.

Encephalopathy   Any degenerative disease of the brain.

Equinovalgus deformity   A condition in which the heel of the foot is everted and turned outward from the midline of the body. Also known as talipes equinovalgus.

Equinovarus deformity   A condition in which the heel of the foot is turned inward from the midline of the leg and the foot is plantar flexed. Also known as talipes equinovarus.

Equinus   A likeness to a horse's leg.

Equinus deformity   A condition in which the heel of the foot is pulled upward and the forefoot downward. Also known as talipes equinus.

Esophageal reflux   A backward or return flow of food up the tube extending from the mouth to the stomach.

Esophagus   Musculomembranous passage extending from the pharynx to the stomach.

Etiology   The cause or origins of a disease or abnormal condition; also, theory and study of the factors that cause diseases or abnormal conditions.

Eversion   Movement of the foot in which the sole turns outward away from the midline of the body.

Expressive language   The ability to speak, to produce symbolic gestures, and/or to write.

Extension The straightening of a joint that diminishes the angle between bones that meet in the joint; the opposite of flexion.

Extensor A general term for any muscle that extends or straightens a joint.

Extensor thrust A reaction in which the neck, back, hips, and knees extend or straighten causing the body to arch backward.

External rotation Turning or rotating of a limb away from the midline of the body.

Extrapyramidal Outside of the pyramidal tracts.

Extremities Arms and legs; also used synonymously with limbs.

Extrinsic Coming from or originating outside; situated on the outside.

Facilitation To make an action or process easier.

Femoral anteversion A forward rotation of the femur.

Femur The thigh bone, extending from the pelvis to the knee.

Fine motor skills Activities using the smaller muscles in the body, such as functional hand activities.

Fixation The act or operation of holding, suturing, or fastening in a fixed position.

Flaccid Floppy; absent or low muscle tone.

Flexion The bending of a joint; the opposite of extension.

Flexor A general term used to describe a muscle that bends a joint.

Forearm Includes elbow through wrist.

Fracture The breaking of a part, usually a bone.

Functional assessment An activity-related test that identifies specific tasks or skills that an individual can perform.

Functional spinal curve A supple abnormal curve or exaggeration of a normal curve of the spine that may be corrected by application of some type of force, such as a brace, traction, or physical manipulation or simple positioning.

Fusion The act or process of melting; the operative formation of an ankylosis or arthrodesis.

Gait The manner or style of walking.

Gastrocnemius Large muscle located on the back of the leg that plantar flexes the ankle joint and flexes the knee joint.

Gastrointestinal Pertaining to or communication with the stomach and intestines.

Gastrostomy The surgical creation of an artificial opening into the stomach.

Gestural language The use of hand motions to form a sign representing a word; a sign method of communication.

Glenohumeral joint Pertaining to the glenoid cavity and to the humerus; shoulder joint.

Goal Broad statement of direction without reference to time or specific behavior.

Goniometer An instrument for measuring angles.

Gross motor skills Activities using the larger muscles in the body (e.g., head control, trunk control, creeping, sitting, standing, running).

Gustatory Pertaining to taste.

Hallux valgus Angulation of the great toe away from the midline of the body or toward the other toes; the great toe may ride under or over the other toes.

Hamstrings Tendons of the muscles located at the back of the thigh and knee.

Head lag   A lack of head control in which the head falls backward into extension when the subject is pulled from a backlying position into a sitting position. This is normal in newborns, but is abnormal after 2–3 months of life.

Heel cord   Tendon and muscle located at the back of the calf from the knee to the ankle.

Hemiplegia   Spastic muscular paralysis involving one side of the body (e.g., right arm and right leg spasticity).

Hiatal hernia   A protrusion of any structure through the esophageal opening of the diaphragm.

Hip abductors   A group of muscles located on the outside of the thigh; primarily responsible for a sideways movement of the leg away from the midline.

Hip adductors   A group of muscles located on the inside of the thigh; primarily responsible for a sideways movement of the leg toward the midline.

Humerus   The bone that extends from the shoulder to the elbow.

Hydrocephalus   A neurological condition in which an abnormal amount of spinal fluid accumulates in and around the brain. The excess fluid can cause increased pressure on the brain and, in the young, enlargement in the circumference of the skull.

Hyperextension   The movement of extension beyond that which is necessary to straighten a part.

Hyperkyphosis   An abnormally increased backward curvature of the spine that causes a hump-like appearance of the upper back in a pathological state.

Hyperlordosis   An abnormally increased forward curvature of the spine that causes a "hollow" or "sway" appearance of the lower back in a pathological state.

Hypermobility   Excessive elasticity of joints that allows them to move beyond their normal limits.

Hypertonia   A condition involving excessive response to stimuli (e.g., tone) by skeletal muscles.

Hypertrophy   The enlargement or overgrowth of an organ or part due to an increase in size of its constituent cells.

Idiopathic   Of unknown causation.

Incision   A cut, or a wound produced by cutting with a sharp instrument.

Incontinence   Inability to control bowel and bladder activity.

Indication   Any condition that renders a treatment or procedure proper or desirable.

Inferior   Pertaining to a lower segment, usually of the body or a body part.

Inhibition   Stopping or slowing an action or a process.

Internal rotation   Turning or rotating of a limb inward toward the center or midline of the body.

Interphalangeal   Situated between two contiguous finger or toe bones.

Intrinsic   Situated entirely within or pertaining exclusively to a part.

Inversion   Movement of the foot in which the sole turns toward the midline of the body.

Inverted prone   Facelying position in which the hips are higher than the head.

Kyphosis   Normal backward curve of the thoracic spine when viewed from the side. Also commonly used synonymously with hyperkyphosis to indicate an abnormal backward curve of the thoracic spine.

Lamina A general term for a thin flat plate or layer, usually referring to the posterior of the vertebrae.

Lateral Pertaining to or toward the sides of the body.

Lordosis The normal forward curve of the lower back. Also commonly used synonymously with hyperlordosis to indicate an abnormal forward curve of the lower back.

Lower extremity A term used to describe the thigh, leg, and foot.

Lumbar Pertaining to the low back.

Luque instrumentation Surgical tools used for a spinal fusion.

Macrocephalic An abnormally large head size.

Mainstreaming Placement of a student with handicaps in a school situation in which he or she may participate in any or all of the regular education programs and activities.

Medial Pertaining to or toward the midline of the body.

Meningitis An inflammation of the membranes that envelop the brain and spinal cord.

Metabolic diseases Abnormal conditions that involve chemical processes within the body.

Metacarpophalangeal joint Pertaining to the metacarpus (i.e., the part of the hand between the wrist and the fingers) and the phalangeals (i.e., finger bones).

Microcephaly A condition involving an abnormally small head.

Midline An imaginary line drawn from head to toes that separates the body into right and left halves.

Midline positioning Placing the body, upper, and lower extremities into an aligned, symmetrical, and neutral posturing.

Monoplegia Paralysis of a limb.

Moro reflex An automatic response that is triggered by sudden removal of support while a person is being lowered from a sitting position to a backlying position.

Motor abilities Meaningful bodily activities, produced by the interaction of muscles, nerves, and joints, such as rolling, sitting, creeping, standing, and walking.

Movement dysfunction Abnormal motion of any body part, a limb, limbs, or the entire body.

Multiple handicaps *Medical Definition*: Severe medical, neurological, and orthopaedic conditions combined with apparent low cognitive functioning usually resulting from damage to or deterioration of the central nervous system. *Educational Definition*: Persons with physical and cognitive problems that cannot be served appropriately in regular education programs or a special education program designed solely to meet needs associated with one impairment.

Muscle belly The fleshy part of a muscle.

Muscle tone The degree of vigor or tension in skeletal muscles.

Musculoskeletal conditions State of affairs affecting the muscles or bones, or both.

Musculotendinous units Pertaining to or composed of muscle and tendon.

Natal Pertaining to birth.

Neonatal Pertaining to the first 4 weeks after birth.

Neurological conditions State of being that pertains to the nervous system.

Neutral position The position indicated at 0 degrees on a goniometer.

Nondominant side   Part of the body (e.g., right or left) used less often; usually has less skill and coordination than the dominant side.

Nonstretch restraint   Strap made of a material with little or no elasticity.

Normalization   A principle stating that treatment and services for persons with handicaps should be provided in such a manner as to enable them to reside in as close as possible to a normal setting within a given society.

Nurse   A person who is especially prepared in the scientific basis of nursing and who meets certain prescribed standards of education and clinical competence to provide services that are essential in the promotion, maintenance, and restoration of health and well-being.

Obligatory   Compulsory.

Obturator nerve   A cord-like structure comprised of a collection of nerve fibers that convey impulses between the central nervous system and the hip adductor muscles.

Occupational therapy   The art and science of directing a person's participation in selected tasks to restore, reinforce, and enhance performance, facilitate learning of those skills and functions essential for adaptation and productivity, diminish or correct pathology, and promote and maintain health. A fundamental concern is the capacity, throughout the life span, to perform with satisfaction to self and others those tasks and roles essential to productive living and to the mastery of oneself and the environment. Occupational therapy includes improving, developing, or restoring functions that are impaired or lost through illness, injury, or deprivation; improving ability to perform tasks for independent functioning when functions are impaired or lost; and preventing, through early intervention, initial or further loss of function.

Olfactory   Pertaining to smell.

Optical righting   Pattern of movement in which vision stimulates the head to rise to a normal position with the face vertical and mouth horizontal when the body is held in a nonvertical position.

Orthopaedist   A medical doctor (e.g., surgeon) specializing in the treatment of bones, joints, and muscles.

Orthosis   An appliance or apparatus used to correct, prevent, support, or align deformities or to improve function of movable body parts.

Orthotist   A person especially trained in making prescribed orthoses and tailoring orthoses to meet an individual's needs.

Os calis   Alternative name for the calcaneus or large bone of the hindfoot or heel.

Palate   The partition separating the nasal and oral cavities.

Palpate   Examine by touch or feel.

Paraplegia   Paralysis of both legs and the lower portion of the trunk.

Passive range of motion   Degrees of excursion that a person manipulates another individual's extremities, head, and trunk.

Patella   The knee cap, a small bone situated at the front of the knee.

Pathological   Pertaining to disease.

Pediatrician   A physician who specializes in that branch of medicine that deals with the development, care, and diseases of children.

Pelvic obliquity   A slanting or inclination of the pelvis such that it is not positioned in a horizontal plane when the person is standing or sitting.

Pelvis Part of the trunk around the hips.

Perceptual skills The ability to mentally register sensory stimuli.

Performance objectives Statement that describes the individual or individuals involved, the behavior to be exhibited, the object or objects employed, the time reference, the technique to be used for measuring the behavior, and the criterion for success.

Pharynx Pertaining to the throat.

Physiatrist A physician who specializes in that branch of medicine that deals with the diagnosis, treatment, and prevention of disease with the aid of physical agents, such as light, heat, cold, water, and electricity, or with a mechanical apparatus.

Physical therapist A physical therapist is a licensed health professional responsible for the promotion of optimum human health and function through the application of scientific principles to prevent, identify, correct, or alleviate acute or prolonged movement dysfunction of anatomic or physiologic origin. Physical therapists evaluate movement dysfunction, identify patient treatment goals, establish and implement individualized treatment programs, direct and supervise support personnel, provide patient and family education, and conduct research to improve treatment techniques. Treatment techniques include therapeutic exercise, postural re-education, joint mobilization and range-of-motion exercises, cardiovascular endurance training, relaxation exercises, therapeutic massage, biofeedback, activities of daily living training, wound debridement, pulmonary physical therapy, ambulation training and modalities such as traction, ultrasound, diathermy, electrotherapy, cryotherapy, and hydrotherapy.

Plantar grasp reflex An automatic curling of the toes when pressure is applied to the ball of the foot.

Plantigrade position The normal standing or walking attitude of the human foot, such that weight is distributed across the full sole of the foot.

Positioning The act of placing or arranging.

Positive support reaction An involuntary action stimulated by pressure on the ball of the foot that causes hip and knee extension.

Posterior Toward the back of the body.

Posterior pelvic tilt Movement in the frontal plane that causes the part of the trunk around the hips (i.e., pelvis) to be positioned backward of its neutral position.

Postnatal After birth.

Postural drainage Positioning that encourages drainage of congestion from the lungs, bronchi, trachea, and throat.

Postural reflex An automatic response to a stimulus that results in a change of attitude of the body.

Posture The position or bearing of the body.

Prognosis A forecast as to the probable outcome of a disease or condition.

Pronation Movement in the forearm that results in turning the palm downward.

Prone Lying horizontally on abdomen with the face turned downward (facelying).

Proprioceptive Receiving stimuli within the tissues of the body (e.g., muscles and tendons).

Protective extension A reaction to loss of sitting or standing balance in which the arms straighten to prevent injury to the head.

Proximal Closer to any point or reference.

Pseudoarthrosis False joint.

Psychologist A qualified specialist in that branch of science that deals with the mind and mental processes, especially in relation to human and animal behavior.

Pyramidal A term applied to two groups of fibers arising chiefly in the sensorimotor regions of the cerebral cortex and descending in the internal capsule, cerebral peduncle, and pons to the medulla oblongata, the corticonuclear fibers synapsing with motor nuclei throughout the brain stem.

Quadriceps A group of muscles located on the front of the upper leg that flex the hip and extend the knee.

Quadriplegia Paralysis of all four limbs.

Radial deviation Motion, occurring at the wrist, that causes a lateral movement of the hand toward the thumb side.

Radiograph A film of internal structures of the body produced by the action of X-rays or gamma rays on a specially sensitized film.

Radius The bone on the outer or thumb side of the forearm.

Range of motion Exercise consisting of moving the parts of the body in specific ways.

Receptive language The ability to understand spoken language.

Reciprocal pattern Alternating motion of similar parts of the body (e.g., creeping pattern, in which movement proceeds from one arm to opposite leg to the other arm to the other leg; or walking pattern, in which movement progresses from one lower extremity to the other).

Reflex Involuntary response to specific stimuli.

Relaxation Any action or condition that causes decreased muscle tension.

Rigidity A stiffness or inflexibility of a body part.

Roentgenogram Photography of various body parts by means of roentgen rays; an X-ray.

Rotation Turning of a body part.

Rotoscoliosis A condition in which a sideways curve of the spine is coupled with a rotation of the ribs and vertebral bodies.

Rumination Regurgitation of swallowed food followed by chewing another time.

Sagittal plane Situated in the direction of the sagittal suture; an anteroposterior plane or section parallel to the median plane of the body.

Sandifer syndrome A combination of hiatal hernia and abnormal posturing of the head and neck.

Scapula A flat, triangular bone in the back of the shoulder; often called the shoulder blade.

Scissoring Crossing of the legs with the knees straight.

Scoliosis An abnormal sideways curvature of the spine.

Sepsis The presence of bacterial infection in the blood or body tissues; blood poisoning.

Shunt A surgically implanted tube that connects two blood vessels, two spaces, or two organs.

Sidelying A position in which a person rests on either the right or left side of the body, usually with legs slightly bent.

Skeletal deformity A distortion of the bones and joints.

Soft tissue surgery Operations that involve lengthening muscles and tendons or releasing tight structures such as ligaments or capsules of joints.

Spasticity Permanently increased muscle tone causing stiffness in movements.

Speech-language pathologist A health professional specially trained and qualified to assist persons in overcoming speech and language disorders.

Spinous processes The projection on the back of the vertebrae.

Splint A rigid or flexible appliance for the fixation of displaced or movable body parts.

Stabilize Provide extra support to secure certain joints.

Staggering reactions Movement (e.g., forward, backward, sideways) of the feet that protects upright posture when the body's position in space is displaced by force.

Structural spinal curve A rigid, abnormal spinal curvature involving permanent changes in alignment of the spinal vertebrae.

Subluxation A condition in which surfaces of the bones forming a joint begin to slip out of alignment.

Superior Pertains to an upper segment, usually of the body or a body part.

Supination Movement in the forearm that turns the palm upward.

Supine A person positioned horizontally on the back with the face upward (backlying).

Symmetrical tonic neck reflex An automatic act in which flexing and extending the head causes changes in muscle tone in arms and legs.

Symmetry Balanced; both sides of the body look similar.

Tactile Pertaining to touch.

Tactile defensiveness Hypersensitivity to touch.

Talus The bone of the foot that interacts with the tibia and fibula to form the ankle joint; often called the ankle bone.

Tendon Fibrous cord at the ends of the muscle that attaches it to the bone.

Thigh Includes hip through knee.

Thoracic Pertaining to or affecting the body cavity that contains the heart and lungs.

Three-point stretch Applying pressure at three points of a joint, limb, or body part to attempt to straighten it. Pressure is applied at the top and bottom of the concave side and at the middle of the convex side.

Tibia The larger bone of the lower leg; the shin bone.

Tone Degree of vigor or tension in a muscle.

Trauma A wound or injury.

Tremor A rhythmic, involuntary movement of certain muscle groups.

Triceps A muscle with three heads (e.g., triceps brachii, a muscle located on the posterior of the humerus that is primarily responsible for extending the elbow joint).

Triplegia Paralysis of three extremities.

Trunk Chest, abdomen, and pelvis of body, excluding head and limbs.

Tube feeding Liquid nourishment administered by means of a tube inserted surgically through a constructed hole in a person's abdomen or inserted through the mouth or nose.

Ulna deviation Movement at the wrist that causes a sideways motion of the hand away from the thumb.

Unilateral Affecting one side.

Upper extremity Arm and forearm; shoulder through hand.

Valleculae Wedge-shaped space formed between the base of the tongue and epiglottis.

Valgus Bent outward; angulation of a part away from the midline.

Varus Bend inward; angulation of a part toward the midline.

X ray A photograph obtained by the use of X-rays.

X-ray Roentgen ray.

Appendix
D

—— . ——

Normal Motion

This appendix provides basic concepts of normal movement. It begins with a brief review of terminology used to describe body positions and movements. Also included are the types and ranges or movement that occur around each major joint.

POSITION AND MOVEMENT

This review of terminology starts by discussing the body's position in space, continues with directional terms applied to parts of the body, and finishes with terms used to describe movement of the limbs.

Spatial Position

Most of the terms used to describe body position or movement in space are familiar ones—rolling, sitting, creeping, crawling, kneeling, and standing. Some of these actions can be performed in different positions, however, and the terminology used to describe the various body positions can become confusing. For instance, a person who is lying down can be said to be supine or prone or in a sidelying position. Understanding what each of these terms means can be important in properly managing a person with physical impairments. The three major kinds of lying position are defined below:

When a person lies on his or her back, the position is called supine. Sometimes, the term backlying may be used to describe this position.
When a person lies on the stomach or abdomen, the position is referred to as prone, or sometimes facelying.
Sidelying describes a person lying on either the right or left side, usually with the legs slightly bent.

285

Directional Terminology

Imaginary lines may be visualized through the body at various angles to identify sections or parts of the body in relation to one another. An imaginary line drawn from head to toes that separates the body into right and left halves establishes the midline. Medial is a term used to describe the body part closer to the midline. Lateral, the opposite of medial, is used to describe the body part further from the midline. For example, the mouth is medial to the ears, and the eyes are lateral to the nose. Similarly, proximal denotes something that is nearer to a point of reference, and distal something that is further away. Thus, the shoulder is proximal to the spine, while the hand is distal.

Now, suppose that the imaginary line were drawn in such a way that it divided the body into front and back halves. The front half is called anterior and the back half, posterior. To illustrate, the nose is anterior to the face, and the ears are posterior to the nose.

Suppose that the imaginary line were drawn horizontally through the middle of the torso so as to divide the body into upper and lower halves. Superior pertains to the upper segment of the body, and inferior to the lower.

Movement Terminology

Bodily motion occurs at a union of two or more bones, called a joint. Much like directional terminology, movement terminology is described by opposing sets of actions. Flexion refers to a bending motion, and extension to a straightening motion. Similarly, abduction is lateral movement, and adduction medial movement of the limbs. Inward rotation and outward rotation describe a turning from the shoulder or hip in which a limb rotates inward or outward, respectively. Inversion and eversion describe foot movement. Inversion occurs when the foot turns inward so that the sole is toward the midline of the body, and eversion describes a situation in which the foot turns outward away from the midline. Supination and pronation refer to motions of the forearm that turn the palm of the hand upward and downward, respectively. Varus indicates an abnormal curving of a part toward the midline, and valgus an angulation away from the midline.

These movements are possible because of three types of joint construction found in the limbs: hinge, pivot, and ball and socket. A hinge joint allows flexion and extension movement only. The knee is an example of this kind of joint. A pivot joint permits a rotary, or pivotal type of motion. This type of joint is located just below the elbow joint. A ball and socket joint allows several movements, including flexion and extension, abduction and adduction, and inward and external rotation. When these motions occur together, creating a circular motion of a limb, circumduction results. The shoulder and hip are examples of ball and socket joints.

Keeping movement terminology in mind, a more detailed explanation of normal limb motion is indicated.

NORMAL JOINT RANGE OF MOTION

Normal joint movement occurs within a certain range that is measured by degrees within a circle or half-circle. The distance of the movement is referred to as range of motion. Therapists and doctors use an instrument called a goniometer that consists of two arms and either a 180-degree or a 360-degree scale, to measure the range of motion of upper extremity or lower extremity joints (see Figure 6.9). For example, a typical reading for normal elbow motion is 0 degrees to 150 degrees. The 180-degree system of measurement used in this text is based on guidelines set by the American Academy of Orthopaedic Surgeons (1965).

Learning how to use a goniometer is a normal part of training for therapists and doctors. The guidelines presented here do not prepare a reader to measure joints. (Readers interested in a detailed description of joint measurement should refer to the text entitled *Measurement of Joint Motion: A Guide to Goniometry* by Norkin and White, 1985.) Rather, these guidelines are presented to help provide an understanding of normal joint motion so that substantial joint limitations may be recognized. The illustration of the human skeleton shown in Figure D.1 can be used as a reference in locating the major bones that form joints of the spine and limbs.

Normal motion of the spine, the upper extremities, and the lower extremities is discussed below. Readers may find it helpful to perform the motions as they read about them.

Spinal Motion

The normal spine is composed of 33 vertebrae (Figure D.2.) The vertebrae work together to allow forward bending (flexion), backward bending (extension), sideways bending (lateral flexion), and rotation. Since flexibility varies greatly in normal persons, measurement of range of motion is not included here.

Upper Extremity Motion

Upper extremity motion occurs at the shoulder, elbow, wrists, fingers, and thumbs.

Shoulder

The shoulder is a ball and socket joint that is capable of both single and combination movements—flexion, extension, abduction, adduction, rotation, and circumduction. The starting position used to measure joint mobility is with the arm resting against the side of the body, the elbow straight, and the

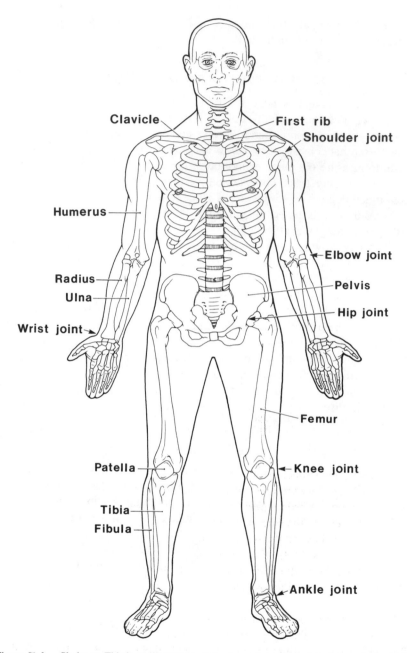

Figure D.1.   Skeleton. This is an illustration of the skeletal structure of the human body. Major bones and joints are indicated.

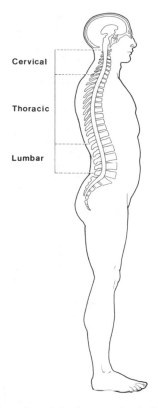

Cervical

Thoracic

Lumbar

Figure D.2. Spine. This illustration of the human spine indicates the location of cervical, thoracic, and lumbar vertebrae. It also shows normal spinal curvature as viewed from the side.

palm of the hand touching the side of the leg. Shoulder flexion involves moving the arm forward and up. In a normal shoulder, it will be possible to raise the arm to a vertical position 180 degrees from the starting point. The return movement to the side is called extension. In a normal shoulder, movement is possible beyond the starting point (i.e., backward extension) for about 60 degrees (Figure D.3). From the same starting position, the arm may be lifted out away from the body to a point above the head (i.e., abduction); or the arm may be moved across the body (i.e., adduction) to about 75 degrees (Figure D.4).

Rotation may be demonstrated in either of two ways. The simplest is directed from the starting position by turning the arm in both directions— inward and outward—until the thumb points either toward or away from the leg. The method used by professionals for measurement purposes involves

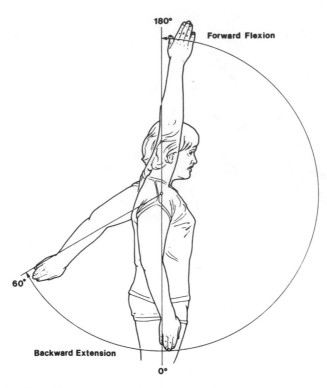

Figure D.3. Normal joint range of motion for shoulder flexion and extension. From a starting point of 0 degrees, the arm can swing forward 180 degrees to a vertical position over the head and backward to 60 degrees.

abducting the arm to 90 degrees, then flexing the elbow 90 degrees with the hand parallel to the floor (if standing), and moving the forearm up toward the head and down toward the hips while holding the upper arm stable. Total rotational range of a normal shoulder should be 180 degrees.

Elbow

The elbow is a hinge joint that allows the arm to flex or extend. As indicated in Figure D.5, normal flexion is approximately 150 degrees. Just below the elbow is a pivot joint that rotates the forearm into a supinated or pronated position (Figure D.6), with normal motion being 90 degrees in each direction.

Wrist

The wrist is comprised of a number of small bones. Motions produced at the wrist include flexion and extension (Figure D.7), and a sideways motion toward the radius bone (i.e., radial deviation) and toward the ulna bone (i.e.,

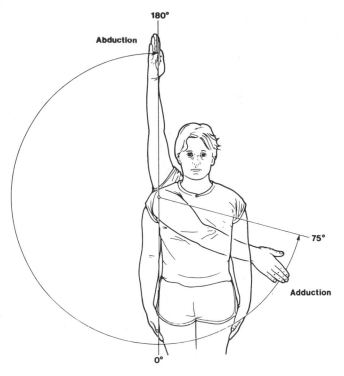

Figure D.4. Normal joint range of motion for shoulder abduction and adduction. From a starting point of 0 degrees, the arm can swing (i.e., abduct) away from the body to a position of 180 degrees above the head and can move across the body to 75 degrees of adduction.

ulnar deviation) (Figure D.8), as well as a combination movement (i.e., circumduction). As indicated in the illustrations, normal flexion approximates 80 degrees; extension, 70 degrees; radial deviation, 20 degrees; and ulnar deviation, 30 degrees.

Fingers and Thumb

The fingers may flex, extend, abduct, or adduct. The thumb is capable of circumduction, allowing performance of finely coordinated and highly skilled tasks (i.e., fine motor skills). Normal range of motion for the fingers is not included here because the focus of this book is on deformities of the larger joints that affect posture.

Lower Extremity Motion

The lower extremity joints are quite similar to those of the upper extremity in construction.

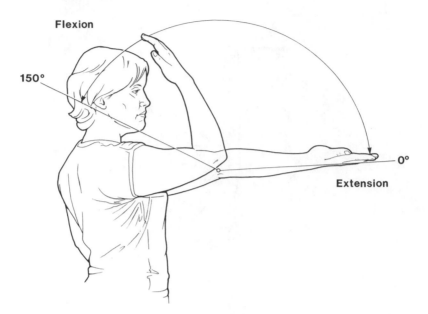

Figure D.5. Elbow flexion and extension. Starting with the arm straight and the elbow fully extended, the forearm can move to a bent angle of about 150 degrees flexion.

Hip

Like the shoulder, the hip is a ball and socket joint. It enables the leg to flex (Figure D.9), extend (Figure D.10), abduct and adduct (Figure D.11), rotate, and circumduct. Normal range for the first four of these motions is indicated in the illustrations. Rotation is demonstrated by sitting on the edge of a table and swinging one lower leg laterally back and forth. Normal range is approximately 45 degrees in each direction.

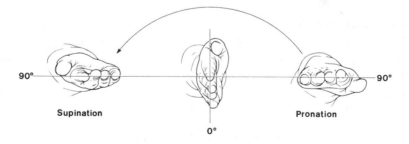

Figure D.6. Forearm supination and pronation. Starting with the forearm in a neutral position indicated as 0 degrees, the forearm can rotate to turn the hand into a palm up position, reflecting 90 degrees of supination. Again starting from the neutral position, the forearm can rotate to turn the hand into a palm down position, reflecting 90 degrees of pronation.

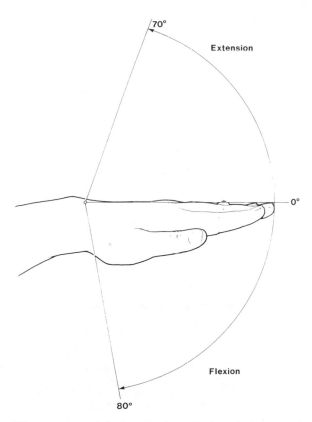

Figure D.7. Wrist extension and flexion. Starting with the wrist in a neutral position of 0 degrees, the wrist can extend to raise the hand 70 degrees and can flex to bend the hand 80 degrees.

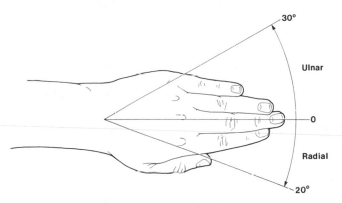

Figure D.8. Wrist radial and ulnar deviation. Starting with the wrist in a neutral position of 0 degrees, radial deviation allows the hand to move 20 degrees sideways toward the thumb and 30 degrees sideways toward the little finger.

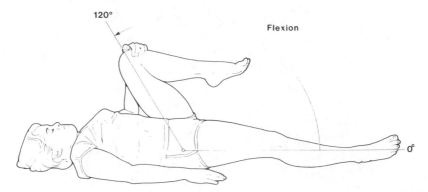

Figure D.9. Normal range of motion for hip flexion. Starting from a neutral position of 0 degrees, the thigh can move to a 120-degree bent position.

Knee

The knee, like the elbow, is a hinge joint. It moves in only two directions, flexion and extension, achieving a normal range of motion, approximately 135 degrees (Figure D.12).

Ankle

The ankle is comprised of several small bones that enable the joint to move in flexion and extension (Figure D.13), inversion and eversion (Figure D.14), and circumduction. Normal ranges of motion are indicated in the illustrations.

Toes

The toes flex and extend, and abduct and adduct. As with the fingers, detail is avoided here inasmuch as toe mobility has a limited effect on posture.

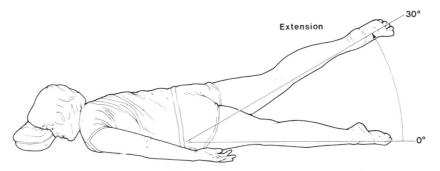

Figure D.10. Normal range of motion for hip extension. From the neutral position of 0 degrees, the leg can move backward to an angle of 30 degrees.

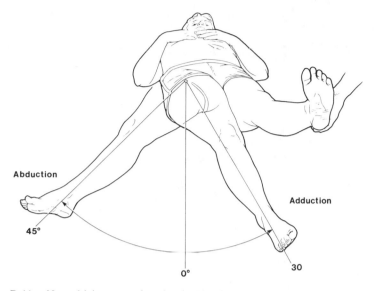

Figure D.11. Normal joint range of motion for hip abduction and adduction. From a 0 degree neutral position, the leg can swing outward to an angle of 45 degrees and across the body to an angle of 30 degrees.

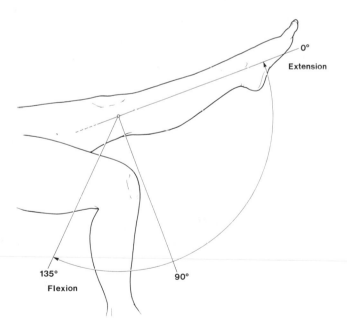

Figure D.12. Normal joint range of motion for knee extension and flexion. Starting with the leg straight and the knee in full (0 degree) extension, the knee can bend the leg to a 135 degree flexed angle.

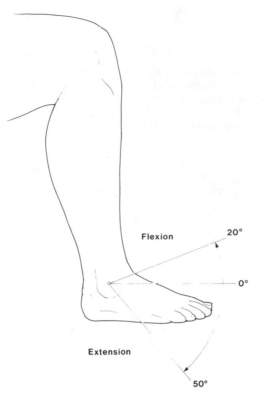

Figure D.13. Normal joint range of motion for ankle extension and flexion. Starting with the foot in a neutral position, the ankle joint allows the foot to move upward into 20 degrees of flexion and downward into 50 degrees of extension.

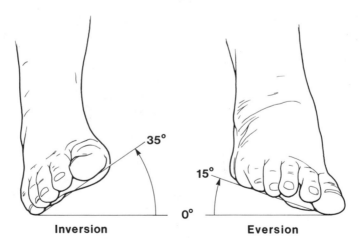

Figure D.14. Normal joint range of motion for ankle inversion and eversion. From a neutral position of 0 degrees, the ankle joint allows the foot to turn inward to 35 degrees of inversion and outward to 15 degrees of eversion.

296

REFERENCES

American Academy of Orthopaedic Surgeons. (1965). *Joint motion method of measuring and recording*. Chicago: Author. (American Academy of Orthopaedic Surgeons, 430 North Michigan Avenue, Chicago, IL 60611)

Norkin, C.C., & White D.J. (1985). *Measurement of joint motion: A guide to goniometry*. Philadelphia: F.A. Davis.

Appendix

E

Related Readings

Related readings are listed according to major subjects discussed in this book: orthopaedics, neurosurgery, orthotics, therapy, transportation safety, and special education and human services. Some of the references cited in the text are listed as well as other current literature pertaining to these subjects. Paper presentations from major meetings and classic references are included in chapter references only.

ORTHOPAEDIC REFERENCES

Bleck, E.E. (1987). Orthopaedic management in cerebral palsy, *Clinics in Developmental Medicine No. 99/100*. Philadelphia: J.B. Lippincott.

Bradford, D.S., & Hensinger, R.N. (Eds.). (1985). *The pediatric spine*. New York: Thieme, Inc.

Chait, L.A., Kaplan, I., Stewart-Loard, B., & Goodman, M. (1980). Early surgical correction in the cerebral palsied hand. *Journal of Hand Surgery, 5,* 122–126.

Hollinshead, W.H. (Ed.). (1985). *Anatomy for Surgeons, Vol. 3*. New York: Harper & Row.

House, J.H., Gwathmey, F.W., & Fidler, M.O. (1981). A dynamic approach to the thumb-in-palm deformity in cerebral palsy. *Journal of Bone and Joint Surgery, 63A,* 216–225.

Louis, D.S., Hankin, F.M., & Bowers, W.H. (1984). Capitate radius fusion in the spastic upper extremity— an alternative to wrist arthrodesis. *Journal of Hand Surgery, 9,* 365–369.

Louis, D.S., Hensinger, R.N., Fraser, B.A., Phelps, J.A., & Jacques, K. (1989). Surgical management of the severely multiply handicapped individual. *Journal of Pediatric Orthopaedics, 9,* 15–18.

Manshe, P.R. (1985). Redirection of extensor pollicis longus in the treatment of spastic thumb-in-palm deformity. *Journal of Hand Surgery, 10A,* 553–560.

Mital, M.A., Beklin, S.C., & Sullivan, R.A. (1976). An approach to head, neck, and trunk stabilization and control in cerebral palsy by use of the Milwaukee brace. *Developmental Medicine and Child Neurology, 18,* 198.

Norkin, C.C., & White, D.J. (1985). *Measurement of joint motion: A guide to goniometry.* Philadelphia: F.A. Davis.

Sakellarides, H.T., Mital, M.A., Lenzi, W.D. (1981). Treatment of pronation contractures of the forearm in cerebral palsy by changing the insertion of the pronator radii teres. *Journal of Bone and Joint Surgery, 63A,* 645–652.

Thompson, G.H., Rubin, I.L., & Bilenker, R.M. (Eds.). (1983). *Comprehensive management of cerebral palsy.* New York: Grune & Stratton.

Turek, S.L. (1984). *Orthopaedics: Principles and their application* (4th ed.). Philadelphia: J.B. Lippincott.

Warwick, R., & Williams, P.L. (Eds). (1979). *Grey's anatomy* (35th ed., British). Philadelphia: W.B. Saunders.

Zancolli, E.A., Goildner, J.L., & Swanson, A.B. (1983). Surgery of the spastic hand in cerebral palsy: Report of the committee in spastic hand evaluation. *Journal of Hand Surgery, 8,* 766–772.

NEUROSURGERY REFERENCES

Fasano, V.A., Broggi, G., & Barolat-Romanan, F. (1979). Surgical treatment of spasticity in cerebral palsy. *Child's Brain, 4,* 289–305.

Laitinen, S., Nilsson, S., & Fugi-Meyer, A.R. (1983). Selective posterior rhizotomy for treatment of spasticity. *Journal of Neurosurgery, 58,* 895–899.

Peacock, W.J., & Ariens, L.J. (1982). Selective posterior rhizotomy for the relief of spasticity in cerebral palsy. *South African Medical Journal, 62,* 119–124.

Peacock, W.J., Ariens, L.J., & Berman, B. (1987). Cerebral palsy spasticity: Selective posterior rhizotomy. *Pediatric Neuroscience, 13,* 61–66.

Staudtl, L.A., & Peacock, W.J. (1989, Spring). Selective posterior rhizotomy for treatment of spastic cerebral palsy. *Pediatric Physical Therapy, 1*(1), 3–9.

Yasuoka, S., Peterson, H.A., & MacCarty, C.S. (1982). Incidence of spinal column deformity after multilevel laminectomy in children and adults. *Journal of Neurosurgery, 57,* 441–445.

ORTHOTIC REFERENCES

Donald, G., & Shurr, M.A. (1984, Spring). The delivery of orthotic and prosthetic services in America. *Orthotics and Prosthetics, 1,* 55–63.

Drennan, J.C., & Gage, J.R. (1983). Orthotics in cerebral palsy. In G.H. Thompson, I.L. Rubin, & R.M. Bilenker (Eds.), *Comprehensive management of cerebral palsy* (pp. 205–213). New York: Grune & Stratton.

Foster, F., & Milani, J. (1979). The genucentric knee orthosis—a new concept. *Orthotics and Prosthetics, 33,* 31.

Harrington, E.D., Lin, R.S., & Gage, M.D. (1983). Use of the anterior floor reaction orthosis in patients with cerebral palsy. *Journal of American Orthotic-Prosthetic Association, 37*(4), 34–42.

THERAPY REFERENCES

General Therapeutic Procedures and Service Delivery References

Bleck, E.E. (1987). Orthopaedic management in cerebral palsy. *Clinics in Developmental Medicine No. 99/100.* Philadelphia: J.P. Lippincott.

Boehme, R. (1988). *Improving upper body control*. Tucson, AZ: Therapy Skill Builders.

Campbell, P.H., McInerney, W.F., & Cooper, M.A. (1984). Therapeutic programming for students with severe handicaps. *American Journal of Occupational Therapy, 38*(9), 594–602.

Cannon, N.M., Foltz, R.W., Koepfer, J.M., Lauck, M.F., Simpson, D.M., & Bromley, R.S. (1985). *Manual of hand splinting*. New York: Churchill Livingstone.

Capute, A.J., Palmer, F.B., Sharpiro, B.K., Wachtel, R.C., Ross, A., & Accardo, P.J. (1984). Primitive reflex profile: A quantitation of primitive reflexes in infancy. *Developmental Medicine and Child Neurology, 26*(3), 375–383.

Cherry, D.B. (1980). Review of physical therapy alternatives for reducing muscle contracture. *Physical Therapy, 60*(7), 877–881.

Connolly, B.H., & Montogomery, P.C. (1987). *Therapeutic exercise in developmental disabilities*. Chattanooga, TN: Chattanoga Corp.

Erhardt, R.P. (1982). *Developmental hand dysfunction*. Laurel, MD: Ramsco.

Farber, S.D. (1982). *Neurorehabilitation: A multisensory approach*. Philadelphia: W.B. Saunders.

Finnie, N.R. (1975). *Handling the young cerebral palsied child at home*. New York: E. P. Dutton.

Howison, M.V. (1983). Occupational therapy with children—cerebral palsy. In G. Hopkins & H.D. Smith (Eds.), *Willard & Spackman's Occupational Therapy* (pp.643–681). Philadelphia: J.P. Lippincott.

Hylton, J., Reed, P., Hall, S., & Cicirello, N. (1987) . *The role of the physical therapist and the occupational therapist in the school setting*. TIES: Therapy in Educational Settings, a collaborative project conducted by Crippled Children's Division—University Affiliated Program, the Oregon Health Sciences University and the Oregon Department of Education, Portland.

Reed, P., Hylton, J., Cicirello, N., & Hall, S. (1988). *A model plan for the supervision and evaluation of therapy services in educational settings*. TIES: Therapy in Educational Settings, a collaborative project conducted by University Affiliated Program of the Child Development and Rehabilitation Center at the Oregon Health Science University, and the Oregon Department of Education, Portland.

Satterfield, J. (1981). *How the physical therapist can help in the educational environment*. White Hall: Pediatric Special Interest Group of Maryland.

Seeger, B.R., Caudrey, D.J., & O'Mara, N.A. (1984). Hand function in cerebral palsy: The effect of hip flexion angle. *Developmental Medicine and Child Neurology, 26*(5), 601–606.

Sommerfeld, D., Fraser, B.A., Hensinger, R.N., & Beresford, C.V. (1981). Evaluation of physical therapy service for severely mentally impaired students with cerebral palsy. *Physical Therapy, 61*(3), 338–343.

von Wendt, L., Ekenberg, L., Dagis, D., & Janlert, U. (1984). A parent-centered approach to physiotherapy for their handicapped children. *Developmental Medicine and Child Neurology, 26*(4), 445–447.

Oral-Motor and Feeding References

American Occupational Therapy Association. (1987). *Problems with eating interventions for children and adults with developmental disabilities*. Rockville, MD: Author.

Logemann, J. (1983). *Evaluation and treatment of swallowing disorder*. San Diego, CA: College-Hill Press.

Morris, S.E. (1982). *The normal acquisition of oral feeding skills: Implications for assessment and treatment*. Central Islip, NH: Therapeutic Media.

Morris, S.E., & Klein, M.D. (1987). *Pre-feeding skills: A comprehensive resource of feeding development*. Tucson, AZ: Therapy Skill Builders.

Ray, S.A., Bundy, A.C., & Nelson, D.G. (1983). Decreasing drooling through techniques to facilitate mouth closure. *American Journal of Occupational Therapy, 37*(11), 749–753.

Stratton, M. (1981). Behavioral assessment scale of oral functions in feeding. *American Journal of Occupational Therapy, 37*, 719–721.

Wilson, J.M. (Ed.). (1978). *Oral-motor function and dysfunction in children*. Chapel Hill: University of North Carolina at Chapel Hill.

Non-Oral Communication

International Action Group for Communication Enhancement. *Where the Action Is*. (Newsletter available from Artificial Language Lab., Computer Science Department, Michigan State University, E. Lansing, MI 48824)

Silverman, F.H., McNaughton, S., & Kates, B. (1978). *Handbook of blissymbolics*. Toronto, Ontario: Blissymbolics Communication Institute.

State Department of Education. (1980). *Non-Oral Communication: A Guide for Training the Child without Speech*. (Available from Fountain Valley School District, P.O. Box 8510, Fountain Valley, CA 92708)

Vanderheiden, G. (Ed.). (1978). *Non-vocal communication resource book*. Baltimore: University Park Press.

Positioning and Seating References

Benson, J., & Schneider, L. (1984). *Improving the crashworthiness of restraints for handicapped children* (SAE Technical Paper Series No. 840528). Warrendale, PA: Society of Automotive Engineers, Inc. (400 Commonwealth Drive, Warrendale, PA 15096)

Bergan, A., & Colangelo, C. (1985). *Positioning the client with central nervous system deficits: The wheelchair and other adapted equipment* (2nd ed.). Valhalla, NY: Valhalla Rehabilitation Publications.

Bock, O. (1988). *Please, be seated: Current trends for the disabled*. Winnipeg, Manitoba: Orthopedic Industry of Canada, LTD. (251 Saulteaux Crescent, Winnipeg, Manitoba, R3J3C7)

Carlson, J.M., Lonstein, J., Beck, K.O., & Wilkie, D.C. (1986). Seating for children and young adults with cerebral palsy. *Clinical Prosthetics and Orthotics, 10*(4), 137–158.

Hobson, D.A. (1986). Research and development considerations in engineering perspective. *Clinical Prosthetics and Orthotics, 10*(4), 122–129.

Jones, S., Clarke, S., & Cook, S. (1985). *Adaptive positioning equipment: Directory of available services*. Atlanta: Georgia Retardation Center. (4770 North Peachtree Road, Atlanta, GA 30338)

Lin, R.S., & Lin, S.S. (1986). Adaptive seating in pediatrics. *Clinical Prosthetics and Orthotics, 10*(4), 130–136.

Nwaobi, O.M. (1986, February). Effects of body orientation in space on tonic muscle activity of patients with cerebral palsy. *Developmental Medicine and Child Neurology, 28*(1), 41–44.

Seeger, B.R., & Caudrey, D.J. (1983). Crashworthiness of restraints for physically disabled children in buses. *Rehabilitation Literature, 44*, 11–12.

Trefler, E. (Ed.). (1984). *Seating for children with cerebral palsy: A resource manual.* Memphis: The University of Tennessee Center for the Health Sciences, Rehabilitation Engineering Program.
Ward, D.E. (1984). *Positioning the handicapped child for function: A guide to evaluate and prescribe equipment for the child with central nervous system dysfunction.* St. Louis: Phoenix Press.
Zacharkow, D. (1988). *Posture, sitting, standing, chair design and exercise.* Springfield, IL: Charles C Thomas.

TRANSPORTATION SAFETY REFERENCES

Benson, J., & Schneider, L.W. (1984). *Improving the crashworthiness of restraints for handicapped children* (SAE Technical Paper Series No. 840528). Warrendale, PA: Society of Automotive Engineers, Inc. (400 Commonwealth Drive, Warrendale, PA 15096)
Brenner, E., & Giangrande, R.V. (1981). *Wheelchair securement systems in transit vehicles: A summary report* (Report No. DOT-TSC-UMTA-81-43). Washington, DC: Transportation Systems Center, U.S. Department of Transportation.
Khadikar, A.V., & Will, E. (1980). *Crash protection systems for handicapped school and transit bus occupants* (Report No. DOT-HS-805-821). Washington, DC: National Highway Traffic Safety Administration, U.S. Department of Transportation.
Linebaugh, P.E. (1988). *Handicapped seating study committee report: Washtenaw Intermediate School District Transportation Report.* Ann Arbor, MI: Washtenaw Intermediate School District.
Petty, S.P.F. (1986). The safe transportation of wheelchair occupants in the United Kingdom. *Proceedings from the 11th International Technical Conference on Experimental Safety Vehicles* (pp. 488–491). Washington, DC: National Highway Traffic Safety Administration.
Schneider, L.W. (1981). *Dynamic testing of restraint systems and tie-downs for use with vehicle occupants seated in powered wheelchairs.* (Report No. UM-HSRI-81-18). Ann Arbor: University of Michigan Transportation Research Institute.
Schneider, L.W. (1981). Protection for the severely disabled: A new challenge in occupant restraint. In R.N. Green & E. Petrucello (Eds.), *The human collision: international symposium on occupant restraint* (pp. 217–231). Morton Grove, IL: AAAM.
Schneider, L.W. (1985). *Sled impact tests of wheelchair tie-down systems for handicapped drivers* (Report No. UMTRI-85-19). Ann Arbor: University of Michigan Transportation Research Institute.
Schneider, L.W., Melvin, J.W., & Cooney, C.E. (1979). *Impact sled test evaluation of restraint systems used in transportation of handicapped children* (SAE Technical Paper Series No. 790074). Warrendale, PA: Society of Automotive Engineers Inc. (400 Commonwealth Drive, Warrendale, PA 15096)
Seeger, B.R., & Caudrey, D.J. (1983). *Crashworthiness of restraints for physically disabled children in buses.* Kilkenny: The Crippled Children's Association of South Australia.
Shelness, A. (1987). Transporting children with special needs, Part II: Protecting handicapped school children. *Safe Ride News, 6*(3), 4.
Standards Association of Australia. (1987). *Wheelchair occupant restraint assemblies for motor vehicles.* (Australian Standard, AS 2942). North Sydney, N.S.W.

Stewart, C.F., & Geinl, H.G. (1981). *Wheelchair securement on bus and paratransit vehicles* (Report No. UMTA-CA-06-0098-81-1). Sacramento: California Department of Transportation.

SPECIAL EDUCATION AND
HUMAN SERVICES REFERENCES

Anastasiow, N.J. (1986). *Development and disability: A psychobiological analysis for special educators.* Baltimore: Paul H. Brookes Publishing Co.

Barringer, M. (1982). *Around the world with S.O.S.: A supplemental education program for students functioning in the sensorimotor stage.* Wayne, MI: Wayne County Intermediate School District.

Batshaw, M.L., & Perret, Y.M. (1986). *Children with handicaps: A medical primer* (2nd ed.). Baltimore: Paul H. Brookes Publishing Co.

Bjorling, B. (Ed.). *Activities file.* Lansing: Midwest Regional Center for Service to Deaf-Blind Children, Michigan Department of Education.

Brown, F., & Lehr. D.H. (1989). *Persons with profound disabilities: Issues and practices.* Baltimore: Paul H. Brookes Publishing Co.

Certo, N., Haring, N., & York, R. (1984). *Public school integration of severely handicapped students: Rational issues and progressive alternates.* Baltimore: Paul H. Brookes Publishing Co.

Copeland, M.E., & Kimmel, J.R. (1989). *Evaluation and management of infants and young children with developmental disabilities.* Baltimore: Paul H. Brookes Publishing Co.

French, J.H., Harel, S., Casaer, P., Gottlieb, M.I., Rapin, I., & DeVivo, D.C. (1989). *Child neurology and developmental disabilities: Selected proceedings of the fourth international child neurology congress.* Baltimore: Paul H. Brookes Publishing Co.

Goetz, L., Guess, D., & Stremel-Campbell, K. (1987). *Innovative program design for individuals with dual sensory impairments.* Baltimore: Paul H. Brookes Publishing Co.

Goldfarb, L.A., Brotherson, M.J., Summers, J.A., & Turnbull, A.P. (1986). *Meeting the challenge of disability or chronic illness: A family guide.* Baltimore: Paul H. Brookes Publishing Co.

Greenberg, S.F., & Valletutti, P.J. (1980). *Stress and the helping professions.* Baltimore: Paul H. Brookes Publishing Co.

Kissinger, E.M. (1981). *A sequential curriculum for severely and profoundly retarded/multiply handicapped.* Springfield, IL: Charles C Thomas.

Linder, T.W. (1983). *Early childhood special education: Program development and administration.* Baltimore: Paul H. Brookes Publishing Co.

Mulliken, R.K., & Buckley, J.J. (1983). *Assessment of multihandicapped and developmentally disabled children.* Rockville, MD: Aspen Publishers Inc.

Scheerenberger, R.C. (1983). *A history of mental retardation.* Baltimore: Paul H. Brookes Publishing Co.

Striefel, S., & Cadez, M.J. (1983). *Serving children and adolescents with developmental disabilities in the special education classroom: Proven methods.* Baltimore: Paul H. Brookes Publishing Co.

Valletutti, P.J., & Sims-Tucker, B.M. (Eds.). (1984). *Severely and profoundly handicapped students: Their nature and needs.* Baltimore: Paul H. Brookes Publishing Co.

Wehman, P., Wood, W., Everson, J.M., Goodwyn, R., & Conley, S. (1988). *Vocational education for multihandicapped youth with cerebral palsy*. Baltimore: Paul H. Brookes Publishing Co.

Wilcox, B., & Bellamy, G. (1982). *Design of high school programs for severely handicapped students*. Baltimore: Paul H. Brookes Publishing Co.

Williamson, G.G. (1987). *Children with spina bifida: Early intervention and preschool programming*. Baltimore: Paul H. Brookes Publishing Co.

Appendix

F

Clothing Resources

Listed below are companies that provide clothing resources and their products.

CLOTHING RESOURCES

Company	Products
Adaptive Fashions 5641 Bartlett Blvd. Mound, MN 55364 (612) 472-4435 (612) 471-9371	Velcro openings Adult jumpsuits Wheelchair leg covers Adult bibs Capes Custom designs
Adaptogs P.O. Box 339 123 N. Washington Otis, CO 80743 (303) 246-3761	Spring cape Adult jogging suits Foot warmers Wheelchair lap covers Bath ponchos Hand, elbow, arm, heel protectors Custom designs
Buck & Buck, Inc. 4115 S. W. Arroyo Drive Seattle, WA 98146 (800) 458-0600	Adult jogging suits Foot warmers Lap warmers Adult bibs
Clothes You-Nique, Inc. P.O. Box 8306 Stockton, CA 95208 (209) 463-3376	Foot warmers Adult jogging suits Bath poncho
Everest & Jennings Avenues 3233 E. Mission Oaks Blvd. Camarillo, CA 93010 (800) 848-2837	Foot warmers Wheelchair leg cover Bath poncho Rain poncho

(*continued*)

Company	Products
Fashion Ease M & M Health Care Apparel Co. 1541 60th Street Brooklyn, NY 11219 (800) 221-8929	Rain poncho Velcro closures Foot warmers Wheelchair leg cover Bibs
Just For You 810 Busch Court Columbus, OH 43229 (614) 846-6133	Foot warmers Wheelchair leg covers Adult bibs Back-snap clothing
Laurel Designs 5 Laurel Avenue, #9 Belvedere, CA 94920 (415) 435-1891	Rain ponchos Adult jogging suits
Maddax, Inc. Pequannock, NJ 07440-1993 (201) 694-0500	Rain ponchos Lap warmers Adult bibs
Smith & Nephew Rolyan, Inc. N93 W14475 Whittaker Way Menomonee Falls, WI 53051 (800) 558-8633 In WI (800) 722-0442	Disposable adult bibs
Special Clothes for Special Children P.O. Box 4220 Alexandria, VA 22303 (703) 683-7343	Capes, child sizes Back-open jackets, child sizes Thumbless mittens Jump suits with snap crotch Snap crotch clothing Gastrostomy tube access
Techni-Flair P.O. Box 40-6 Cotter, AR 72626 (800) 643-5656	Personal shopper service Rain ponchos Adapted fasteners Adult jumpsuits
Wheelie's Bentwear P.O. Box 455 Roseburg, OR 97470 (503) 673-8726	Clothing for wheelchair users Back-open coats Wheelchair leg covers Fasteners clients can't undo Clothing "bent" for comfort in wheelchairs
Wheelmates Designs by Vicki Wade 611 East Washington Pittsfield, IL 62363 (217) 285-6520	Special needs capes & ponchos (e.g., spring and winter weight, child and adult sizes) Leg warmers Nose and face covers Muffs for hands

GENERAL RESOURCES/PATTERNS

The following supply general resources and patterns.

Clothing Designs for the Handicapped
Anne Kernaleguen
The University of Alberta Press
Edmonton, Alberta, Canada 1978

PAM Pepeater No. 49 Wearables
Arselia S. Ensign, Editor
PAM Assistance Center
601 W. Maple Street
Lansing, MI 48906
(800) 274-7426

P.R.I.D.E. Foundation, Inc.
71 Plaza Court
Groton, CT 06340
(203)445-1448

Appendix
G

Adaptive Devices

Listed below are companies that provide commercially available switches, toys, and related products; computer-related hardware and software; and communication products.

COMMERCIALLY AVAILABLE SWITCHES, TOYS, AND RELATED PRODUCTS

Company	Typical products
ABLENET 1081 10th Avenue, S.E. Minneapolis, MN 55414 (612) 379-0956	Push switch String switch Timer Slide projector control Mounting systems Adapters Newsletter
The Able Child P.O. Box 250 Bohemia, NY 11716 (800) 356-1564	Plate switch Tactile touch switch Squeeze switch Toys adapted with jacks Adapted knobs and handles
Adaptive Aids, Inc. P.O. Box 57640 Tucson, AZ 85732-7640 (800) 223-5369	Control unit Pressure pad switch Ring stack switch Tilt switch Squeeze switch

(continued)

Company	Typical products
Arroyo & Associates, Inc. 2549 Rockville Centre Parkway Oceanside, NY 11572-1626 (516) 763-1407	Control unit Adjustable pressure switch Plate switch Vibrating plate switch Tilt switch Timer Mounting hardware
Creative Switch Industries P.O. Box 5256 Des Moines, IO 50306 (515) 287-5748	Pull switch Wobble switch Pinch switch Mat switch Timer Fireman's hat
Crestwood Company 6625 N.Sidney Place Milwaukee, WI 53209 (414) 352-5678	Touch switch Switch mountings TASH switches Beeper Toys adapted with sandwich interfaces
Don Johnston Developmental Equipment, Inc. P.O. Box 639 1000 N. Rand Road Bldg. 115 Wauconda, IL 60084 (708) 526-2682	Plate switch Light touch switch Sensor switch Mounting kits Adaptive firmward card
Handicapped Childrens Technological Services, Inc. P.O. Box 7 Foster, RI 02825 (401) 861-3444	Control unit Timer Push switch Barrel switch Puzzle switch Joy stick Toys adapted with jacks (large selection) Adapted toys appropriate for adolescents
Hugh MacMillan Medical Centre 350 Rumsey Road Toronto, Ontario M4G-1R8 (416) 425-6220	Adapted remote control toys Mounting for head switches Latching switch interface
Jessana, Ltd. P.O. Box 17 Irvington, NY 10533 (914) 591-5539, (800) 443-4728	Various switches/toys from Steven Kanor, Ph.D., Inc. and Therapeutic Toys, Inc. Squeeze switch
Maddax Pequannock, NJ 07440-1993	Plate switch Squeeze switch Music box TV

(continued)

Company	Typical products
Steven Kanor, Ph.D., Inc. 8 Herkimer Avenue Hewlett, NY 11557 (914) 478-0960	Control unit Timer module Photo cell switch Voice activated switch Tilt switch Button switch Pull switch Wobble switch Leaf switch Grasp switch Puzzle switches Rocking plate switch Vertical plate switch Vibrating plate switch Lighted plate switches Plate switch Adapted radios/tape players Activity centers Large variety of toys adapted with jacks Adapters Simple communications devices
T.A.S.H., Inc. 70 Gibson Dr., Unit 12 Markham, Ontario, Canada L3R-4C2 (416) 475-2212	Touch switches Cup, mini cup switches Pillow switch Soft switch Leaf switch Tilt switch Dual switches Mounting devices Adapters Environmental control system Grasp switch
Therapeutic Toys, Inc. 91 Newberry Road East Haddam, CT 06423 (203) 873-9509, (800) 638-0676	Multi-sensory motivator Treadle switch Tiltswitch Adapters

COMPUTER-RELATED HARDWARE AND SOFTWARE

Company	Product
Hardware	
ADAMLAB W.C.I.S. D. 33500 Van Boarn Road Wayne, MI 48184 (313) 467-1610	AICES

(continued)

Company	Typical products
Adaptive Peripherals 4529 Bagley Avenue, N. Seattle, WA 98103 206) 623-6190	Adaptive firmware card

Software

R. J. Cooper & Assoc.
24843 Del Prado, Suite 283
Dana Point, CA 92629
(714) 240-1912

Dunamis Inc.
3620 Highway 317
Suwanee, GA 30174
(800) 828-2443

Laureate Learning Systems
110 E. Spring Street
Winooski, VT 05404
(802) 655-4755

Peal Software
South Tower, Suite 1207
3200 Wilshire Blvd.
Los Angeles, CA 90010
(213) 739-9062

Project ACTT
Western Illinois University
27 Horrabin Hall
Macomb, IL 61455
(309) 298-1014

UCLA/LAUSD
Microcomputer Software
1000 Veterans Avenue
Suite 23-10
Los Angeles, CA 90024
(213) 825-4821

COMMUNICATION PRODUCTS FOR PERSONS WITH SEVERE MULTIPLE IMPAIRMENTS

Company	Product
Adaptive Communication Systems, Inc. Box 12440 Pittsburgh, PA 15231 (412) 264-2288	ACS Speech Pac/Scan Pac/Epson All talk

(continued)

Company	Product
ADAMLAB W.C.I.S. D. 33500 Van Born Road (313) 467-1300	Super WOLF Scan WOLF Kanor WOLF AIPS WOLF
APCOM Industries Detroit Institute for Children 5447 Woodward Detroit, MI 48202 (313) 832-1100	Audioscan
Prentke-Romich 1022 Heyl Road Wooster, OH 44691 (216) 262-1984	Touch Talker Light Talker Express Minspeak
Shea Products 1042 W. Hamlin Rochester, MI 48063 (313) 656-2281	Special Friend
Zygo Industries P.O. Box 1008 Portland, OR 97207 (503) 297-1724	16+100 Model Scan Boards

RESOURCES FOR ADAPTIVE DEVICES

ABLENET Newsletter, 1081 10th Avenue, S. E., Minneapolis, MN 66414.

Burkhart, L.J. (1980). *Homemade battery powered toys and educational devices for severely handicapped children.* (Available from Linda J. Burkhart, 8503 Rhode Island Avenue, College Park, MD 20740.)

Burkhart, L.J. (1982). *More homemade battery devices for severely handicapped children with suggested activities.* (Available from Linda J. Burkhart, 8503 Rhode Island Avenue, College Park, MD 20740.)

Casby, M.W. (1984, July). Simple switch modifications for use in augmentative communication. *Language, Speech, and Hearing Services in Schools, 15,* 216–220.

Closing the Gap Newsletter, P. O. Box 68, Henderson, MN 58044.

Coker, W.B. (1984, January). Homemade switches and toy adaptation for early training with nonspeaking persons. *Language, Speech, and Hearing Services in Schools, 15,* 32–36.

Handicapped Children's Technological Services, Active Stimulation Program and Technical Newsletters, Box 7, Foster, RI 02835.

Higgins, J. (1982). *Guidelines for adapting battery operated toys for the physically handicapped.* Vista, CA: California Avenue School. (215 West California Ave., Vista, CA)

Levin, J., & Scherfenberg, L. (1986). *Breaking barriers.* Minneapolis, MN: ABLENET.

Levin, J., & Scherfenberg, L. (1987). *Selection and use of simple technology in home, school, work, and community settings.* Minneapolis, MN: ABLENET.

PAM Assistance Center and Living and Learning Resource Centre, 601 West Maple, Lansing, MI 48906

Project Access Newsletter, W.C.I.S.D., 33500 Van Born Road, Wayne, MI 48184.

Project ACTT. (1986). *Curriculum for use of switches and computers*. Macomb, IL: Western Illinois University.

RESNA. (1982). A guide to controls, selection, mounting applications. Washington, DC: Author. (1101 Connecticut Avenue, NW, Suite 700, Washington, DC 20036)

Shein, G.F., & Mandel, A.R. (1982, February). Large area flap switch to control battery operated toys. *American Journal of Occupational Therapy, 36*(2), 107–110.

Appendix
H
—·—
Wheelchair Tie-Down/ Restraint System Resources

Lawrence W. Schneider

Listed below are companies that market passenger tie-down/restraint systems that have demonstrated effectiveness in 48 km/hr (30 mph), 20g impacts.

Creative Controls Inc.
32450 DeQuindre
Warren, MI 48092
(313) 979-3500
Product Name: Strap-LOK

Q-Straint
A Division of Giram, Inc.
4248 Ridge Lea Road
Buffalo, NY 14226
(716) 831-9959
Product Name: Q-Straint

Aeroquip Corp.
Transportation Products Division

2901 Lakeview Road
Lawrence, KS 66044
(913) 841-4000

Gresham Driving Aids
30800 Wixon Road
Wixon, MI 48096
(313) 624-1533
Product Name: Sure-Lock

Ortho Safe Systems, Inc.
P.O. Box 9435
Trenton, NJ 08650
(609) 587-3859
Product Name: Protector

Lawrence W. Schneider, Ph.D., is a research scientist and Head of the Biosciences Division, The University of Michigan Transportation Research Institute, Ann Arbor.

Index

Obligatory, defined, 280
Obligatory postural reflex activity,
    21–26
  asymmetrical tonic neck reflex, 22,
    23
    see also Asymmetrical tonic neck
      reflex (ATNR)
  feeding and, 240–241
  Galant reflex, 25–26
  symmetrical tonic neck reflex, 22–25
  tonic labyrinthine reflex, 25
Obligatory synergy patterns, 27
Observation, orthopaedic management
    and, 40–41
Obturator nerve, defined, 280
Occupant protection systems, for trans-
    portation, 152–161
  see also Transportation
Occupational therapists
  and feeding program, 232
  and physical management, 12–13
    PL 94-142 effects on, 17
Occupational therapy
  defined, 280
  service delivery model resources, 267
Occupational therapy assessment,
    41–42
Olfactory, defined, 280
Optical righting, defined, 280
Oral assessment, 229
Oral hygiene, 263–265
Oral hypersensitivity, 245
Oral-motor abnormalities
  drooling and, 264
  feeding and, 242–245
Oral-motor reflexes, feeding and,
    241–242
Orientation and mobility specialists, and
    physical management, 13
Orthopaedic assessment, 41–45
Orthopaedic examination, 45–46, 48
  of lower extremity deformities,
    88–94
    foot, 94
    hip, 89–91
    knee, 91–93, 94
  of spinal curvatures
    hyperkyphosis, 76
    hyperlordosis, 75–76
    scoliosis, 61–65
    see also Spinal curvatures

Orthopaedic treatment, 29, 37–52
  control/support phase of, 38–39
  goal planning in, 48–49
  hospitalization and, 50
  of lower extremity deformities,
    94–98
    bracing in, 95
    footwear in, 95
    surgery in, 95–98
  observation in, 40–41
  philosophy of, 38–39
  preliminary screening in, 39–40
  prevention phase of, 38
  prognosis and, 49–50
  of spinal curvatures
    hyperkyphosis, 76–77
    hyperlordosis, 76
    scoliosis, 65–74
    see also Spinal curvatures
  surgery in, 39, 50–51, 95–98
  of upper extremity deformities,
    104–107
Orthopaedist(s)
  defined, 280
  and physical management, 12
Orthoplast, 139
Orthosis(es), 137–150
  categories of, 138
  defined, 280
  lower extremity, 146–148, 149, 150
  materials for, 138–140
  naming systems for, 138
  seating, 128, 129
    materials for, 139–140
  spinal, 141–145
    casting of, 144
    clamshell, 142
    CTLSO, 66
    evaluation for, 142–143
    fabrication of, 144–145
    jacket, 141
    modifications of, 145
    TLSO, 65–66, 67, 68
  see also Orthotics
Orthotics
  defined, 137
  practice settings for, 138
  see also Orthosis(es)
Orthotist, 137, 280
Os calis, 280
Osteoporosis, 98